Default Reasoning

ACM Doctoral Dissertation Awards

1982
Area-Efficient VLSI Computation
by Charles Eric Leiserson

1983
Generating Language-Based Environments
by Thomas W. Reps

1984
Reduced Instruction Set Computer Architectures for VLSI
by Manolis G.H. Katevenis

1985
Bulldog: A Compiler for VLIW Architectures
by John R. Ellis

1986
Computational Limitations of Small Depth Circuits
by Johan Hastad

Full Abstraction and Semantic Equivalence
by Ketan Mulmuley

1987
The Complexity of Robot Motion Planning
by John F. Canny

1988
Communication Complexity: A New Approach to Circuit Depth
by Mauricio Karchmer

1989
Concurrent Constraint Programming
by Vijay Saraswat

1990
Probabilistic Similarity Networks
by David E. Heckerman

Default Reasoning: Causal and Conditional Theories
by Hector Geffner

Default Reasoning

Causal and Conditional Theories

Hector Geffner

The MIT Press
Cambridge, Massachusetts
London, England

This book was printed and bound in the United States of America.

Library of Congress Cataloging-in-Publication Data

Geffner, Hector.
Default reasoning : causal and conditional theories / Hector Geffner.
p. cm. — (ACM doctoral dissertation awards ; 1990)
Includes bibliographical references (p.) and index.
ISBN 0-262-07137-1
1. Default reasoning. 2. Artificial intelligence—Data processing. I. Title.
II. Series: ACM doctoral dissertation award ; 1990.
Q339.G44 1992
006.3—dc20

91-46489
CIP

Contents

Preface

A main goal of research in Artificial Intelligence (AI) is the construction of programs capable of displaying commonsense behavior. Default reasoning is a branch of AI aiming to explain the common behavior in which beliefs are established and retracted on the basis of default assumptions.

Defaults are important because they permit us to act in the absence of complete information. For example, when we plan to drive home after work, we are implicitly assuming that the car is where we last parked it, that the battery works, that the road is not blocked, and so on. Yet, these expectations hold by default only, and we must be ready to reassess our beliefs when they are violated.

The ubiquity of defaults has been underlined by the CYC project — a long term AI effort aimed at creating a large body of commonsense knowledge. Guha and Lenat assess that 95% of CYC's knowledge base consists of defaults (AI Magazine, Fall 1990). Defaults are used for representing actions (e.g., 'if a block is pushed the block will move'), for encoding typical properties of objects, (e.g., 'birds fly'), and for describing normal modes of behavior (e.g., 'the output of an adder is the sum of the inputs'), among other things.

To represent and reason with defaults we need to address three issues. First, we need a *language* for expressing default information. Second, we need a formal *semantics* to specify the inferences that defaults legitimize. And third, we need *inference procedures* to capture these inferences efficiently. The main difficulty in addressing these issues is that defaults interact not only with facts and observations but also with other defaults (e.g., 'people work on weekdays, people don't work on holidays; today is Monday and Labor Day'). This raises the question of what to do when one default supports one conclusion and a second default supports another conclusion, incompatible with the first. We call this the problem of *default interactions.*

One approach to the problem of default interactions is to accept a default only when there is no conflicting information and no conflicting defaults. Formally, this amounts to accepting as many defaults as is consistently possible, or alternatively, accepting only models that violate a minimal set of defaults. The problem with this approach, though, is that it does not explain why people so often prefer one default over another when defaults are in conflict. For example, if Tim is a penguin, we invoke the default 'penguins don't fly' but not the default 'birds fly'. The reason is that first default takes into account more information.

Similarly, if I left the lights of the car on last night, it will be reasonable to believe that the battery will be dead and that the car will not start, in spite of the otherwise expected conclusion that the car will start when the key is turned.

The non-monotonic logics developed in AI — so called because, as in default reasoning, additional axioms may invalidate old theorems — have addressed the problem of default interactions by providing devices in which the user is expected to specify how defaults are supposed to interact. For example, the user may be expected to express in one way or the other that the default 'birds fly' is not applicable to penguins, that a car will not start when there is evidence that the battery is dead, and so on. The problem is that as the size of the knowledge base grows, anticipating how defaults are supposed to interact becomes increasingly difficult, and expressing those interactions in terms of the devices offered by the underlying logic is not trivial (e.g., the above encoding may not work if we suspect that Tim is a penguin but are not completely sure).

In this book we approach the problem of default interactions in a different way. Rather than burden the user with the intricacies of specifying default interactions, we focus closer on what defaults say about the world and develop an interpretation that accounts for the intended default interactions automatically. The proposed interpretation is based on two notions: *conditionals* and *explanations*. Whereas non-monotonic logics view a default like "if p then normally q" as a soft reason to believe q given the truth of p, we view it as a hard but context-dependent assertion that q is true (or highly probable) in the context determined by p and possibly some background knowledge. We also introduce a distinction between causal and evidential relations and replace the idea of minimizing default violations underlying non-monotonic logics by the idea of minimizing *unexplained* default violations. We test the resulting interpretation of defaults on several domains of interest in AI, including theories for reasoning about change, inheritance hierarchies, logic programs, and abductive reasoning, and sketch an implementation based on the ideas of *argument systems*.

Acknowledgments

This monograph is a revised version of the doctoral dissertation that I completed at UCLA in November 1989. I want to thank first my uncle Jacobo Sclarsky, who started all this. He got me interested in science before I ever went to school and has been my best teacher ever since. I also want to thank my parents and my Bobe, for their love, their example and their dedication.

For my years at UCLA, I owe the most to Judea Pearl, my thesis advisor. Everything I know about doing research, I learned from Judea. His intuitions, his methods and his work couldn't have a stronger influence on me. He is also responsible for making probability theory into a powerful conceptual framework from which the main ideas of this work are drawn. Judea also provided valuable comments on an earlier draft and suggested significant improvements. I am also grateful to the other members of my dissertation committee: Michael Dyer, Kit Fine, Keith Holyoak and Stott Parker. Kit Fine was especially generous with his time, providing many insightful comments. I also thank Gina George, Verra Morgan, Rosemarie Murphy, Doris Sublette and Judy Williams from the CSD staff, for bearing with me during all my years at UCLA, and the many friends my wife and I met there, for their warm companionship (at the risk of missing someone, I want to mention Leon Alkalaj, Olga Barrios, Bonnie Chiu, Rina Dechter, Bill Dolan, Danny Geiger, Miquel Huguet, Jaime Moreno, Dorab Patel, TM Ravi, Frank Schaffa, and Tom Verma).

Many other people provided useful comments, encouragement or both. I want to thank specially Matt Ginsberg, Ramiro Guerreiro, Ronald Loui, Don Nute, Alberto Torres, and my friends — too numerous to mention — at the Universidad Simón Bolívar in Caracas. Ramiro and Alberto, in particular, carefully read some chapters, discovering bugs and suggesting improvements.

Since my graduation in November 1989, I have been in the Knowledge Representation group at the IBM Thomas J. Watson Research Center, benefiting from the company of Leora Morgenstern, Benjamin Grosof, Wlodek Zadrozny, and Francisco Corella. At IBM I also had the opportunity to delve further into some of the issues raised in my dissertation and to work out this revised version.

If I have kept my sanity after all these years, it is only because of my wife, Maria Eugenia Fuenmayor. She has been a constant source of support and inspiration. To her, to Ivan and to my family in Argentina who kept asking me "How come you haven't finished yet?" my deepest thanks of all.

El libro esta dedicado a la memoria de mi madre, Sara Sclarsky, y de mis amigos Judith Goldberg, Mario Geffner y Ruben Gerenschtein.

Default Reasoning

- And where is the bellybutton?
- He doesn't have a bellybutton, Gille; because he hatched from an egg.

- And then his wings?
- He doesn't have wings either.
- How come. Didn't he hatch from an egg?

Yes, right, but not everything that hatches from an egg has wings. Lots of things come from eggs, like fish and spiders, and snakes, and birds, and ants, and frogs, and who knows what else.

Gee, eggs are really mixed up!

1 Introduction

1.1 Overview

The comic strip on the opposite page illustrates two pervasive aspects of commonsense inference: the elaboration of predictions in the absence of complete information and the ability to revise and explain predictions found to be wrong. Both aspects are so entrenched in common discourse that normally we forget that most of our actions are adopted on the basis of partial information and tentative beliefs. We get up in the morning and expect to find the coffee machine in the same place, the newspaper under the door, and the car in the garage. Yet not always is the coffee machine in the same place, the newspaper under the door, and the car in the garage. Still, these predictions are usually true and permit us to make plans that work most of the time. When they are not true, we adopt new beliefs and plans, and discard the old predictions.

Ubiquitous as these forms of reasoning are, they have resisted a satisfactory explanation. Why are both expectations "animal hatched from eggs have wings" and "reptiles have no wings" right, even though reptiles do hatch from eggs? Clearly, there is a high proportion of winged animals among those that hatch from eggs, yet a low proportion among reptiles. Still, the explanation of such expectations in terms of probabilities is not completely satisfying. These expectations rather appear to rely on *qualitative default rules* that express what is normally the case without ruling out the possibility of exceptions: turtles which are hatched from eggs but do not have wings, pterodactyls which are reptiles but do have wings, and so on.

In Artificial Intelligence (AI), it has been natural to express commonsense knowledge in terms of defaults. Inheritance hierarchies, for instance, encode the prototypical properties of classes by means of defaults. In reasoning about change, defaults encode the tendency of properties to remain invariant in the absence of relevant changes. In diagnostic reasoning, defaults encode the absence of pathological behavior, whose presence must be explained by postulating appropriate hypotheses. Even deductive databases usually embed default assumptions to fill in information not in the database.

However, attempts to represent and reason with defaults in AI have encountered the problem of spurious arguments: arguments which rely on acceptable defaults but which support unacceptable conclusions. For instance, the argument that penguins fly, on the grounds that penguins are birds and birds normally fly, is not acceptable. Still, the same argument is acceptable about canaries. Therefore, if defaults are to be represented and reason with, criteria for distinguishing 'good' default arguments from 'bad' ones are needed.

Classical logic appears to be the most suitable language for formulating these criteria. Precise and clear, a logical account of default inference will make explicit the features that distinguish good default arguments from bad ones, independently of domains and implementations. Logic itself was developed to describe sound argumentation. However, while logic is concerned with arguments that yield true conclusions form true premises, default reasoning is concerned with arguments that yield likely conclusions from likely premises.

In AI, the first attempts to provide a logical account of default reasoning had to face the problem of *non-monotonicity*. Default reasoning is *non-monotonic* in the sense that default predictions often need to be revised in the light of new information. For example, if I turn the ignition key, I expect the car will start. Yet, if before turning the key I notice that the lights don't work, I'll certainly be less sure. In default reasoning, thus, more information might mean less conclusions. *Deductive reasoning,* on the other hand, is *monotonic:* a valid deductive argument remains so no matter what else is learned.

Accommodating non-monotonic forms of inference in a logical framework presents a number of mathematical difficulties. The so-called non-monotonic logics have addressed these difficulties by extending classical logic with devices and constructs that allow new premises to invalidate old theorems. These formalisms, for example, can support the conclusion that somebody must be at home when the lights are on, switch to the opposite conclusion when nobody answers the bell, and switch once again to the original conclusion when voices are heard through the window; all without incurring an inconsistency.

In addition to mathematical difficulties, default reasoning presents also the epistemological problem of accounting for how defaults are used in common discourse. As we have seen before, this involves distinguishing 'good' default arguments from 'bad' ones. An example of a bad argument is the argument that penguins fly on the grounds that penguins are birds and birds fly. This argument is bad because information about penguins must take precedence over information about the more general class of birds. However, other classes of bad default arguments are possible. For instance, in reasoning in the so-called blocks world, we may want to conclude that if a block A is on a table at time t_1, then it is likely to remain on the table until time t_2. Yet, if the block, say, is blue, and we are told that, *by default*, all blue blocks were moved between times t_1 and t_2, we do not want the initial prediction that A would remain on the table to count as evidence against A being moved; we expect the second default to override the first.

The non-monotonic logics developed in AI address the mathematical difficulties that arise in default reasoning but not the epistemological ones. In particular, they do not tell us which defaults arguments are 'good' or 'bad', but leave that up to the user, who must indicate how defaults are supposed to interact by means of priorities, exceptional conditions and so on. For instance, in the first example above, a user may be expected to say, in one way or the other, that the default 'birds fly' is not applicable to penguins. A similar caveat would have to be made explicit in the second example.

This 'linguistic' approach for representing and reasoning with defaults, however, is not fully general. As the knowledge base grows, anticipating how defaults are supposed to interact becomes increasingly difficult, and expressing those interactions in terms of the devices offered by the underlying logic is no longer trivial. A more promising approach would be to study those interactions and build an interpretation of defaults which automatically accounts for them. For that, however, we need to go beyond the non-monotonicity of defaults, focus closer on what defaults say about the world, and figure out why and when certain defaults are preferred to others.

This work is an attempt in this direction. The aim is to build an interpretation which accounts for the way defaults are used in common discourse, uncovering default preferences and distinguishing 'good' default arguments from 'bad' ones.

The interpretation we will develop is built around two notions which we have found essential for understanding defaults. The first is the notion of *conditionals*. Conditionals are expressed in English by the form 'if A then B', and are understood as context-dependent assertions; namely, that B is true in a scenario defined by A and some relevant context.[1] Conditionals with false antecedents, such as: "if I were not writing these lines I would be watching Crimes and Misdemeanors," are called *counterfactuals*. While counterfactuals are bound to be trivially true in classical logic, they may be false when analyzed conditionally. In such a case, the truth of the counterfactual results from evaluating the truth of its consequent in a context which is as 'close' as possible to the current one, but in which the counterfactual antecedent is true.[2]

Here we will adopt a *conditional interpretation of defaults:* a default 'if A then B' will be understood as asserting that B is true in the context that results from the assimilation of A in a given *background context*. For a example, if "birds fly" is a default, we will be allowed to jump to the conclusion that a particular bird flies, if that is all the factual information available, *even if other defaults suggest otherwise.* As we will show, this view will have a definite impact on the type of default behavior which is legitimized; a behavior which will be made precise by appealing to probability theory and logic.

The second thread in the proposed interpretation of defaults is the notion of *explanation*. Defaults encode expectations, and violations of defaults represent expectation failures. The task of default reasoning is normally associated with the minimization of expectation failures. This is most explicit in McCarthy's [McC86] account of defaults, where default violations are encoded by means of "abnormality" predicates whose extensions are assumed minimal. Here we will take a slightly different approach. Rather than treating all expectation failures in the same way, we will distinguish between those which are *explained* from those which are *not explained.* The task of default inference will then be associated with the minimization of *unexplained* expectation failures. In terms of McCarthy's abnormality formulation, this amounts to considering the "abnormality" of scenarios as opposed to the "abnormality" of individuals. So, for instance, no penalty will be associated with a scenario involving a *dead* non-flying bird, say Tim, because even though Tim might be an abnormal bird, he is certainly not an abnormal *dead* bird, and that is what we claim matters.

The notions of *conditionals* and *explanations* will be at the center of the interpretation of defaults that we will develop in this thesis. We aim

[1] See [Nut84] for a survey on conditional logics.

[2] There are a number of well-known problems in determining this 'closeness' relation; see [Goo55].

to show that the proposed interpretation provides a reasonable account for how defaults are used in common discourse, and by freeing the user from having to explicate how defaults are supposed to interact, that it renders a more suitable framework for representing and reasoning with defaults.

1.2 Representing Knowledge

Programs capable of reasoning about the world must embed large amounts of knowledge. Knowledge, however, can be embedded in programs in many ways. At one extreme, knowledge can be embedded in procedures, as in operating systems and communication programs. At the other extreme, knowledge can be encoded in declarative chunks with no commitment at all about its potential uses, like in logics of various types. The first choice leads to programs that are more efficient, but which are also less flexible (the goals are fixed) and extensible (it is difficult to add new knowledge); the second choice leads to programs that are less efficient (they must 'think' about what to do next), but which are more flexible and incremental.

In AI, unlike in most of computer science, *declarative* representations of knowledge have been favored. AI programs normally contain a set of expressions, called the *knowledge base*, and a general purpose interpreter, called the *inference engine*, which assembles the expressions in the knowledge base according to the goals at hand. This organization of programs originated from the desire to make AI programs extensible and the need to deal with ill-understood problems for which conventional top-down software techniques were not adequate [McC87, Doy85].

The behavior of programs which are organized in this fashion is a function of both the *content* of the knowledge-base and the way the knowledge-base is *interpreted.* According to the way each of these two aspects have been addressed, two clearly different approaches in AI can be distinguished.

The so-called "scruffy" approach, best represented by Schank's school, emphasizes the organization of the knowledge base for simulating how people process high-level information (see, for instance, [SA77]). Given a particular task, certain knowledge structures are postulated, and an interpreter is designed which handles these structures in an intuitively satisfying way. Programs in this tradition have illustrated the psychological appeal and the computational importance of the organization of knowledge in memory (e.g., [Dye83, Kol84]).

Proponents of the "neat" approach, on the other hand, have argued that interpreters tailored to particular tasks are likely to lack the flexibility needed to endow programs with commonsense [McC68]. They say that the range of reasoning patterns should not be wired a priori by a 'knowledge engineer,' but rather that it should be implicit in the correspondence between the expressions in the knowledge base and the world being represented. Work along the "neat" track has thus proceeded with the development of *formal languages* in which fragments of world knowledge can be encoded, and *formal semantics* in which the meaning of such encodings can be made precise. The interpreter is to derive new expressions from old ones in ways compatible which such meanings. For its precision and clarity, classical logic has constituted the language of choice, often extended to accommodate temporal and epistemic notions, and non-monotonicity (see [Moo85a, Lev87]; [McD82, All84]; [McC80, MD80, Rei80]).

A limitation of the "neat" approach is that the different logical formulations do not determine what is *useful* for the interpreter to do, but only what is *valid*. What is valid, however, may be often useless, and sometimes what is useful may be invalid. Even determining validity may be out of the question at times [LB87]. Therefore, it is reasonable to believe that programs capable of displaying commonsense will require both semantic and architectural considerations to be taken into account.

In this work we tackle the problem of default reasoning using a 'neat' methodology but motivated by 'scruffy' goals. The goal is an architecture for default reasoning which computes the 'right' conclusions in the 'right' manner. For that, we will use formal methods: we will define a semantics that characterizes which default inferences are 'valid', and obtain the architecture by imposing restrictions on what we want to be able to express and what we want to be able to infer. The role of the semantics will be to distinguish good default arguments from bad ones, making it intelligible why an argument belongs to one or the other class. The role of the architecture will be to capture most inferences of interest in a reasonable fashion. For the architecture to be useful, though, it does not have to be complete or even sound; what we will demand is that its approximations be understandable in terms of the semantic framework.

1.3 A Reader's Guide

In the standard non-monotonic logics, defaults are regarded rules for *extending* a set of beliefs in the absence of conflicting evidence. This view is enforced by means of *consistency* notions in logics which are defined proof-theoretically, and by means of *minimality* notions in logics which are defined model-theoretically. In the reminder of this chapter we review some of these logics and the systems (databases, truth maintenance systems, logic programs, etc.) from which they draw their main intuitions.

There is however more to default reasoning than non-monotonicity, and more to defaults than the 'extensional' view. In Chapter 2 we show that it is possible to build an alternative interpretation of defaults by regarding defaults of the form "normally, if p then q" as licenses to assume the conditional probability of q given p to be arbitrarily high, short of being one. Such an interpretation, called *ϵ-semantics,* leads to a qualitative set of inference rules called the *core*, which has virtues and limitations that are practically orthogonal to those of the standard non-monotonic logics. In particular, as a result of the context-sensitivity of conditional probabilities, the core resolves arguments of different 'specificity' (e.g., "penguins don't fly in spite of being birds"), but fails to account for arguments involving "irrelevance" assumptions (e.g., concluding "*red*-birds fly" from "birds fly"). Arguments involving irrelevance assumptions are later accounted by extending the core with an additional rule of inference, called the *irrelevance* rule, whose purpose is to derive sensible assumptions about conditional independence. We show that the core augmented with the irrelevance rule combines the advantages of the probabilistic and the extensional interpretations of defaults, and illustrate the resulting behavior with several examples.

Chapter 3 focuses on a non-probabilistic semantics of defaults. The semantics is structured around the notion of preferential entailment advanced by Shoham [Sho88], and further developed by Kraus *et al.*, Makinson, and Lehmann and Magidor [KLM90, Mak89, LM88]. The idea is to interpret defaults as constraints on preference relations on models, and to identify the valid predictions of a theory as those that hold in its preferred models. A default $p \rightarrow q$, for example, asserts that q is true in the preferred models of p. We show that that the resulting semantics is equivalent to the probabilistic semantics developed in Chapter 2 and that both semantics are correctly and completely captured by the five inference rules in the core.

The goal of Chapter 4 is the development of an extended interpretation to validate both the core and the *irrelevance rule.* This is accomplished within the framework of preferential entailment, except that now preferences on models are determined by means of *priorities* on defaults. The resulting semantics, called *conditional entailment*, has many elements in common with McCarthy's prioritized circumscription [McC86], except that priorities do not need to be given by the user but are automatically extracted from the knowledge base. A proof-theory for conditional entailment is also developed which, unlike the core, is both sound and complete. The proof-theory has the form of an argument system (e.g., [Pol87, Lou87a]), in which arguments for and against propositions compete, and 'strongest' arguments win. An implementation of this argument system based on an assumption-based truth-maintenance system [dK86] is also sketched.

Conditional entailment integrates the *conditional* interpretation of defaults based on probabilities and preferential structures, with the *extensional* interpretations based on the standard non-monotonic logics. Still, examples can be constructed — the most notorious being the "Yale shooting problem" [HM87] — in which conditional entailment fails to deliver the intuitive results. In Chapter 5 we argue that what is still missing is an account of the *causal* aspects of defaults.

The causal aspects of defaults are addressed by extending the language of default theories with a *causal operator* 'C' which is used for distinguishing explanatory from non-explanatory relations. For example, to assert that a cold *explains* fever, we will write `cold` $\Rightarrow$ `Cfever`, while to assert that high temperature is an *indication* of fever, we will write `high_temp` $\Rightarrow$ `fever`. Thus, while `high_temp` will make `fever` true, only `cold` will *explain* `fever`.

The distinction between propositions which are *true* and propositions which are *explained* is essential for *abductive reasoning* in which the aim is to *explain* a body of observations and not simply to make them true. The same distinction, we argue, is crucial in the context of *default reasoning.* We appeal to this distinction to define a new preference relation on classes of models in which roughly only the most *coherent* classes of models are preferred. The resulting framework provides a language for encoding defeasible knowledge in a natural way, a semantics which sanctions the intended conclusions, and procedures which compute these conclusions in a reasonable way.

In Chapter 6 we consider applications in the areas of general logic programs, inheritance hierarchies, reasoning about change, and abduction. Finally, in Chapter 7, we summarize the main contributions and discuss some open problems.

1.4 Non-Monotonic Systems

In this section we will review some systems and tasks which involve forms of reasoning which can be regarded as non-monotonic. These systems, while not always based on clear logical foundations, are sufficiently simple and well-understood as to provide a flavor of the type of inferences that we want to capture. We consider databases, inheritance hierarchies, general logic programs, truth-maintenance systems, and time map management systems.

Databases

Databases are systems designed for the efficient storage and retrieval of information about objects and their relations. A departmental database, for example, may contain a relation `teach` with two tuples $\langle \texttt{grey}, \texttt{c} \rangle$ and $\langle \texttt{kay}, \texttt{lisp} \rangle$, indicating that Prof. Gray teaches C and Prof. Kay, Lisp. Relations and tuples are understood as encoding ground atoms in classical first order logic; in this case, $\texttt{teach}(\texttt{grey}, \texttt{c})$ and $\texttt{teach}(\texttt{kay}, \texttt{lisp})$. Thus, if queried about who teaches `c` or `pascal`, the answer `grey` can to be understood from the fact that $\texttt{teach}(\texttt{grey}, \texttt{c}) \vee \texttt{teach}(\texttt{grey}, \texttt{pascal})$ logically follows from those atoms.

The logic of databases, however, involves more than atoms. For example, answers like "`kay` does not teach `c`" and "only `grey` teaches `c`", are not logical consequences of the database. To account for such answers, the logical encoding of the database must be augmented with certain assumptions about the names of the objects and the world that the database is supposed to represent. These are the *unique names assumption*, by which individuals with distinct names are assumed distinct, the *domain closure assumption*, by which all individuals are assumed named, and the *closed world assumption*, by which all instances of a relation are assumed to be deducible from the database [Rei84].

For the database above, the unique names, domain closure and closed world assumptions amount to extending the database with the formulas:[3]

$$\texttt{grey} \neq \texttt{kay}\,,\ \texttt{c} \neq \texttt{lisp}\,,\ \texttt{grey} \neq \texttt{c}\,,\ \ldots$$
$$\forall x.\ x = \texttt{grey} \vee x = \texttt{kay} \vee x = \texttt{c} \vee x = \texttt{lisp}$$
$$\forall x, y.\, \texttt{teach}(x, y) \Rightarrow (x = \texttt{grey} \wedge y = \texttt{c}) \vee (x = \texttt{kay} \wedge y = \texttt{lisp})$$

Provided with these assumptions, the answers that can be obtained from the database will be theorems of the logical encoding. As assumptions, however, these formulas may turn out to be false. For instance, a second c class taught by kay, may be opened, rendering the above closed world assumption false. In such a case, the database will no longer support the conclusion "kay does not teach c" but rather, its negation.

The logical encoding of the database is not incremental: the addition of new information not only translates in the addition of new formulas but also in the replacement of old ones. This outcome, though, is not surprising: while the behavior of the database changes *non-monotonically*, the behavior of its logical encoding can only change *monotonically*. Yet, if we were able to express a closed world assumption capable of adapting itself to a changing database, we would be able to have a logical encoding supporting non-monotonic behavior. As we will see in Section 1.5 below, that is indeed the intuition behind circumscription.

Inheritance Hierarchies

Databases are designed with efficiency as a main concern. They usually store large amounts of data in a few fixed formats that permit fast storage and retrieval. Semantic networks, on the other hand, focus both on computational and representational issues, providing languages which are more expressive (e.g., [Fah79, Sow84, BS85b]). The central idea of semantic networks is to represent knowledge in terms of directed graphs, with links representing relations among concepts. Here we will be concerned with a restricted form of semantic networks, commonly referred to as inheritance networks, in which the only relation is that of class inclusion [Tou86].

Figure 1.1 depicts a simple inheritance network. The network involves two types of links: positive links ($\rightarrow$), which assert that one class is a

[3]The symbol '$\Rightarrow$' is used to denote material implication.

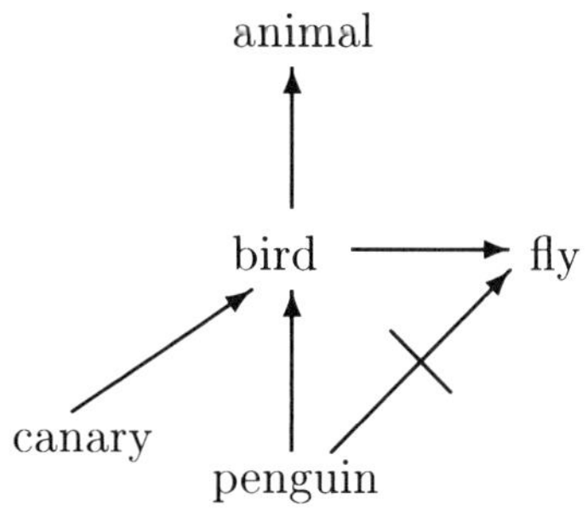

Figure 1.1
Simple inheritance hierarchy

(not necessarily strict) subclass of another (e.g., birds are flying things), and negative links ($\not\rightarrow$) which assert that one class is a (not necessarily strict) subclass of the *complement* of another (e.g., penguins are *not* flying things).

Classes are assumed to *inherit* the properties of their superclasses unless otherwise specified. In the net depicted in Fig. 1.1, for instance, canaries are assumed to inherit the property 'fly' from birds, as 'birds' is a superclass of 'canaries'. Similarly, penguins inherit the property 'animal'. On the other hand, penguins do not inherit the property 'fly' because the link from penguins to the *negation* of 'fly,' being more "specific" than the link from birds to 'fly', *overrides* the inheritance path 'penguin $\rightarrow$ bird $\rightarrow$ fly'.[4]

Inheritance reasoning is also non-monotonic: a bird is assumed to fly, although a penguin, which is also a bird, is not; more information thus may result in the retraction of conclusions. Compared to databases, inheritance hierarchies point to another aspect of non-monotonic reasoning that an adequate account of default reasoning must accommodate; in this case, the preference for more "specific" defaults over more "general" ones.

[4]The problem of determining "specificity" conditions in more general networks has been a subject of some debate. See [Tou86], [HTT87], and [GV89] among others.

Logic Programs

Logic programs are collections of rules of the form $A \leftarrow L_1, L_2, \ldots, L_n$, where A is an atom and each L_i, $i = 1, \ldots, n$, $n \geq 0$, is a positive or negative literal. Unlike common programming language constructs, the rules in a logic program accept both a procedural and a declarative reading. When all literals are positive, a rule $A \leftarrow L_1, L_2, \ldots, L_n$ can be understood both as stating that the goal A is *derivable* when each of the subgoals L_i, $i = 1, \ldots, n$, is *derivable*, and that A is *true* when each of the literals L_i, $i = 1, \ldots, n$ is *true* [Kow79].

When some of the literals L_i are negative, however, things are not so simple and the declarative reading of logic programs is usually dropped. The resulting programs are commonly understood in procedural terms, with the proviso that negative literals $\neg A_i$ are assumed to be derivable when every derivation for the atom A_i fails (see [Rou75, Cla78]). This form of negation, called *negation as failure,* has turned out to be particularly useful in programming [Hew72]. Since a derivation that fails in a given context may succeed when more information becomes available, negation as failure also produces a behavior that is *non-monotonic*. In a program containing a single rule $\mathtt{p} \leftarrow \neg\mathtt{q}$, for example, negation as failure yields $\mathtt{p}$, but when the rule $\mathtt{q} \leftarrow$ is added, $\mathtt{p}$ follows instead.

While the straightforward declarative reading of logic programs does not legitimize the behavior of negation as failure, more adequate logical accounts have recently been developed. We will consider some of these accounts in Chapter 6, when we analyze the relation between logic programs and a class of 'causal' default theories.

Truth Maintenance Systems

Truth maintenance systems (TMSs) are systems which keep track of dependencies among propositions, often performing some type of inference [Doy79, dK86]. In Doyle's TMS, a user expresses justifications among propositions in a restricted propositional language and the TMS generates a labeling where each proposition is believed (IN) or not (OUT) according to whether the proposition has a valid justification or not. Each justification is made in turn of two lists of propositions, an IN-list and an OUT-list, and is valid when each proposition in the IN-list and no proposition in the OUT-list has a valid justification. To break circularities, admissible labelings are also required to be *well-founded*, or what amounts to the same, to be *minimal* in the set of believed propositions.

A TMS may contain, for example, the following justifications (syntax is "IN-list | OUT-list → atom"):

$$\begin{array}{lcl} \texttt{J}_1 & : & \texttt{D} \mid \texttt{H} \rightarrow \texttt{W} \\ \texttt{J}_2 & : & \texttt{C} \mid \ \rightarrow \texttt{H} \\ \texttt{J}_3 & : & \rightarrow \texttt{D} \end{array}$$

The justification $\texttt{J}_1$ says that if today is a weekday and it is not believed that John is at home, then John is at work; $\texttt{J}_2$ says that if John's car is in the garage, then John is at home, and $\texttt{J}_3$ says that today is a weekday.

Given these justifications, the TMS will label the atoms D and W as IN and H as OUT. If a new justification → C ("John's car is in the garage") is added, however, H would become IN, defeating the default justification for W and thus forcing W to go OUT.

Although understood in procedural terms for a long time, some declarative accounts of the TMS belief revision process have been recently advanced [Elk88, RDB89]. These accounts reveal that a Doyle's TMS is not very different from a propositional logic program, and that the admissible TMS labelings correspond to the *stable models* of the logic program that results from mapping each TMS justification of the form $p_1, \ldots, p_n \mid q_1, \ldots, q_m \rightarrow p$ into a rule $p \leftarrow p_1, \ldots, p_n, \neg q_1, \ldots, \neg q_m$.[5]

Time Map Management Systems

Time map management systems (TMMs) [DM87] are systems for efficiently reasoning about propositions whose status changes over time. In one of its simplest forms, given a set of propositions which hold at a given time, a TMM infers the propositions that will hold at a later time, after a sequence of events has occurred [DB87]. All such propositions are assumed to persist in the absence of relevant changes, and changes are the result of events whose effects are described by means of causal rules. A causal rule may indicate, for example, that after checking a book out of the library, the book is no longer at the library; another one may say that if the borrower has checked a book at a some time t and has not returned it for a certain period of time T, s/he will get a fine at time $t+T+\triangle$, and so on.

[5]For the stable semantics of logic programs, see [GL88]. We will say more about stable models and TMSs in Section 6.1.

In the simple case described, the task of the TMM is straightforward (see also [HM85]). The algorithm starts at the time for which it has complete information, and moves forward along the time axis looking for causal rules which may be triggered. If found, all such rules are inspected and the status of the temporal database is updated accordingly.

Simple as the example may seem, this projection task is very instructive of what a system of default reasoning must be able to do. We will come back to these issues in Section 6.2 when we will analyze some of the general requirements that an adequate framework for reasoning about change must meet.

1.5 Non-Monotonic Logics

The systems reviewed in the previous section all behave non-monotonically, yet this behavior is the result of well-crafted algorithms which are tailored to specific languages and tasks. Non-monotonic logics were developed with the aim of providing a general framework for studying and defining non-monotonic forms of reasoning. We will review three of the now standard non-monotonic formalisms: Reiter's default logic [Rei80], McCarthy's circumscription [McC80, McC86], and Moore's autoepistemic logic [Moo85b].[6]

Default Logic

Reiter's default logic extends classical first order logic with tentative rules of inference of the form:

$$\frac{\alpha(x) : \beta(x)}{\gamma(x)}$$

where $\alpha(x)$, $\beta(x)$ and $\gamma(x)$ are formulas with free variables among those of $x = \{x_1, x_2, \ldots\}$, called the precondition, the test condition and the consequent of the default, respectively. For a tuple a of ground terms, such a rule permits one to derive $\gamma(a)$ from $\alpha(a)$, *provided that* $\neg\beta(a)$ *is not derivable.* For instance, a default

$$\frac{\texttt{bird}(x) : \texttt{flies}(x)}{\texttt{flies}(x)}$$

[6]For more detailed surveys on non-monotonic reasoning, see [Gin87], and [Rei87a]. [McD87] reviews some of these issues within the broader context of logic in AI.

yields the conclusion flies(Tim) from bird(Tim). However, if the negation of flies(Tim) is observed, the default gets blocked and flies(Tim) is no longer supported.

The appeal to non-derivability in the body of defaults together with their use to extend the set of derivable sentences leads in certain cases to conflicts among defaults. For instance, given a second default:

$$\frac{\texttt{injured}(x) : \neg\texttt{flies}(x)}{\neg\texttt{flies}(x)}$$

and that Tim is injured, two defaults would be applicable. However, if the first default is applied, the second one becomes blocked, and if the second default is applied, the first one becomes blocked. Reiter deals with these situations by introducing the notion of *extensions* of a default theory $T = \langle W, D \rangle$, where W is a set of well-formed formulas (wffs) and D a set of defaults. In this case, there would be two extensions, one which corresponds to the application of the first default, and one which corresponds to the application of the second default.

Formally, if we say that $\Gamma(S)$ *expands* a set of wffs S according to T when $\Gamma(S)$ denotes the minimal deductively closed set of wffs which includes W and every consequent γ of defaults $\alpha : \beta / \gamma$ in D for which $\alpha \in \Gamma(S)$ and $\beta \notin S$, then an *extension* of T is a collection E of wffs that expands into itself, i.e., E is an extension if $E = \Gamma(E)$.

A default theory $T = \langle W, D \rangle$ may give rise to one, none, or many extensions, and each one is supposed to reflect a possible 'completion' of the classical theory W according to the defaults in D. In the example above, two different extensions arise, one in which Tim flies and another in which he does not.

Reiter's default logic extends classical first order logic with non-monotonic features by means of a simple and yet flexible formal device. Such an extension is sufficient to account for the forms of inference that arise in databases, and, if carefully encoded, other forms of reasoning as well (see [ER83] and [BF87], for encoding inheritance reasoning and logic programs, respectively). As a framework for representing and reasoning with defaults, however, default logic is too weak. The natural encoding of a body of knowledge in the form of a default theory often gives rise to unreasonable extensions, which the user must prune by properly selecting the test conditions of the defaults [RC83]. In this regard, Reiter's logic is more a precise language for specifying non-monotonic behavior than an interpretation for uncovering the meaning of databases containing defaults. Yet, it is such an interpretation, what we are looking for.

Circumscription

Circumscription is a formal device, which, added to a first order theory, asserts that the objects that satisfy a predicate P are exactly the objects which can be *shown* to satisfy P [McC80, McC86, Lif88a]. For instance, from a database which only includes the fact $\mathtt{Q(a)}$, the circumscription of $\mathtt{Q}$ yields the formula $\forall \mathtt{x}.\, \mathtt{Q(x)} \Rightarrow \mathtt{x} = \mathtt{a}$, which says that $\mathtt{a}$ is the only object that satisfies $\mathtt{Q}$. Thus, if $\mathtt{b}$ is an object different from $\mathtt{a}$, the circumscription of $\mathtt{Q}$ will permit us to jump to the conclusion $\neg\mathtt{Q(b)}$. If $\mathtt{Q(b)}$ is learned, however, the previous conclusion would no longer hold, and the new conclusions would correspond to those derivable from the formula $\forall \mathtt{x}.\, \mathtt{Q(x)} \Leftrightarrow \mathtt{x} = \mathtt{a} \vee \mathtt{x} = \mathtt{b}$. Circumscription thus behaves as an 'adaptable' closed world assumption, capable of dealing with theories richer than those expressible in databases.

Formally, if we let A(P) stand for a first order sentence containing the predicate P, and let A(Φ) denote the sentence that results from replacing all the occurrences of P by a predicate Φ with the same arity as P, the circumscription Circ[A(P); P] of P in A(P) can be expressed as the second order schema [McCarthy, 80]:

$$\mathrm{A(P)} \wedge \mathrm{A}(\Phi) \wedge \forall \mathbf{x}.\, [\Phi(\mathbf{x}) \Rightarrow \mathrm{P}(\mathbf{x})] \Rightarrow \forall \mathbf{x}.\, (\mathrm{P}(\mathbf{x}) \Rightarrow \Phi(\mathbf{x}))$$

The schema can be understood as stating that among the predicates Φ that satisfy the constraints in A(Φ), P is the strongest.

In order to see how circumscription works, consider the sentence $\mathrm{A}(\mathtt{Q})$: $\mathtt{Q(a)}$, and let us substitute the predicate $\Phi(\mathbf{x})$ by $\mathbf{x} = \mathtt{a}$. Such substitution yields the closed first order formula:

$$\mathtt{Q(a)} \wedge \mathtt{a} = \mathtt{a} \wedge \forall x.\, [x = \mathtt{a} \Rightarrow \mathtt{Q}(x)] \Rightarrow \forall x.\ \mathtt{Q}(x) \Rightarrow x = \mathtt{a},$$

which simplifies to:

$$\mathtt{Q(a)} \wedge [\forall x.\, \mathtt{Q}(x) \Rightarrow x = \mathtt{a}]$$

from which a minimal definition of $\mathtt{Q}$ follows:

$$\forall x.\mathtt{Q}(x) \Leftrightarrow x = \mathtt{a}$$

The predicate $\Phi^*(x) \stackrel{\text{def}}{=} x = \mathtt{a}$ is indeed the strongest predicate which satisfies $\mathrm{A}(\Phi)$, and thus, the effect of circumscribing $\mathtt{Q}$ in $\mathrm{A}(\mathtt{Q})$ is to set $\mathtt{Q}$ to Φ^*.

Circumscription can be understood from a model-theoretic perspective as well. In classical logic, a sentence s is said to be entailed by a sentence A(P) if s holds in every model of A(P). Circumscription weakens this condition: a proposition s is entailed by Circ[A(P); P] if s holds in every model of A(P) which is *minimal* in P [McC80, Lif85]. A model M is minimal in P when there is no other model which assigns a strictly smaller extension to P and which preserves from M the same domain and the same interpretation of symbols other than P.

Notice how circumscription produces non-monotonic behavior: given a set of axioms, circumscription picks up a minimal interpretation for some predicate(s) *subject to the constraints imposed by the axioms.* As the base of axioms changes, so does the minimal interpretation circumscription selects, and thus, the inferential import of the circumscriptive schema.

For instance, given $\mathrm{A}(\mathtt{Q}) : \mathtt{Q}(\mathtt{a})$, the circumscriptive schema reduces to the formula $\forall x. \mathtt{Q}(x) \Leftrightarrow x = \mathtt{a}$. Similarly, for $\mathrm{A}(\mathtt{Q}) = \mathtt{Q}(\mathtt{a}) \wedge \mathtt{Q}(\mathtt{b})$, the circumscriptive schema reduces to $\forall x. \mathtt{Q}(x) \Leftrightarrow x = \mathtt{a} \vee x = \mathtt{b}$. In either case, provided that $\mathtt{c}$ is different from $\mathtt{a}$ and $\mathtt{b}$, $\neg\mathtt{Q}(\mathtt{c})$ can be inferred. On the other hand, if $\mathtt{b}$ is different from $\mathtt{a}$, $\neg\mathtt{Q}(\mathtt{b})$ follows in the first case, but not in the second.

This way of 'jumping to conclusions' stands in contrast with the way Reiter's default logic achieves the same effect. In default logic, the situation above would be represented by means of a default:

$$\frac{: \neg\mathtt{Q}(x)}{\neg\mathtt{Q}(x)}$$

which, given $\mathtt{Q}(\mathtt{a})$, will permit us to jump to $\neg\mathtt{Q}(\mathtt{c})$ directly, independent of whether, say, $\mathtt{Q}(\mathtt{b})$ holds or not. On the other hand, while Reiter's default logic permits inferring $\neg\mathtt{Q}(t)$, for *each* term t, $t \neq \mathtt{a}$, it does not authorize the conclusion allowed in circumscription that $\mathtt{Q}$ does not hold for *all* individuals different from $\mathtt{a}$, i.e., $\forall x. x \neq \mathtt{a} \Rightarrow \neg\mathtt{Q}(x)$.

Circumscription adds non-monotonic features to first order logic, but does not uniquely specify how defeasible knowledge should be encoded. For that purpose, McCarthy introduced a convention by which defaults like "birds fly" are encoded in circumscription as formulas

$$\forall x.\texttt{bird}(x) \land \neg\texttt{ab}_\texttt{i}(x) \Rightarrow \texttt{flies}(x)$$

read as "every *non-abnormal* bird flies" [McC86]. Once defaults are so expressed, the expected behavior follows from circumscribing the predicates $\texttt{ab}_\texttt{i}$, or as McCarthy says, from "minimizing abnormality." Nevertheless, before this can be done effectively, a more powerful form of circumscription is needed.

To illustrate this need, consider the default above, and a bird called Tim. We would expect the circumscription of $\texttt{ab}_\texttt{i}$ to yield $\neg\texttt{ab}_\texttt{i}(\texttt{Tim})$ and therefore, flies(Tim). However, circumscription as presented so far, does not yield such a conclusion. To show that, consider a model M in which $\neg$flies(Tim) holds and Tim is the only abnormal individual. If M is not a minimal model in $\texttt{ab}_\texttt{i}$, there must be a model M' which assigns a smaller extension to the predicate $\texttt{ab}_\texttt{i}$, and which preserves the same interpretation for all other symbols. This however amounts to requiring that M' satisfy the rules about birds together with the literals bird(Tim), $\neg$flies(Tim), $\neg\texttt{ab}_\texttt{i}(\texttt{Tim})$, which is not possible. Thus, M is a minimal model, and therefore the soundness of circumscription guarantees that the sentence flies(Tim) will not be sanctioned.

What is needed in such cases is a form of circumscription in which certain predicates can be minimized *at the expense* of others. The form of circumscription proposed in [McC86] permits precisely that. The circumscription Circ[A(P, Z); P, **Z**] of the predicate P in the sentence A(P, **Z**), where **Z** stands for a tuple of predicates allowed to vary in the minimization of P, is defined by the second order formula:

$$\mathrm{A}(\mathrm{P}, \mathbf{Z}) \land \forall \Phi, \mathbf{\Psi}\ \mathrm{A}(\Phi, \mathbf{\Psi})\ \land \forall \mathbf{x}.\,[\Phi(\mathbf{x}) \Rightarrow \mathrm{P}(\mathbf{x})] \Rightarrow \forall \mathbf{x}.\,[\mathrm{P}(\mathbf{x}) \Rightarrow \Phi(\mathbf{x})]$$

This formula is stronger than the previous schema, permitting not only substitutions in place of P, but also in place of the predicates in **Z**.

The expected conclusion flies(Tim) in the example above follows by circumscribing the predicate $\texttt{ab}_\texttt{i}$, allowing the predicate flies to vary . To see that, it suffices to substitute $\Phi(x)$ by $x \neq x$, and $\mathbf{\Psi}(x)$ by $x = x$.

This extended form of circumscription also accepts an appealing model theoretic interpretation. The circumscriptive schema Circ[A(P, **Z**); P, **Z**] sanctions as theorems the sentences that hold in all models of the sentence A(P, **Z**) which are *minimal in* P *with respect to* **Z** [Lif85, Eth88]. A model M of A(P, **Z**) is minimal in P with respect to **Z**, if there are no other models M' of A(P, **Z**) which assign a smaller extension to P, and which preserve from M the same domain and the same interpretation of symbols other than P and **Z**.

While the discussion above focused on the circumscription of a single predicate, the generalization to many predicates, known as *parallel circumscription,* is straightforward. More interesting is the case of *prioritized circumscription*, in which the user is allowed to specify a priority ordering among the circumscribed predicates [McC86, Lif85, Lif88a]. For instance, the circumscription Circ[A; $P_1 > P_2 > \ldots > P_n$;Z] of predicates P_1,P_2, ..., P_n in decreasing order of priority, translates into $n-1$ circumscriptions of the form Circ[A; P_i;$\mathbf{Z} \cup \{P_{i+1}, \ldots, P_n\}$] together with Circ[A; P_n;**Z**]. That is, predicates with higher priority are circumscribed at the expense of predicates with lower priority. Although there are no general guidelines for selecting the priorities among the predicates, some selection guidelines for specific domains have been advanced (see [Lif88b] and [KKW89] for the domains of logic programs and inheritance hierarchies, respectively).

Circumscription has found wide appeal due to its power and mathematical tractability. As a framework for reasoning with defaults, however, circumscription shares the limitation of default logic: the distinction between good and bad default arguments is left to the user who remains responsible for explicating the relevant preferences. Moreover, the treatment of equality and universals is often less appealing in circumscription than in default logic. For instance, circumscription will legitimize counterintuitive conclusions, such as "all birds fly" given a default "birds fly," which are not allowed by default logic. Similarly, if Tim is a bird who does not fly, circumscription, unlike default logic, will not jump to the expected conclusion that Tweety flies, unless Tim and Tweety are known to be different individuals.[7] On the other hand, circumscription provides devices such as priorities, which are very convenient for expressing preferences among defaults. We will analyze the role of priorities in default reasoning in Chapter 4.

Autoepistemic Logic

Autoepistemic logic is a non-monotonic extension of classical logic, originally proposed by Moore [Moo85b] as a reconstruction of McDermott's

[7]Both problems could be solved if rather than minimizing the *extension* of circumscribed predicates P, we would minimize the set of atoms $P(a)$, for all tuples a of ground terms in the language. See the discussion in Section 4.9.

and Doyle's [MD80] non-monotonic logic. Since then, autoepistemic logic has received growing attention and has been studied by Marek, Konolige, and Gelfond among others [Mar86, Kon88, Gel89a].

Autoepistemic logic deals with *autoepistemic theories:* propositional theories[8] augmented by a belief operator L, where sentences of the form Lα are read as "α is believed". The *stable expansions* of an autoepistemic theory T are defined as the sets of formulas $S(T)$ which satisfy the equation

$$S(T) = \mathrm{Th}(T + \{\mathrm{L}p : p \in S(T)\} + \{\neg\mathrm{L}p : p \notin S(T)\})$$

where Th(X) stands for the set of tautological consequence of X. Stable expansions are supposed to reflect possible states of belief of an ideal rational agent, closed both under positive and negative introspection [Moo85b].

The default 'if it is a bird, it flies', which in McCarthy's 'abnormality' formulation would be encoded as a sentence $\mathtt{bird} \wedge \neg\mathtt{ab_i} \Rightarrow \mathtt{flies}$ with a circumscribed predicate $\mathtt{ab_i}$, can be encoded in autoepistemic logic as a sentence $\mathtt{bird} \wedge \neg\mathrm{L}\mathtt{ab_i} \Rightarrow \mathtt{flies}$. Then, given `bird`, the only autoepistemic expansion will contain the autoepistemic sentence $\neg\mathrm{L}\mathtt{ab_i}$, and therefore, the target sentence `flies`.

An autoepistemic theory may have one, none or many stable expansions. For instance, a theory such as $T = \{\neg\mathrm{L}p \Rightarrow p\}$ has no stable expansions, while a theory such as $T' = \{\neg\mathrm{L}p \Rightarrow q, \neg\mathrm{L}q \Rightarrow p\}$ has two.

Autoepistemic logic regards literals of the form $\neg\mathrm{L}\alpha$ as assumptions, and unless a proof for α can be constructed from other beliefs, those assumptions will appear in every expansion. Under certain circumstances, as in a theory $T = \{\mathrm{L}p \Rightarrow p\}$, literals of the form L$\alpha$ also act as assumptions, although whether they should act in this way has been debated [Kon88].

Autoepistemic logic has been successfully applied to characterize the semantics of general logic programs [Gel87, GL88] and truth maintenance systems [RDB89, Elk88]. Both characterizations are natural and simple, requiring only to replace logic negation by autoepistemic negation; i.e., literals of the form $\neg p$ by literals of the form $\neg\mathrm{L}p$.

Other appealing features of autoepistemic logic follow from its epistemic character: no other non-monotonic logic can distinguish between

[8]See [Kon88] and [Lev87] for first order extensions.

belief on a proposition from lack of belief on its negation.[9] Autoepistemic logic does so, and makes the lack of belief the preferred belief state.

On the negative side, there two kinds of problems with autoepistemic logic as a framework for default reasoning. On the technical side, exceptions often give rise to theories which lack stable expansions. For instance, the autoepistemic encoding $\texttt{bird} \wedge \neg \mathrm{L}\texttt{ab}_{\texttt{i}} \Rightarrow \texttt{flies}$ of a default "if it is a bird, it flies" will lack stable expansions given the exception $\texttt{bird} \wedge \neg \texttt{flies}$.[10] On the conceptual side, autoepistemic logic has some of the shortcomings of default logic and circumscription. In particular, none of these formalisms is able to account for the preference of a default "if p and r then $\neg q$" over a conflicting default "if p then $\neg q$," nor can they detect any inconsistency between two defaults "birds fly" and "birds not fly." Indeed, these formalisms provide no insight in the empirical basis for declaring the first default good and the second one bad.

To account for these aspects of defaults, the notion of defaults needs to be taken more seriously; not merely as rules for extending beliefs, but as declarative constraints over states of affairs. The nature and logic that governs those constraints will then provide us with an interpretation which better reflects the use of defaults in common discourse.

---

[9] Except for approaches such as [San88] and [Gin88], which are based on partial models and multivalued logics respectively.

[10] Some proposals for dealing with such difficulties have been advanced recently. See [Mor89, KM89].

2 Defaults and High Probabilities

2.1 Introduction

Belief commitment and belief revision are two central features of default reasoning: beliefs are adopted in the absence of complete information and are revised when new, conflicting information becomes available. Accounting for both aspects of defaults, however, presents a number of problems. Classical logic, for example, cannot accommodate belief revision; new information can only add new theorems but never remove old ones. Probability theory, on the other hand, while able to revise old beliefs in the light of new evidence, does not accommodate belief commitment: propositions are believed only to a certain degree, never accepted as true for practical purposes.

Recently, there have been efforts to overcome these problems both by proponents of logic and by proponents of probability theory. As we have seen in Chapter 1, those working within the framework of logic have developed 'non-monotonic' extensions of classical logic in which new 'axioms' may defeat old 'theorems'. Likewise, those working within the framework of probabilities have developed 'rules of acceptance' which work on top of a body of probabilistic knowledge to create a body of believed, though defeasible, propositions (see [Lou87b] for a review).

The probabilistic approach has enjoyed a significant advantage over the logical approach. Given a body of probabilistic knowledge there is in general no question about what its consequences are. The issue is rather what constitutes an adequate acceptance rule. Non-monotonic logics have lacked such a clear empirical basis. Not only it has been difficult to account for the conclusions implicit in a body of defaults (e.g. [HM86]), but even more so to identify what these conclusions ought to be (see, for instance, [THT87], "A clash of intuitions ...").

Yet, on the positive side, as noted in [GT84] and [Lou87b], the logical approach has shown that a *qualitative* account of non-monotonic reasoning not requiring 'acceptance rules' or the expense and precision of computing with numbers is possible, and has even suggested ways in which such an account may proceed.

The goal of this chapter is to show that it is possible to combine the best of both worlds. We will develop a system of defeasible inference which operates like a natural deduction system in logic but which can be justified on probabilistic grounds. The system is closely related to a logic of conditionals developed by Adams [Ada66], as defaults $p \rightarrow q$ are interpreted as asserting that the conditional probability of q given p is arbitrarily high, short of one. However, high probabilities are not sufficient for our purposes. In order to account for patterns of inference, like deriving that *red* birds fly, given that birds fly, *assumptions about independence* are also needed. We therefore extend the probabilistic interpretation with a syntactic account of *irrelevance* which captures those assumptions. This notion of irrelevance gives the proposed system the flavor of *argument* systems, in which defeasible reasoning emerges from the interaction of competing arguments (e.g., [Lou87a, Nut88b, Pol87]).

Viewing defaults as statements about conditional probability augmented with independence assumptions has two advantages. The first advantage is pragmatic: given a body of default knowledge, the probabilistic interpretation produces a behavior which is in closer correspondence with intuition. This is important as we want the interpretation to be faithful to the information encoded in the knowledge base. The second advantage is more theoretical: we can appeal to the empirical grounds of a probabilistic semantics for *understanding* potential disagreements between what is sanctioned and what is intended. This is particularly relevant in scenarios like the "Yale shooting" in which different solutions have often been motivated by different conceptions of where the problem lies.

Actually, the framework for defeasible inference to be developed in this chapter does not handle the Yale shooting scenario properly because the notion of irrelevance used does not take causal considerations into account. Those aspects of default reasoning will be treated in full detail in Chapter 5.

2.2 Language: Default Theories

The system of defeasible inference to be introduced accepts as input a context composed of sentences and defaults, and implicitly characterizes the conclusions that legitimately follow from that context. Sentences and defaults are expressed in terms of an underlying first order language $\mathcal{L}$.

We use the object-level connective '$\Rightarrow$' for material implication, and the meta-level connective '$\rightarrow$' for defaults. The sentence '$p \Rightarrow q$' thus reads as 'if p then q,' while the expression '$p \rightarrow q$' as 'if p, then *normally* q.' The symbols '$\vdash$' and '$\nvdash$' stand for derivability and non-derivability in classical first order logic with equality, respectively.

Letters p, q, ... possibly indexed, will be used as variables ranging over sentences, while expressions in typewriter style will denote object-level sentences (e.g., `dog(fido)`). Likewise, letters in italics from the end of the alphabet x, y, ... will denote variables (sometimes tuples of variables), while letters in italics from the beginning of the alphabet a, b, ... will denote ground terms (sometimes tuples of ground terms). Free variables will be assumed to be universally quantified, so we often write $\texttt{dog}(x) \Rightarrow \texttt{animal}(x)$ instead of $\forall x.\texttt{dog}(x) \Rightarrow \texttt{animal}(x)$.

Default theories $T = \langle K, E \rangle$ have two parts: a *background context* K containing generic information, and an *evidence set* E containing information specific to the situation at hand. Intuitively, K contains the relevant *rules*, while E contains the relevant *facts*. For instance, in the "birds fly, penguins don't" example, we would include the strict and defeasible generics, "penguins are birds," "birds fly," and "penguins don't fly" in K, leaving the facts such as "Tweety is a bird," "Tim weights three pounds," etc., in E.

The distinction between background and evidence, although not widely acknowledged, appears in one way or the other in most systems that implicitly handle 'specificity' preferences among defaults. It appears as a distinction between necessary and contingent facts in [Poo85], [Del87], and [SL90], between strict rules and facts in [Nut88b], and between reified predicates (rules) and terms (facts) in [Gin90]. From a probabilistic point of view, as we will see, including a sentence s in the background amounts *to setting its prior* to one, while including it in the evidence set amounts *to conditionalizing* on it.

The background context $K = \langle L, D \rangle$ of a default theory $T = \langle K, E \rangle$ has also two components: a set of sentences L (the 'strict' rules) and a set of *defaults* D (the 'defeasible' rules). Defaults are encoded by expressions of the form $p \rightarrow q$, where p and q denote sentences in $\mathcal{L}$, called the default antecedent and consequent, respectively. The expression $\texttt{dog(fido)} \rightarrow \texttt{can\_bark(fido)}$, for instance, represents a default stating that "normally, if Fido is a dog, Fido can bark." We use *default schemas* of the form $p(x) \rightarrow q(x)$, where p and q are wffs with free variables among those of x, to denote the collection of defaults $p(a) \rightarrow q(a)$ that results from replacing x by all tuples a of ground terms in the language.

For a particular domain, the background K normally remains fixed while the evidential set E changes. Together they will also be referred to as a *context*, which we often denote as E_K.

2.3 Rules of Inference: The Core

The system of defeasible inference below, called **P** for "probabilistic," is characterized by a set of rules of inference in the style of natural deduction systems. The first five rules constitute what we call the *core*. We will later introduce an additional rule of inference which extends the power of the core significantly. The reason for isolating the first five rules as the core of **P** is because these rules admit a precise and pure probabilistic interpretation. The power and limitations of the core will thus be a good indication of the power and limitations of the underlying probabilistic interpretation. The sixth rule will supplement the core with assumptions about independence. We will show in Chapters 3 and 4 that both **P** and its core can be given a *non-probabilistic* semantics as well.

The rules of **P** implicitly define the set of conclusions that follow from a given context. We write $E \mid\!\approx_K p$ to denote that the sentence p is derivable in **P** from a context $T = \langle K, E \rangle$ with background K and evidence set E. Likewise, $E, \{q\} \mid\!\approx_K p$, abbreviated $E, q \mid\!\approx_K p$, states that p is derivable from the context that results from adding the sentence q to E. We will use the notation $E \vdash_K p$ as an abbreviation of $E, L \vdash p$. It should be kept in mind that the consequence operator '$\mid\!\approx_K$,' unlike '$\vdash_K$,' is *non-monotonic*, so the expression $E, q \mid\!\approx_K p$ does not necessarily follow from $E \mid\!\approx_K p$.

Definition 2.1 The *core* of **P** is defined by the following set of rules:

Rule 1 (Defaults) If $p \rightarrow q \in D$ then $p \mid\!\approx_K q$

Rule 2 (Deduction) If $E \vdash_K p$ then $E \mid\!\approx_K p$

Rule 3 (Augmentation) If $E \mid\!\approx_K p$ and $E \mid\!\approx_K q$ then $E, p \mid\!\approx_K q$

Rule 4 (Reduction) If $E \mid\!\approx_K p$ and $E, p \mid\!\approx_K q$ then $E \mid\!\approx_K q$

Rule 5 (Disjunction) If $E, p \mathrel{\mid\!\approx_K} r$ and $E, q \mathrel{\mid\!\approx_K} r$ then $E, p \vee q \mathrel{\mid\!\approx_K} r$

The **defaults** rule permits us to conclude the consequent of a default when its antecedent represents all the available evidence. **Deduction** states that whatever the context, what is derivable by the rules of classical logic is also derivable in **P**. **Augmentation** permits the assimilation of an established conclusion to the current evidence set without affecting the status of any other derived conclusion. **Reduction** is the inverse of augmentation: it permits us to remove information from the evidence set if such information is derivable from the reduced set. Finally, **disjunction** permits reasoning by cases.

Rules 2–5 can be shown to share the inferential power of the system proposed by Adams [Ada66] for deriving what he calls the probabilistic consequences of a set of conditionals. Some of these rules also appear, in different forms, in several logics of conditionals (see [Nut84]), and in a "minimal" non-monotonic logic proposed by Gabbay [Gab85]. More recently Gabbay's system has been further investigated by Kraus *et al.* [KLM90] and Makinson [Mak89] who arrive at a system which is equivalent to the core above, and which is justified on model-theoretic grounds (see Chapter 3).

We will now investigate some of the properties of the system defined by Rules 1–5. Later on we will discuss some of its limitations as we enhance the system with an additional rule for drawing assumptions about independence.

Some Useful Derived Rules of Inference

The following derived rules illustrate some of the properties of **P**:

Theorem 2.1 The following rules are derived rules of **P**:

Deductive Closure If $E \mathrel{\mid\!\approx_K} p$, $E \mathrel{\mid\!\approx_K} q$, and $E, p, q \vdash_K r$, then $E \mathrel{\mid\!\approx_K} r$

Context Equiv If $E, p \mathrel{\mid\!\approx_K} q$, $E, q \mathrel{\mid\!\approx_K} p$, and $E, p \mathrel{\mid\!\approx_K} r$, then $E, q \mathrel{\mid\!\approx_K} r$

Weak Reduction If $E, q \mathrel{\mid\!\approx_K} p$ then $E \mathrel{\mid\!\approx_K} \neg q \vee p$

Presuppositions If $E \mathrel{\mid\!\approx_K} p$ and $E, q \mathrel{\mid\!\approx_K} \neg p$ then $E \mathrel{\mid\!\approx_K} \neg q$

Parallel Reduction If $E, p, q \mathrel{\mid\!\approx_K} r$, $E \mathrel{\mid\!\approx_K} p$, and $E \mathrel{\mid\!\approx_K} q$, then $E \mathrel{\mid\!\approx_K} r$

OR-transitivity If $E, p \vee q \mathrel{\mid\!\approx_K} q$ and $E, q \vee r \mathrel{\mid\!\approx_K} r$, then $E, p \vee r \mathrel{\mid\!\approx_K} r$

OR-monotonicity If $E, p \vee q \mathrel{\mid\!\approx_K} \neg q$, then $E, p \vee q \vee r \mathrel{\mid\!\approx_K} \neg q$

To illustrate how derivations proceed, we include the proofs.

Proof We start with **deductive closure**. From $E \mid\!\sim_K q$ and $E \mid\!\sim_K p$, we can obtain $E, p \mid\!\sim_K q$ by augmentation. Similarly, from $E, p, q \vdash_K r$ we get $E, p, q \mid\!\sim_K r$ by deduction. Applying reduction twice then, the target result follows. For **context-equivalence**, $E, p \mid\!\sim_K q$ permits us to augment $E, p \mid\!\sim_K r$ into $E, p, q \mid\!\sim_K r$, while $E, q \mid\!\sim_K p$ permits us to reduce the latter into the desired conclusion $E, q \mid\!\sim_K r$. For **Weak reduction** note that $E, \neg q \mid\!\sim_K \neg q \vee p$ and $E, q \mid\!\sim_K \neg q \vee p$ follow by deduction and deductive closure respectively. Thus, reasoning by cases and reducing $q \vee \neg q$ from the evidence set, the final result follows. **Presupposition** is a consequence of weak reduction on $E, q \mid\!\sim_K \neg p$ and the deductive closure of $E \mid\!\sim_K \neg q \vee \neg p$ and $E \mid\!\sim_K p$. **Parallel reduction** follows from the augmentation of $E \mid\!\sim_K p$ into $E, q \mid\!\sim_K p$, and the reduction of $E, q, p \mid\!\sim_K r$ into $E, q \mid\!\sim_K r$, and further into $E \mid\!\sim_K r$. To prove **Or-transitivity**, note that by deduction we can obtain $E, q \vee r \mid\!\sim_K p \vee q \vee r$, while from the hypothesis $E, p \vee q \mid\!\sim_K q$ and reasoning by cases we get $E, p \vee q \vee r \mid\!\sim_K q \vee r$. Similarly, we obtain $E, p \vee r \mid\!\sim_K p \vee q \vee r$ and $E, p \vee q \vee r \mid\!\sim_K p \vee r$. Finally, from the hypothesis $E, q \vee r \mid\!\sim_K r$, one application of context-equivalence yields $E, p \vee q \vee r \mid\!\sim_K r$, and a second one $E, p \vee r \mid\!\sim_K r$. The last derived rule, **Or-monotonicity**, is a consequence of augmenting the hypothesis $E, p \vee q \mid\!\sim_K \neg q$ into $E, p \vee q, p \vee q \vee r \mid\!\sim_K \neg q$, from which $E, p \vee q \vee r \mid\!\sim_K \neg q$ follows by weakly reducing $p \vee q$ from the premises, and by deductive closure.

Some non-theorems:

$E \vdash p$ and $p \mid\!\sim_K q$ do necessarily imply $E \mid\!\sim_K q$
$E \mid\!\sim_K p$ and $E' \mid\!\sim_K p$ do not necessarily imply $E, E' \mid\!\sim_K p$

Note that the first non-theorem is clearly undesirable. If accepted, it would endow our system with the monotonic characteristics of classical logic, precluding exceptions like non-flying birds, etc. The second rule would authorize conclusions such that John will be happy when married to both Jane and Mary on the grounds that he will be happy when married to either one of them.

Rules 1–5 define an extremely conservative non-monotonic logic. In fact, the inferences sanctioned by these rules do not invoke any assumptions regarding information absent from the background context. For while the core is *non-monotonic* in the evidence set E, it is *monotonic* in the background context K. More precisely, if for two background contexts $K = \langle L, D \rangle$ and $K' = \langle L', D' \rangle$ we write $K \subseteq K'$ for $L \subseteq L'$ and $D \subseteq D'$, the following result holds:[1]

Theorem 2.2 (K-monotonicity) If $E \,\vert\!\!\approx_K p$ and $K \subseteq K'$ then $E \,\vert\!\!\approx_{K'} p$.

2.4 Semantics: ϵ-entailment

As indicated above, it is possible to construct a probabilistic interpretation under which Rules 1–5 are *sound* and, as we will later see, *complete*. The idea is to associate the expression $E \,\vert\!\!\approx_K p$ with the statements $P_K(p \,|\, E) \approx 1$ for probability distributions $P_K(\cdot)$ which comply with the constraints in K in a suitable manner. Note the different roles that *background* and *evidence* will play: the background K delimits the space of probability distributions, while the set E represents the information upon which those distributions are *conditioned.*[2] The distributions P_K that comply with the constraints in K, for a given parameter ϵ, are called ϵ-admissible and are defined as follows:

Definition 2.2 A probability distribution P_K is *ϵ-admissible* relative to a background $K = \langle L, D \rangle$ when P_K assigns unit probability to every (strict) sentence s in L, i.e. $P_K(s) = 1$, and probabilities $P_K(q \,|\, p) > 1 - \epsilon$ and $P_K(p) > 0$ to each default $p \rightarrow q$ in D.

In other words, a probability distribution P_K is ϵ-admissible when it renders the sentences in L *certain*, while leaving a range ϵ of uncertainty for the defaults in D.

If the conditional probability of a proposition p given a body of evidence E approaches one, as the uncertainty associated with the defaults in D is reduced to zero, the proposition will be said to be *ϵ-entailed:*

Definition 2.3 A proposition p is ϵ-entailed by $T = \langle K, E \rangle$ when for any $\epsilon' > 0$, there exists an $\epsilon > 0$, such that $P_K(p \,|\, E) > 1 - \epsilon'$ for any ϵ-admissible probability distribution P_K.

As showed by Adams [Ada66, Ada75], ϵ-entailment makes Rules 1–5 sound:

[1] Proofs can be found in the appendix.

[2] For an introduction to probabilities, see [Pea88b].

Theorem 2.3 (Adams) If $E \mathrel{|\!\!\approx_K} p$ then p is ϵ-entailed by $T = \langle K, E\rangle$.

Like deductive inference preserves truth, Rules 1–5 preserve high-probability. Note, however, that unlike classical model-theory, the probabilistic interpretation does not provide a semantics for defaults but for default *inference.* We cannot evaluate whether a default is true in given a world, but only whether a proposition should be accepted provided that (1) only conclusions with arbitrarily high conditional probability (short of one) are accepted, and (2) defaults are accepted.[3]

Rules 1–5 are not only sound with respect to ϵ-entailment but also *complete.* The proof is somewhat intricate and will be presented step by step in the next chapter. Below we will focus on examples that will permit us to assess the virtues and limitations of Rules 1–5 as a system of default inference.

Example 2.1 (Specificity) Let us consider a background context K with information about birds (B), red birds (RB), penguins (P) and flying things (F) expressed as follows (see Fig. 2.1):

$$\mathtt{B}(x) \rightarrow \mathtt{F}(x)$$

$$\mathtt{P}(x) \Rightarrow \mathtt{B}(x)$$

$$\mathtt{P}(x) \rightarrow \neg\mathtt{F}(x)$$

$$\mathtt{RB}(x) \Rightarrow \mathtt{B}(x)$$

Then it is possible to prove that an arbitrary bird `tim` is likely to fly by a single application of Rule 1:

1. $\mathtt{B(tim)} \mathrel{|\!\!\approx_K} \mathtt{F(tim)}$; Defaults, $\mathtt{B}(x) \rightarrow \mathtt{F}(x) \in D$

The same rule yields the opposite conclusion if Tim is a penguin:

2. $\mathtt{P(tim)} \mathrel{|\!\!\approx_K} \neg\mathtt{F(tim)}$; Defaults $\mathtt{P}(x) \rightarrow \neg\mathtt{F}(x) \in D$

There is no contradiction between the two conclusions since they hold in different contexts: $\{\mathtt{B(tim)}\}_K$ and $\{\mathtt{P(tim)}\}_K$. Nonetheless, since penguins are known to be birds, the latter context subsumes the former one:

[3] For alternative probabilistic semantics of plausible reasoning, see [Wel90], [NP88], [Bac89], and the recent survey [Pea89a].

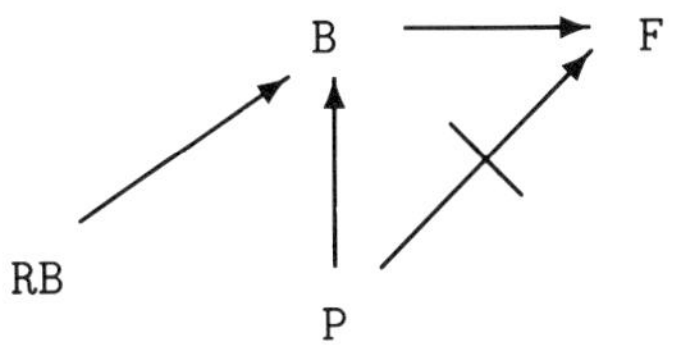

Figure 2.1
Standard example

   3. $\text{P}(\texttt{tim}) \mathrel{\vdash\!\!\!\!\sim}_K \text{B}(\texttt{tim})$; Deduction

enabling us to *augment* 2 above to yield:

   4. $\text{P}(\texttt{tim}), \text{B}(\texttt{tim}) \mathrel{\vdash\!\!\!\!\sim}_K \neg\text{F}(\texttt{tim})$; Augmentation 2,3

This is how properties of subclasses override properties of superclasses in this system. Unlike default logic or circumscription, the 'abnormality' of subclasses does not have to be explicated; the expected behavior emerges automatically from the probabilistic interpretation embodied in the rules and from the distinction made between formulas in the background K and those in the evidence set E.

It is important to emphasize this last distinction. The behavior we have just illustrated would not be sanctioned if we had included the fact that 'penguins are birds' in E rather than in K. In such a case, we would have to show that the expression $\text{P}(x) \Rightarrow \text{B}(x)$ can be assimilated into the left hand side of the non-monotonic consequence operator '$\mathrel{\vdash\!\!\!\!\sim}_K$' without affecting the status of the intended conclusion $\neg\text{F}(\texttt{tim})$. This is not possible, however.

On the other hand, when the expression $\text{P}(x) \Rightarrow \text{B}(x)$ is included in the background context, it does not have to be assimilated; if $p \rightarrow q$ is a default in K, Rule 1 permits us to derive q from p *regardless of what else is in K*. If, for example, K was augmented with the fact that $\texttt{tim}$ is an exceptional bird, namely $\text{B}(\texttt{tim}) \wedge \neg\text{F}(\texttt{tim})$, we would be able to conclude both $\text{B}(\texttt{tim}) \mathrel{\vdash\!\!\!\!\sim}_K \text{F}(\texttt{tim})$ and $\text{B}(\texttt{tim}) \mathrel{\vdash\!\!\!\!\sim}_K \neg\text{F}(\texttt{tim})$. Indeed, such a background would be ϵ-*inconsistent*, i.e., no probability distribution would be able to make the probability of $\text{F}(\texttt{tim})$ given $\text{B}(\texttt{tim})$ arbitrarily high, while making the probability of $\text{B}(\texttt{tim}) \wedge \neg\text{F}(\texttt{tim})$ one and the

probability of B(tim) greater than zero.[4] This is one of the reasons for including only *generic information* in the background context, leaving the information specific to the situation at hand in the evidence set.[5]

The interpretation of defaults embedded in Rules 1–5 captures certain pattern of reasoning that escape more traditional formulations, but falls short in other aspects. For instance, in the example above, we would expect that a *red* bird will be likely to fly. But while the expression $\mathtt{B(tim)} \mathrel{|\!\!\approx_K} \mathtt{F(tim)}$ ("a bird flies") is derivable, the expression $\mathtt{RB(tim)}, \mathtt{B(tim)} \mathrel{|\!\!\approx_K} \mathtt{F(tim)}$ ("a *red* bird flies") is not.

This limitation of Rules 1–5 is serious and prevent us from drawing default conclusions in the presence of *irrelevant* information. This is not surprising though: Rules 1–5 are probabilistically sound, and therefore, only 'jump' to conclusions $E \mathrel{|\!\!\approx_K} p$ whose high conditional probability $P_K(p \mid E)$ can be guaranteed in *every* probability distribution P_K admissible with K. Since there are probability distributions admissible with K in which red birds do not fly (as much as penguins do not fly), the conclusion that a red bird is likely to fly is *not* probabilistically sound, and therefore, not derivable from the core.

To account for these inferences, additional restrictions on the space of admissible probability distributions are needed. A natural restriction is to require these distributions to comply with certain assumptions about independence; namely, that the probability of q given p *and* E be equal to the probability of q given p alone, when $p \rightarrow q$ is a default in K and E does not provide conflicting information. This is the intuition that the irrelevance account below aims to capture.

---

[4]We will study this form of probabilistic consistency in Section 3.4.

[5]This raises the question of how to encode defaults about particular *individuals*. These defaults do not encode general information, but as defaults, can only be included in the background context. The trick is to create new generic classes as follows. For instance, let us say that we want to encode a default stating that a specific person, say Tom, normally gets up late in the afternoon. Then, rather than encoding this as a default **true** → **gets_up_late**(**tom**) we will write it as the generic default "people like Tom get up late", i.e. Tom(x) → **gets_up_late**(x), together with the evidential fact that tom is one of this people. Not only does this 'reified' encoding abide by the principle that only generic information gets into the background context, but it also yields the right behavior in situations in which the simpler encoding does not. For example, if there is another default stating that 'most people don't get up late in the afternoon,' the simpler encoding would incorrectly conclude that Tom does *not* get up late in the afternoon, given that Tom is a person. On the other hand, the 'reified' encoding would correctly infer the opposite conclusion, provided that the background includes the information that 'people like Tom are people', i.e. Tom(x) → people(x). For other reasons for construing defaults as originating from classes and not from individuals, see [Kyb83, Bac90].

2.5 Irrelevance

Our account of irrelevance extends Rules 1–5 with assumptions about independence. The intent is to make defaults $p \rightarrow q$ in K applicable in all contexts $T = \langle K, E \rangle$ which do not provide evidence for p and the *negation* of q. We will find convenient to treat defaults as material conditionals. So when we say that a default $p \rightarrow q$ is applicable in a context T we mean that the material conditional $p \Rightarrow q$ can be asserted in T. Similarly, we will say that a set D of defaults $p_i \rightarrow q_i$, $\mathsf{D} \subseteq D$ *supports* a proposition p in a context $T = \langle K, E \rangle$ with $K = \langle L, D \rangle$, when p is a logical consequence of L, E and the material conditionals $p_i \Rightarrow q_i$. When D does not support both p and $\neg p$, for some p, we will say that D is *consistent* in T.

The main difference between a default $p \rightarrow q$ and the material conditional $p \Rightarrow q$ is that the latter, unlike the former, can be applied in any context. Defaults, on the other hand, are context-dependent and can only be asserted when the information which has been gathered does not suggest otherwise.

In our framework the conditions for adopting a default will depend on whether there are *arguments* against the default. Arguments are reasons for belief which are formalized as follows:

Definition 2.4 An *argument* for a proposition p in a context T with background $K = \langle L, D \rangle$, is a collection of defaults D, $\mathsf{D} \subseteq D$, such that 1) D supports p in T and 2) D is consistent in T.

For example, if T contains a default $\mathtt{p} \rightarrow \mathtt{q}$ and two sentences $\mathtt{q} \Rightarrow \mathtt{r}$ and $\mathtt{p}$, then the singleton $\{\mathtt{p} \rightarrow \mathtt{q}\}$ would be an argument for $\mathtt{r}$, as $\{\mathtt{p}, \mathtt{p} \Rightarrow \mathtt{q}, \mathtt{q} \Rightarrow \mathtt{r}\} \vdash \mathtt{r}$ and $\{\mathtt{p}, \mathtt{p} \Rightarrow \mathtt{q}, \mathtt{q} \Rightarrow \mathtt{r}\} \not\vdash \mathbf{false}$.

Arguments are required to be consistent to prevent conflicting defaults from supporting any proposition in the language. When an argument supports the negation of a proposition will say that the argument is *against* the proposition. Likewise, an argument *against a default* $p \rightarrow q$ is an argument against the material conditional $p \Rightarrow q$:

Definition 2.5 D is an argument against a default $p \rightarrow q$ if D is an argument for $p \wedge \neg q$.

If there are no arguments against a default $p \rightarrow q$ it is reasonable to adopt the default and regard the evidence as *irrelevant.* This is precisely the intuition underlying most non-monotonic logics, where a default $p \rightarrow q$ is viewed as a reason for concluding q from p in the absence of conflicting evidence. However, adopting a default only when there is no conflicting evidence is not enough; sometimes there are arguments against a default and yet we prefer to adopt the default and reject the counterarguments. For instance, in a context in which all we know is that Tim is a penguin, i.e. $E = \{\texttt{P(tim)}\}$, there is an an argument against the default $\texttt{P(tim)} \rightarrow \neg\texttt{F(tim)}$, given by $D = \{\texttt{B(tim)} \rightarrow \texttt{F(tim)}\}$; yet, Rule 1 permits us to apply the default $\texttt{P(tim)} \rightarrow \neg\texttt{F(tim)}$ and derive $\neg\texttt{F(tim)}$.

More generally, whenever K contains a default $p \rightarrow q$ and E *contains only the proposition* p, Rule 1 will permit us to apply the default and derive q, *regardless of the other information in* K. In particular, if D is a collection of defaults in K that support the *negation* of q, the argument D against the default $p \rightarrow q$ will be implicitly ignored.

We will say that a set D of defaults is *in conflict* with a default $p \rightarrow q$ when D supports the negation of q in the context $\{p\}_K$.[6] Since legitimizing the default $p \rightarrow q$ then amounts to establishing a preference of $p \rightarrow q$ over D, we will say that $p \rightarrow q$ *dominates* D:

Definition 2.6 (Dominance) If D is in conflict with $p \rightarrow q$, then the default $p \rightarrow q$ *dominates* D. D is *in conflict* with $p \rightarrow q$ if D supports the negation of q in the context $\{p\}_K$.

To test then whether a default $p \rightarrow q$ can be applied in a given context, the arguments D which are dominated by $p \rightarrow q$ will be excluded. If no arguments against $p \rightarrow q$ are left, we will assume that the evidence is irrelevant and that the default can be adopted.

For example, given that Tim is a penguin and also a red-bird, i.e. $E = \{\texttt{RB(tim)}, \texttt{P(tim)}\}$, $D = \{\texttt{B(tim)} \rightarrow \texttt{F(tim)}\}$ is the single (minimal) argument against the default $\texttt{P(tim)} \rightarrow \neg\texttt{F(tim)}$. D, however, is dominated by $\texttt{P(tim)} \rightarrow \neg\texttt{F(tim)}$ as D supports $\texttt{F(tim)}$ in the context $\{\texttt{P(tim)}\}_K$. As a result, by the above criterion, the conflicting argument D can be ignored, the default $\texttt{P(tim)} \rightarrow \neg\texttt{F(tim)}$ can be adopted, and $\neg\texttt{F(tim)}$ can be derived.

Yet the irrelevance criterion that results from the exclusion of dominated arguments is still not powerful enough. Consider for instance the

[6] Recall that $\{p\}_K$ stands for the theory $T = \langle K, E\rangle$ with $E = \{p\}$.

theory that results from replacing the *strict* inclusion $\mathtt{P}(x) \Rightarrow \mathtt{B}(x)$ by the *defeasible* inclusion $\mathtt{P}(x) \rightarrow \mathtt{B}(x)$. In the resulting background, the singleton $D = \{\mathtt{B(tim)} \rightarrow \mathtt{F(tim)}\}$ is no longer in conflict with the default $\mathtt{P(tim)} \rightarrow \neg\mathtt{F(tim)}$. Thus, given the evidence $E' = \{\mathtt{P(tim)}, \mathtt{RB(tim)}\}$, D prevents the default $\mathtt{P(tim)} \rightarrow \neg\mathtt{F(tim)}$ from being applied and $\neg\mathtt{F(tim)}$ from being derived. However, the replacement of a strict 'link' by a defeasible 'link' should make no difference here. In fact, we can still conclude that the default 'birds fly' is not applicable to 'penguins' because both $\mathtt{P(tim)} \succapprox_K \mathtt{B(tim)}$ and $\mathtt{P(tim)} \succapprox_K \neg\mathtt{F(tim)}$ are derivable. So, although the default 'birds fly' is no longer dominated by the default 'penguins don't fly', it certainly carries less weight.

These intuitions about the 'strength' of defaults can be justified in a different way as well. Let us assume that whenever a default d dominates a set D of defaults, d must be *stronger* than some default in D, and let d_1, d_2 and d_3 stand for the defaults $\mathtt{B(tim)} \rightarrow \mathtt{F(tim)}$, $\mathtt{P(tim)} \rightarrow \neg\mathtt{F(tim)}$ and $\mathtt{P(tim)} \rightarrow \mathtt{B(tim)}$. Then, since d_2 dominates the set $\{d_1, d_3\}$, and d_3 dominates the set $\{d_1, d_2\}$, d_2 has to be stronger than either d_1 or d_3, and d_3 has to be stronger than either d_1 or d_2. If d_2 is *not* stronger than d_1, then d_2 has to be stronger than d_3. This, however, means that d_3 has to be stronger than d_1 (because d_3 cannot be stronger than d_1), and therefore, by transitivity, that d_2 has to be stronger than d_1 as well, in contradiction with our original assumption. So d_2 has to be stronger than d_1 and, by analogous arguments, d_3 has to be stronger than d_1 as well.

This line of reasoning actually suggests how the dominance relation should be extended to better reflect the preferences among defaults which are implicit in a given background context. We will call the extended form of dominance, *preemption*, and define it as follows:[7]

Definition 2.7 (Preemption) A default $p \rightarrow q$ *preempts* a set D of defaults if 1) $p \rightarrow q$ dominates D, or 2) $p \rightarrow q$ preempts $D + \{p' \rightarrow q'\}$, for some default $p' \rightarrow q'$ in K, and $p' \rightarrow q'$ preempts $D + \{p \rightarrow q\}$.

Provided with this notion of preemption, a body E of evidence will be regarded as *irrelevant* to a default $p \rightarrow q$ when all arguments against $p \rightarrow q$ are preempted:

[7] The notion of preemption can also be found in inheritance networks (e.g., see [HTT87, THT87]), although defined in a different way.

Definition 2.8 (Irrelevance) A body of evidence E is *irrelevant* to a default $p \rightarrow q$ in a background K, written $I_K(p \rightarrow q \mid E)$, when $p \rightarrow q$ preempts all arguments D against $p \rightarrow q$ in the context $T = \langle K, E \rangle$.

Note that the preemption relations are established in the contexts E'_K in which only the antecedents of the defaults $p \rightarrow q$ are known, i.e., $E' = \{p\}$, but they are used for testing the relevance of arbitrary bodies of evidence E.

When E is irrelevant to a a default $p \rightarrow q$ in K, a rule of inference will allow us to conclude the *material conditional* $p \Rightarrow q$ in the context $T = \langle K, E \rangle$:

Rule 6 (Irrelevance) If $I_K(p \rightarrow q \mid E)$ then $E \mathrel{|\!\!\sim_K} p \Rightarrow q$

The formal justification of this rule will be given in Chapter 4. In the remainder of this chapter we will illustrate the motivation for the rule and how the rule is used.

Often we will say that a default $p \rightarrow q$ is *applicable* in a context E_K when p can be derived from E but E is irrelevant to the default. In such cases, by the irrelevance rule and deductive closure, we will be able to apply the default and derive q. Since this pattern will be common we will capture it in a derived rule of inference which we call *Default Transitivity:*

Default Transitivity If $E \mathrel{|\!\!\sim_K} p$ and $I_K(p \rightarrow q \mid E)$ then $E \mathrel{|\!\!\sim_K} q$

Default transitivity will allow us to chain defaults, and to conclude, for instance, r from p, given two defaults $p \rightarrow q$ and $q \rightarrow r$. In Example 2.1, default transitivity permits us to prove that a red bird is expected to fly as follows:

1.	$\mathtt{RB(t)} \mathrel{|\!\!\sim_K} \mathtt{B(t)}$	; Deduction
2.	$I_K(\mathtt{B(t)} \rightarrow \mathtt{F(t)} \mid \mathtt{RB(t)})$	; No args against $\mathtt{B(t)} \rightarrow \mathtt{F(t)}$
3.	$\mathtt{RB(t)} \mathrel{|\!\!\sim_K} \mathtt{F(t)}$	; Default Transitivity, 1,2

2.6 Examples

In this section we will illustrate the behavior of the system of defeasible inference defined by Rules 1–6.

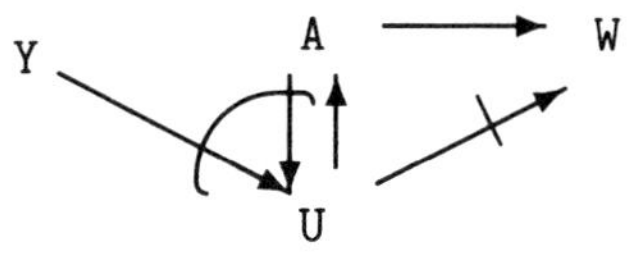

Figure 2.2
Implicit preferences among defaults

Example 2.2 (Default Preferences) Let the background context K contain the following defaults: "adults (A) work (W)," "university students (U) are adults but do not work," and "adults which are young (Y) are university students" (Fig. 2.2):

$$A(x) \rightarrow W(x)$$

$$U(x) \rightarrow A(x)$$

$$U(x) \rightarrow \neg W(x)$$

$$A(x) \wedge Y(x) \rightarrow U(x)$$

We show first that an adult, say Ken (k), who is also a university student, is likely not to work, i.e., $A(k), U(k) \mathrel{\vdash\!\!\!\sim}_K \neg W(k)$:

1. $U(k) \mathrel{\vdash\!\!\!\sim}_K \neg W(k)$; Defaults, $U(x) \rightarrow \neg W(x)$
2. $U(k) \mathrel{\vdash\!\!\!\sim}_K A(k)$; Defaults, $U(x) \rightarrow A(x)$
3. $U(k), A(k) \mathrel{\vdash\!\!\!\sim}_K \neg W(k)$; Augmentation 1,2

The inference rules in **P** yield again a *preference* for more 'specific' defaults. In fact, in the context $\{U(k)\}_K$, the defaults $U(k) \rightarrow A(k)$, and $U(k) \rightarrow \neg W(k)$ hold, while the default $A(k) \rightarrow W(k)$ does not hold:

4. $U(k) \mathrel{\vdash\!\!\!\sim}_K U(k) \Rightarrow A(k)$; Deductive closure, 2
5. $U(k) \mathrel{\vdash\!\!\!\sim}_K U(k) \Rightarrow \neg W(k)$; Deductive closure, 1
6. $U(k) \mathrel{\vdash\!\!\!\sim}_K \neg(U(k) \Rightarrow W(k))$; Deductive closure, 1

If we refer to these three defaults as d_1, d_2, and d_3, respectively, we will find that d_1 *dominates* the set $\{d_2, d_3\}$, d_2 *dominates* the set $\{d_1, d_3\}$, and thus, both d_1 and d_2 preempt $\{d_3\}$. In light of the definition of irrelevance this implies that arguments against either $U(x) \rightarrow \neg W(x)$ or

$\mathtt{U(k)} \rightarrow \mathtt{A(k)}$ involving the default $\mathtt{A(k)} \rightarrow \mathtt{W(k)}$, will be ignored. As a result, we can establish the conclusion that 'a young adult is likely not to work' as follows:[8]

7.	$\mathtt{Y(k)}, \mathtt{A(k)} \mathrel{\vert\!\!\sim_K} \mathtt{U(k)}$	; Defaults, $\mathtt{A(k)} \wedge \mathtt{Y(k)} \rightarrow \mathtt{U(k)}$
8.	$I_K(\mathtt{U(k)} \rightarrow \neg\mathtt{W(k)} \mid \mathtt{Y(k)}, \mathtt{A(k)})$	; $\mathtt{U(k)} \rightarrow \neg\mathtt{W(k)} > \{\mathtt{A(k)} \rightarrow \mathtt{W(k)}\}$
9	$\mathtt{Y(k)}, \mathtt{A(k)} \mathrel{\vert\!\!\sim_K} \neg\mathtt{W(k)}$	; Default Transitivity

The irrelevance rule extends the core but does not introduce inconsistencies (see Chapter 4 for a proof). In this case, for example, there is no way of proving the opposite conclusion $\mathtt{A(k)}, \mathtt{Y(k)} \mathrel{\vert\!\!\sim_K} \mathtt{W(k)}$; the evidence $E = \{\mathtt{A(k)}, \mathtt{Y(k)}\}$ is indeed *relevant* to the default $\mathtt{A(k)} \rightarrow \mathtt{W(k)}$ as the argument $D = \{\mathtt{A(k)} \wedge \mathtt{Y(k)} \rightarrow \mathtt{U(k)}\,,\, \mathtt{U(k)} \rightarrow \neg\mathtt{W(k)}\}$ is not preempted.

The irrelevance rule permits us also to contrapose defaults. For instance, if Ken does not work, we can derive that he is likely not be an adult as follows:

10.	$I_K(\mathtt{A(k)} \rightarrow \mathtt{W(k)} \mid \neg\mathtt{W(k)})$	; Definition + No counterargs
11.	$\neg\mathtt{W(k)} \mathrel{\vert\!\!\sim_K} \mathtt{A(k)} \Rightarrow \mathtt{W(k)}$	; Irrelevance 10
12.	$\neg\mathtt{W(k)} \mathrel{\vert\!\!\sim_K} \neg\mathtt{A(k)}$	; Deductive Closure

However, if it is learned that Ken is a university student, the former derivation no longer applies, and the conclusion changes:

13.	$\mathtt{U(k)} \mathrel{\vert\!\!\sim_K} \mathtt{A(k)}$	; Defaults
14.	$\mathtt{U(k)} \mathrel{\vert\!\!\sim_K} \neg\mathtt{W(k)}$	; Defaults
15.	$\mathtt{U(k)}, \neg\mathtt{W(k)} \mathrel{\vert\!\!\sim_K} \mathtt{A(k)}$	; Augmentation 13,14

The former derivation no longer applies because the irrelevance assertion $I_K(\mathtt{A(k)} \rightarrow \mathtt{W(k)} \mid \mathtt{U(k)}, \neg\mathtt{W(k)})$ is false: $\{\mathtt{U(k)} \rightarrow \mathtt{A(k)}\}$ is an argument against the default $\mathtt{A(k)} \rightarrow \mathtt{W(k)}$ in the context $\{\mathtt{U(k)}, \neg\mathtt{W(k)}\}_K$ which is not preempted.

Example 2.3 (Cases) Let us consider now a background context K with defaults "quakers (q) are doves (d)," "republicans (r) are hawks (h)" and "both doves and hawks are politically motivated (p)," together

[8] We use the notation $d_i > D$ to indicate that d_i preempts D.

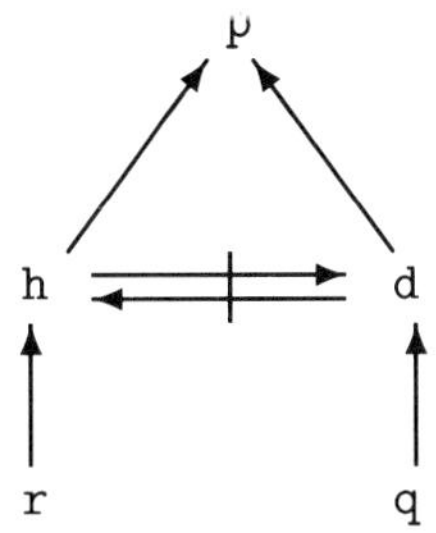

Figure 2.3
Reasoning by cases

with the fact that nobody is both a hawk and a dove:[9]

$$\begin{aligned} &\texttt{r}(x) \rightarrow \texttt{h}(x) \\ &\texttt{q}(x) \rightarrow \texttt{d}(x) \\ &\texttt{h}(x) \rightarrow \texttt{p}(x) \\ &\texttt{d}(x) \rightarrow \texttt{p}(x) \\ \neg\, &(\texttt{d}(x) \wedge \texttt{h}(x)) \end{aligned}$$

We want to show that if somebody, say Nixon ($\texttt{n}$), is a quaker and a republican, then he is likely to be politically motivated. Reasoning by cases yields $\texttt{q(n)}, \texttt{r(n)} \mid\!\approx_K \texttt{d(n)} \vee \texttt{h(n)}$ because $\texttt{q(n)}, \texttt{r(n)}, \texttt{d(n)} \mid\!\approx_K \texttt{d(n)} \vee \texttt{h(n)}$ follows from deduction, and $\texttt{q(n)}, \texttt{r(n)}, \neg\texttt{d(n)} \mid\!\approx_K \texttt{d(n)} \vee \texttt{h(n)}$ follows from the irrelevance of $E = \{\texttt{q(n)}, \texttt{r(n)}, \neg\texttt{d(n)}\}$ to $\texttt{r(n)} \rightarrow \texttt{h(n)}$. Then since by irrelevance $\texttt{q(n)}, \texttt{r(n)} \mid\!\approx_K \texttt{h(n)} \Rightarrow \texttt{p(n)}$ and $\texttt{q(n)}, \texttt{r(n)} \mid\!\approx_K \texttt{d(n)} \Rightarrow \texttt{p(n)}$ also follow, the target conclusion $\texttt{q(n)}, \texttt{r(n)} \mid\!\approx_K \texttt{p(n)}$ can be proven by deductive closure. Note that neither $\texttt{q(n)}, \texttt{r(n)} \mid\!\approx_K \texttt{d(n)}$ or $\texttt{q(n)}, \texttt{r(n)} \mid\!\approx_K \texttt{h(n)}$ are sanctioned by **P** since neither of the required irrelevance conditions, $I_K(\texttt{r(n)} \rightarrow \texttt{h(n)} \mid \texttt{q(n)})$ and $I_K(\texttt{q(n)} \rightarrow \texttt{d(n)} \mid \texttt{r(n)})$, hold.

Example 2.4 (Inconsistency) Defaults in **P** may give rise to inconsistent conclusions even in theories which are *logically* consistent. For instance, a background containing two defaults "birds fly" and "birds do not fly" yields two contradictory conclusions $\texttt{bird(tim)} \mid\!\approx_K \texttt{fly(tim)}$ and

9. This example is due to Matt Ginsberg.

bird(tim) $\not\vdash_K$ ¬fly(tim). This behavior does not arise in most default reasoning frameworks which regard these defaults as *conflicting* rather than as *inconsistent.* The present framework separates the two notions. The distinction is useful because, usually, inconsistent default theories reveal something wrong about the encoding. We will say more about the consistency of default theories in Chapter 3.

The examples above illustrate some of the characteristics of the system of defeasible inference **P** defined by Rules 1–6. This system accounts for what we call the *conditional* aspects of defaults, which includes *specificity* preferences and *cumulative* behavior (i.e. the equivalence between the contexts $T = \langle K, E \rangle$ and $T' = \langle K, E + \{p\} \rangle$, when p is a defeasible consequence of T [Mak89]). These features are present in most *logics of conditionals* [Nut84], although these logics do not address the distinction between *background* and *evidence*, nor the need for assumptions about independence.

The system **P** says little, however, about other aspects of defaults which surface in scenarios involving *causal relations.* The Yale shooting scenario [HM86], for instance, belongs to such class. In Chapter 5 we will analyze several such examples in detail and construct a more refined account of defeasible inference in which both the *causal* and *conditional* aspects of default are taken into consideration.

2.7 Related Work

As we mentioned earlier, Rules 2–5 are essentially equivalent to the logic of indicative conditionals developed by Adams [Ada66, Ada75]. These rules appear in somewhat different form in most logics of conditionals as well (see [Nut84]), where they are usually justified in terms of possible worlds rather than high probabilities. More recently, Makinson [Mak89] and Kraus *et al.* [KLM90] developed a system that is equivalent to the core of **P**, which is derived on model-theoretic grounds. None of these systems, however, goes beyond the core. So, while they display *non-monotonic* behavior in the evidence set, they remain *monotonic* in the set of defaults (conditionals); i.e., the more defaults, the more inferences that are sanctioned (see Theorem 2.2). However, the fact that the core can also be justified on model-theoretic grounds is by itself interesting, and as we will see in the next two chapters, fruitful.

Most non-monotonic logics in AI require the explicit addition of preferences in order to deal with interacting defaults [RC83]. In recent years, however, several novel systems of defeasible inference have been proposed which attempt to uncover such preferences.

In this regard, the closest formalism to **P** is perhaps the one proposed by Pollock [Pol88a]. Pollock also combines probabilities and arguments, although in a different manner. He relates defeasible inference to what philosophers have called direct inference: the inference of *definite probabilities* relating members of certain classes from *indefinite probabilities* relating the classes themselves. For an instance a of a class A, the conditional indefinite probability $P(\mathrm{B}|\mathrm{A}) \geq \mathtt{r}$, for some r reasonably high, is regarded as a *prima facie reason* (i.e., defeasible reason) for believing a to be a member of the class B. Prima facie reasons combine to form arguments, and undefeated arguments support what Pollock calls the warranted conclusions. The rest of Pollock's account is concerned with the conditions for argument defeat.

The main feature that distinguishes **P** from Pollock's framework is its syntactic form. Unlike Pollock's account, **P** constitutes a *calculus* of defeasible inference. Its simplicity is a result of the focus on arbitrarily high and low probabilities, and the limited use of arguments for identifying *independence assumptions* only. Also, by distinguishing 'primitive' from 'derived' defaults, there is no need for the notion of 'projectibility' (see [Pol88a]).

Delgrande's [Del87] system is also close to the one proposed here. The system's core is a variant of the logics of counterfactuals developed by Lewis [Lew73], and is based on a possible worlds semantics rather than on probabilities. The possible worlds semantics, however, does not circumvent the need for assumptions about independence, which are captured by means of a fixed point construction which adds new defaults and assertions to the original set.

Loui [Lou87a] bases his default reasoning system on dialectical argumentation. Arguments supporting and rebutting propositions of interest are evaluated in terms of a number of syntactic attributes, like 'has more evidence', 'is more specific', and so on, and superior arguments are allowed to defeat inferior arguments. The criteria for evaluating arguments embed most of the inference rules that define our system and can be mostly justified in terms of them. Still, it is possible to find differences. One such difference is that Loui's system is not deductively closed. It is possible to believe propositions A and B, and still fail to believe their conjunction [Lou87a]. In our scheme, the deductive closure of believed propositions is established by Theorem 2.1. Similarly, Loui's preference for arguments based on 'more evidence' sometimes contradict our augmentation rule, as the confirmation of facts expected to hold might lead to changes in belief.

Touretzky [Tou86] was the first to suggest the use of specificity relations for filtering spurious ambiguities in default theories. His work was motivated by the problems caused by the presence of redundant paths in inheritance networks. His 'inferential distance' criterion, however, is not a calculus of defeasible inference but a criterion for pruning spurious extensions. In order to determine whether a proposition follows from a network, it is still necessary to test whether the proposition holds in all 'legitimate' extensions. Similar observations apply to Poole's [Poo85] proposal.

Nute [Nut88b] and Horty *et al.* [HTT87] define defeasible inference inductively, with special attention paid to 'specificity' relations. Horty *et al.* define a skeptical inheritance scheme for homogeneous (defaults only) inheritance hierarchies, while Nute's system deals with linear arguments comprised of both defeasible and undefeasible rules. The specificity relations are established by means of defaults in Horty *et al.*'s scheme, and by means of strict rules in Nute's. The difference between 'strict' rules and facts in Nute's system is reminiscent of the distinction made in [Poo85] and [Del87] between necessary and contingent facts, and the one made here between background and evidence.

3 High Probabilities and Model-Preference

3.1 Introduction

In the previous chapter we described a system of defeasible inference made up of six rules. We showed that the fives rules of the core can be given a probabilistic interpretation that guarantees that only highly probable conclusions can be derived from highly probable premises. The *irrelevance* rule supplements the core with assumptions about independence. The resulting system captures a variety of patterns of default inference and provides a new vantage point for understanding default reasoning.

Interestingly, the core of **P** can also be justified on non-probabilistic grounds. In this chapter we will present a validation of the core that rests on model-theoretic grounds and show that ϵ-entailment is equivalent to a form of *preferential entailment.* Preferential entailment is a generalization of classical entailment in which only the *preferred* models of the premises are considered [Sho88]. The semantics of circumscription as proposed by McCarthy [McC80, McC86] as well as the notion of subimplication due to Bossu and Siegel [BS85a], can both be understood in terms of preferences of models of this sort. Preferential entailment is also closely related to the possible world semantics of counterfactual logics, and, in particular, to Lewis' [Lew73] comparative similarity formulation.

The correspondence between ϵ-entailment and preferential entailment will help us to understand better the potentials and limitations of interpretations of defaults based on high probabilities and preferred models, and will also provide us with a completeness characterization of the inference rules that constitute the core.

This chapter is largely a reformulation of results that can be traced back to [Ada66, Ada75] and greatly benefits from the recent developments in the area of preferential logics [LM88, Mak89, KLM90, Pea90].

3.2 Preferential Structures and p-entailment

As discussed in Section 1.5, the circumscription of a predicate P in a theory T is a second order formula that asserts that the tuples that can be shown to comply with P in T are the *only* tuples that do. Model-theoretically, the effect of circumscription is to exclude from consideration all models of T which assign to P an extension larger than necessary. The models which are left assign to P a *minimal* extension, thus the name *minimal models*. Entailed by the circumscription of P in T are the formulas that hold in the minimal models of T relative to P. These formulas are said to be *minimally entailed* by T, where the minimality criterion is understood relative to the extension of P.

Minimal entailment can be regarded as a generalization of classical entailment. While a proposition A *logically* entails a proposition B when B is true in all models of A, A *minimally* entails B when B is true in all models of A considered *minimal* in some sense. The notion of minimality underlying circumscription is a function of the extension of the circumscribed predicates and the interpretation of fixed predicates and function symbols [Lif85, Eth88]. However, other minimality criteria which do not necessarily translate into a simple circumscriptive axiom are also possible. Shoham [Sho86], for instance, developed an alternative minimization criterion motivated by the apparent limitations of circumscription for handling problems in the temporal domain [HM86].

Shoham [Sho88] himself later investigated the properties associated with the form of entailment that results from an abstract 'minimality' criterion; namely, a simple strict partial order on interpretations. Shoham found that the resulting form of entailment, called preferential entailment, preserves certain traits of classical entailment, while being non-monotonic. Other properties of preferential entailment have been established by Kraus *et al.* [KLM90] and Makinson [Mak89]. In the summary below our notation and terminology is closest to Kraus *et al.*

We start with the notion of preferential structures. These are pairs which establish a preference order on non-empty sets of interpretations. We will denote by $\mathcal{I}_{\mathcal{L}}$ the set of all interpretations over the language $\mathcal{L}$. An interpretation I is a model of a default theory $T = \langle K, E \rangle$ with a background $K = \langle L, D \rangle$, when I satisfies the sentences in both L and E. The role of D, as we will see, will be to constrain the *order* of those models.

Definition 3.1 A *preferential structure* (p-structure) is a pair $\langle \mathcal{I}, < \rangle$, where $\mathcal{I}$ denotes a non-empty collection of interpretations, $\mathcal{I} \subseteq \mathcal{I}_{\mathcal{L}}$, and '$<$' denotes an irreflexive and transitive order relation over $\mathcal{I}$.

Within a particular p-structure $\langle \mathcal{I}, < \rangle$, we read the notation $M < M'$ for two interpretations M and M' in $\mathcal{I}$ as indicating that M is *preferred* to M'. Furthermore, when M is a model of $T = \langle K, E \rangle$ and there is no model of T preferred to M in $\mathcal{I}$, we will say that M is a *preferred model* of T. If K is understood, we will also say that M is a preferred model of E.

Definition 3.2 A model M of a default theory T is a *preferred* model of T in a p-structure $\langle \mathcal{I}, < \rangle$, iff $M \in \mathcal{I}$ and there is no model M' of T in $\mathcal{I}$ such that $M' < M$.

The semantics of circumscription can be understood in terms of a particular type of preferential structure $\langle \mathcal{I}_{\text{circ}}, <_{\text{circ}} \rangle$, in which $\mathcal{I}_{\text{circ}}$ corresponds to the set of all logically possible interpretations, and the ordering '$<_{\text{circ}}$' on interpretations is such that an interpretation M is preferred to an interpretation M' when both M and M' coincide on the domains and the interpretation of fixed predicate and function symbols, but M yields a smaller extension for the circumscribed predicates [Lif85, Eth88].

Preferential structures will play a role analogous to probability distributions in ϵ-semantics (see Chapter 2). First of all, among all possible preferential structures, a background $K = \langle L, D \rangle$ will pick out those structures which comply with the information in L and D in the following way:

Definition 3.3 A well-founded[1] preferential structure $\langle \mathcal{I}, < \rangle$ is *admissible* relative to a background $K = \langle L, D \rangle$ iff every interpretation in $\mathcal{I}$ satisfies L, and for every default $p \rightarrow q$ in D, (a) q is true in all preferred models of p in $\mathcal{I}$, and (b) there is an interpretation in $\mathcal{I}$ that satisfies p.

Thus, while ϵ-admissible probability distributions P render q *likely* given p for defaults $p \rightarrow q$ in D (provided that ϵ is small), admissible p-structures make q *true* in the preferred models of p. Furthermore, while for the former we require the probability $P(p)$ to be greater than zero, here we require that p be true in some interpretation.[2]

Preferential entailment is defined in terms of the preferred models of the *admissible* preferential structures:

---

[1] A preferential structure $\langle \mathcal{I}, < \rangle$ is well-founded relative to a background K, when for any theory $T = \langle K, E \rangle$, and any model M of T, $M \in \mathcal{I}$, either M is a *preferred* model of T, or there is a preferred model M' of T, $M' \in \mathcal{I}$, such that M' is preferred to M (see also [Eth88]).

[2] This is different from the account in [KLM90].

Definition 3.4 A default theory $T = \langle K, E\rangle$ *preferentially entails (p-entails)* a proposition p iff p is true in all the preferred models of E in every preferential structure admissible with K.

Note again that while in ϵ-entailment the background K picks the admissible probability distributions which are then conditioned upon the evidence E, in p-entailment, the background K picks the admissible preferential structures from which the preferred models of E are selected. Furthermore, p-entailment provides an alternative validation of Rules 1–5:

Theorem 3.1 (Soundness) If p is is derivable from T by means of Rules 1–5, then p is also preferentially entailed by T.

The simple nature of Rules 1–5, together with the existence of natural justifications in terms of both probabilities and models, have led some researchers to present Rules 1–5, or equivalent ones, as a minimal core for default reasoning (e.g. [Pea89a]). Yet, the core is too weak an account of default inference. The main obstacle is that it remains *semi-monotonic:* although non-monotonic in the evidence set E, it is *monotonic* in the background K. This makes the resulting account too conservative. For example, given *only* two defaults $a \rightarrow b$ and $b \rightarrow c$, we do not get c from a (defeasible transitivity). This is to be expected though; if we did, by the semi-monotonicity of the core, we would still have to conclude c from a when a new, more 'specific' default $a \rightarrow \neg c$ were added, in contradiction with the conclusion $\neg c$ which would be derivable from Rule 1.

One way to overcome this limitation is by means of a criterion for distinguishing relevant from irrelevant evidence (see Chapter 2). A second way is suggested by the results above: instead of defining a preferential entailment relation which depends on *all* the structures that are admissible, we could define a *stronger* preferential entailment relation in which only *some* of those structures are considered. Since any admissible structure satisfies Rules 1–5, any set of admissibly structures will satisfy Rules 1–5 and possibly other rules as well. In Chapter 4, we will show that the two approaches are intimately related and that the 'irrelevance' approach can be validated by a suitable selection of the admissible structures.

In this chapter we will focus instead on the features that make a probabilistic and a model-theoretic interpretation of defaults legitimize a common body of inference rules. In particular, we would like to know whether these rules are *complete* with respect to either ϵ-entailment and p-entailment, and whether these two entailment relations are in fact equivalent. As we will show, several interesting relations among key notions in default reasoning will be revealed from this analysis.

3.3 Layered Structures and l-entailment

To get a deeper insight into the relation between p-entailment and ϵ-entailment we need to relate the structures on which both notions rely. Preferential structures deal with fully fledged *interpretations* which are *partially ordered*; probability distributions deal with *worlds* (truth-valuations) which are ordered by their probability ranks. We will find it useful to introduce an intermediate class of structures, called *layered structures*, consisting of non-empty sets of worlds $\mathcal{W}$, ordered according to a ranking function $\kappa(\cdot)$ (see also [LM88]):

Definition 3.5 A *layered structure* (l-structure) is a pair $\langle \mathcal{W}, \kappa \rangle$, where $\mathcal{W}$ is a non-empty set of worlds, and κ is a function which assigns a non-negative integer to each world in $\mathcal{W}$.

Layered structures are thus collection of worlds organized in layers $\mathcal{W}_0$, $\mathcal{W}_1, \ldots \mathcal{W}_i, \ldots$, where a world W belongs to a layer $\mathcal{W}_i$ if and only if its rank $\kappa(W)$ is equal to i. Worlds in lower layers are preferred to worlds in higher layers.

The definition of preferred worlds within a given l-structure is analogous to the definition of preferred models within a given p-structure, and so are the definitions of *admissible* layered structures and *l-entailment:*

Definition 3.6 A layered structure $\langle \mathcal{W}, \kappa \rangle$ is *admissible* with a background $K = \langle L, D \rangle$ iff every world in $\mathcal{W}$ satisfies L, and for every default $p \rightarrow q$ in D, (a) q is true in all preferred worlds of p in $\mathcal{W}$, and (b) there is a world in $\mathcal{W}$ that satisfies p.[3]

Definition 3.7 A default theory $T = \langle K, E \rangle$ *l-entails* a proposition p iff p is true in all the preferred worlds of T of every layered structure admissible with K.

[3]Layered structures are always well-founded and in this respect they are different from Lehmann's and Magidor's [LM88] ranked models. A notion similar to layered structures also appears in [Ada66] and [Spo88] under the names of "P-orderings" and "ordinal conditional functions," respectively.

We also follow the convention of saying that a world W satisfies a default theory $T = \langle K, E\rangle$ with a background $K = \langle L, D\rangle$, when W satisfies the sentences in both L and E.

3.4 Equivalences

Admissible layered structures will play the role of a bridge between admissible preferential structures and admissible probability distributions. For the sake of simplicity we will assume throughout that the underlying language $\mathcal{L}$ and the theories $T = \langle K, E\rangle$ are such that they give rise to a *finite* number of worlds (for example, $\mathcal{L}$ may be a finite propositional language, or the theories may be universal, and contain a finite number of constants and no function symbols). Some of the results depend on this assumption (see proofs in the appendix), although weaker assumptions would suffice. The assumption of a finite number of worlds will permit us to concentrate on the main issues and to avoid a number of subtle technical problems.

We have three types of structures corresponding to each of the entailment relations considered: ϵ-entailment, p-entailment and l-entailment. We want to show first that if there is an admissible structure of one type, there will always be an admissible structure of the other types. For that purpose, let us introduce the following notion of consistency:

Definition 3.8 A background K is *ϵ-consistent* when for every positive ϵ there is a probability distribution which is ϵ-admissible relative to K; otherwise K is ϵ-inconsistent. Similarly, K is *p-consistent* (resp. *l-consistent*) when there is a p-structure (resp. l-structure) admissible relative to K, and p-inconsistent (resp. l-inconsistent) otherwise.

Then, the correspondences between the three types of structures can be formulated as follows:

Lemma 3.1 K is p-consistent if and only if K is l-consistent.

Lemma 3.2 K is ϵ-consistent if and only if K is l-consistent.

The importance of these correspondences is twofold. First, they show us that the structures defined by model-preference or infinitesimal probabilities are, in an important sense, equivalent. Second, since the notions

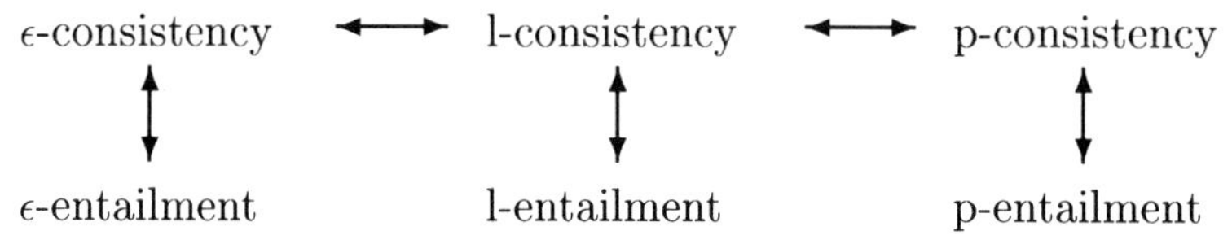

Figure 3.1
Equivalence between various forms of entailment

of entailment and consistency are intimately related, they establish a close connection between the entailment relations that both structures define. Consistency and entailment are related as follows:

Lemma 3.3 A default theory $T = \langle K, \{p\} \rangle$ ϵ-entails (resp. p-entails, l-entails) a proposition q, if and only if the background obtained by adding the default $p \rightarrow \neg q$ to K, is ϵ-inconsistent (resp. p-inconsistent, l-inconsistent).

The equivalence between the three forms of entailment is immediate:

Theorem 3.2 A default theory T ϵ-entails a proposition p iff T p-entails p iff T l-entails p.

Figure 3.1 illustrates the resulting relations. It is clear now *why* the core, justified originally in terms of probabilities, is valid under a preferential interpretation: there is a two way correspondence between the structures that underlie both accounts, and whenever one structure renders a given inference invalid, a corresponding structure can be constructed in the other interpretation which renders the same inference invalid too. Because of the equivalence between the three forms of entailment, we can now prove the core to be *complete* with respect to ϵ-entailment or p-entailment by proving the core complete with respect to l-entailment. This is what we are about to do. First we will introduce the notion of *default rankings* which will be essential in the proof.

3.5 Default Rankings

A *default ranking* over a background context $K = \langle L, D \rangle$ is a function that assigns a non-negative integer to each default in D. The rank of a default is a measure of its strength, and thus ranks are like priorities in prioritized circumscription [McC86]. However, rather than as a means for *expressing* preferences on defaults, default rankings will be used to *read* those preferences from the knowledge base. For example, in a background containing two defaults $\mathtt{p} \rightarrow \mathtt{q}$ and $\mathtt{p} \wedge \mathtt{r} \rightarrow \neg\mathtt{q}$, the more 'specific' default $\mathtt{p} \wedge \mathtt{r} \rightarrow \neg\mathtt{q}$ will automatically receive a higher rank than the less 'specific' default $\mathtt{p} \rightarrow \mathtt{q}$. Such a use of default rankings was implicit in the original work of Adams [Ada66], and has been exploited by Pearl [Pea90] in a recent extension of Adams' work.

We will refer to default rankings that comply with the preferences implicit in K as *admissible default rankings*. To make these preferences explicit, we will first recall a notion introduced in Section 2.5. We said that a set D of defaults is *in conflict* with a default $p \rightarrow q$ when D supports the negation of q in the context $\{p\}_K$ with background K and evidence $E = \{p\}$. Model-theoretically, this means that every model that *verifies* the defaults in D and satisfies the sentences in K, must violate the default $p \rightarrow q$ (a default $p \rightarrow q$ is *verified* in a model if *both* p and q are satisfied, and is *violated* in a model if p is satisfied but q is not).

Since Rule 1 permits us to apply a default $p \rightarrow q$ even in the presence of sets D in conflict with $p \rightarrow q$, it is reasonable to assume that the violation of a default from D is preferable to the violation of the default $p \rightarrow q$. Admissible default rankings capture this intuition by constraining the rank of $p \rightarrow q$ to be higher than the rank of some default in D:

Definition 3.9 A default ranking σ over a background $K = \langle L, D\rangle$ is *admissible* if every set of defaults $\mathsf{D} \subseteq D$ in conflict with a default $p \rightarrow q$ in D contains a default $p' \rightarrow q'$ such that $\sigma(p' \rightarrow q') < \sigma(p \rightarrow q)$.

We appealed to this intuition before for defining dominance and preemption relations among defaults (Section 2.5). Default rankings, and later on default priorities (Chapter 4), will provide the formal justification for these notions.

As an example, if $K = \langle L, D\rangle$ contains a default $\mathtt{p} \rightarrow \mathtt{q}$ and a second default $\mathtt{p} \wedge \mathtt{r} \rightarrow \neg\mathtt{q}$, then σ will be admissible only if $\sigma(\mathtt{p} \rightarrow \mathtt{q}) < \sigma(\mathtt{p} \wedge \mathtt{r} \rightarrow \neg\mathtt{q})$. This is because the set $\mathsf{D} = \{\mathtt{p} \rightarrow \mathtt{q}\}$ is in conflict with $\mathtt{p} \wedge \mathtt{r} \rightarrow \neg\mathtt{q}$, as $L, \mathtt{p} \wedge \mathtt{r}, \mathtt{p} \Rightarrow \mathtt{q} \vdash \mathtt{q}$. More generally, whenever $\mathtt{p} \rightarrow \mathtt{q}$ and $\mathtt{p}' \rightarrow \neg\mathtt{q}$ are two defaults in K, such that $\mathtt{p}$ is 'more specific' than $\mathtt{p}'$, i.e. $L \vdash \mathtt{p} \Rightarrow \mathtt{p}'$, $\mathtt{p} \rightarrow \mathtt{q}$ will get a higher rank than $\mathtt{p}' \rightarrow \neg\mathtt{q}$.

It is easy to come up with backgrounds which do not accept *any* admissible default ranking. For instance, no default ranking will be admissible with K if K contains a pair of defaults $p \rightarrow q$ and $p \rightarrow \neg q$. In fact, the existence of admissible rankings is a sufficient and necessary condition for the existence of admissible structures:[4]

Theorem 3.3 A background $K = \langle L, D \rangle$ is consistent if and only if there is a default ranking admissible with K.

More precisely, given an admissible default ranking σ, we can build an admissible layered structure $\langle \mathcal{W}_L, \kappa \rangle$ by setting $\mathcal{W}_L$ to the worlds that satisfy the sentences in L, and $\kappa(W)$ to zero if W violates no default, and to one plus the rank of the highest ranked default violated by W otherwise. Similarly, we can build an admissible default ranking function σ given an admissible layered structure $\langle \mathcal{W}, \kappa \rangle$ by setting $\sigma(p \rightarrow q)$ to the rank of the lowest ranked world in $\mathcal{W}$ which satisfies both p and q. We will use these correspondences later on.

Due to the relation between entailment and consistency expressed by Lemma 3.3 (page 49), default rankings provide an alternative method for evaluating entailment. Default rankings will be particularly convenient for this task because of the explicit relation between the admissibility conditions and the syntactic form of K. The notion of *default clashes* will make this advantage more overt:

Definition 3.10 A non-empty set of defaults D, $\mathsf{D} \subseteq D$, constitutes a *clash* in a background $K = \langle L, D \rangle$, iff every default $p \rightarrow q$ in D is in conflict with D. Likewise, a default $p \rightarrow q$ *clashes* with D, if the set $\mathsf{D} + \{p \rightarrow q\}$ constitutes a *clash*.

The defaults $p \rightarrow q$ and $p \rightarrow \neg q$, for instance, clash in every background context. Indeed, clashes of defaults are the only reason for inconsistency. In other words, we can test the consistency of a background context by simply testing for the presence of default clashes:[5]

Lemma 3.4 A background is consistent if and only if it does not contain a clash.

---

[4]We are assuming that the background $K = \langle L, D \rangle$ is logically consistent.

[5]We are assuming that the background K contains a finite number of default schemas $p(x) \rightarrow q(x)$ and no ground terms, so that any two default instances give rise to the same conflicts except for term substitutions. This permits us to assign the same rank to all the potentially infinite instances of a given default schema.

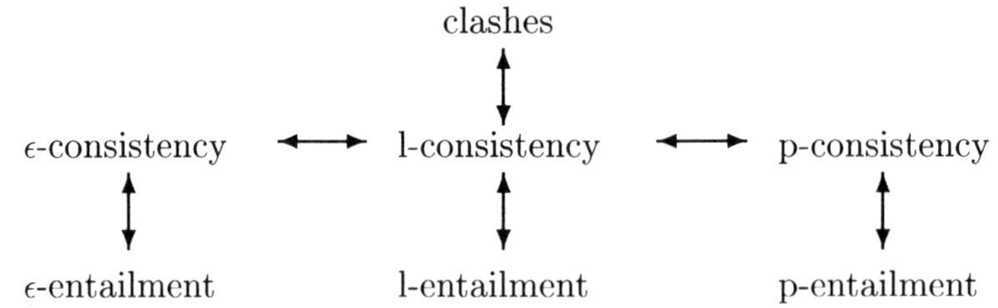

Figure 3.2
Entailment and default clashes

Due to the relation between consistency and entailment (Lemma 3.3), clashes yield a *syntactic method for testing entailment* (Fig. 3.2):

Lemma 3.5 p entails q in a background context $K = \langle L, D \rangle$ if and only if the background $K' = \langle L, D + \{p \rightarrow \neg q\} \rangle$ contains a clash.

The presence of clashes can be tested for in a 'greedy' fashion whether a background context $K = \langle L, D \rangle$ contains a clash. For if D itself is a clash then every default $p \rightarrow q$ in D must be in conflict with D; otherwise, every default *not* in conflict with D is guaranteed not to participate in any clash, and thus can be removed, leaving a smaller set D' which can be tested by similar means. As originally noted by Pearl [Pea90], such a procedure, together with Lemma 3.5, permits us to compute entailment in time polynomial in the number of defaults in D:

Theorem 3.4 (Pearl) For a background context $K = \langle L, D \rangle$ with n defaults, there is a $\mathcal{O}(C(n) \times n^2)$ procedure for testing whether a sentence q is entailed by a sentence p in K, where $C(n)$ is the complexity associated with testing the satisfiability of n sentences in the language that contains the sentences in L, the material counterparts of the defaults in D, and the sentence $p \Rightarrow \neg q$ (e.g., $C(n) = \mathcal{O}(n)$ for Horn clauses).

3.6 Completeness of the Core

We are now almost ready to show the completeness of the core relative to ϵ-entailment and p-entailment. The notion of *quasi-conjunctions,* originally introduced in [Ada75], will help us to tie everything together.

The quasi-conjunction $C(D)$ of a collection D of defaults $p_i \rightarrow q_i$, $i = 1, \ldots, n$, is the default:

$$p_1 \vee p_2 \vee \cdots \vee p_n \rightarrow (p_1 \Rightarrow q_1) \wedge (p_2 \Rightarrow q_2) \wedge \cdots \wedge (p_n \Rightarrow q_n)$$

Quasi-conjunctions permit us to map the problem of whether a sentence q is entailed by a sentence p in a background $K = \langle L, D \rangle$ into the problem of testing the consistency of a simpler background $K' = \langle L, D' \rangle$ containing only *two* defaults: the quasi-conjunction $C(D)$ of D, and the denial $p \rightarrow \neg q$ of the default $p \rightarrow q$. This feature is a consequence of results established in Section 3.5 and the following lemma:

Lemma 3.6 Let $p \rightarrow q$ be a default in D, let D' be a subset of D, and let $C(D')$ be the quasi-conjunction of D'. Then, $p \rightarrow q$ clashes with D' in a background context $K = \langle L, D \rangle$, if and only if $p \rightarrow q$ clashes with $C(D')$ in the background context $K' = \langle L, D'' \rangle$ with $D'' = \{C(D'), p \rightarrow q\}$.

Lemma 3.6 is a simple consequence of the logical equivalence between the sentence

$$\neg(p_1 \Rightarrow q_1) \vee \cdots \vee \neg(p_n \Rightarrow q_n)$$

and the sentence

$$\neg(p_1 \vee p_2 \vee \cdots \vee p_n \Rightarrow (p_1 \Rightarrow q_1) \wedge (p_2 \Rightarrow q_2) \wedge \cdots \wedge (p_n \Rightarrow q_n))$$

We are now ready to prove that the core is *complete* with respect to all three forms of entailment considered. This proof is the guarantee that Rules 1–5 in Chapter 2 do not miss any inference sanctioned by either ϵ-entailment or p-entailment. We will use the expression $p \mathrel{\vdash\kern-0.5em\sim}_K q$ to indicate that q is derivable from the theory $T = \langle K, E \rangle$ with $E = \{p\}$, by means of Rules 1–5, viz. without relying on the irrelevance rule.

Theorem 3.5 (Completeness) If p entails q in a *consistent* background $K = \langle L, D \rangle$, then $p \mathrel{\vdash\kern-0.5em\sim}_K q$.

Proof Note first, that if p entails q in K, the background context K' that results from the addition of $p \rightarrow \neg q$ to K must be inconsistent. Furthermore, since K is assumed to be consistent, the results above imply that the default $p \rightarrow \neg q$ must clash with a subset D' of D in L, and therefore, that $p \rightarrow \neg q$ must clash with the quasi-conjunction $C(D')$ of D'. The rest of the proof is a straightforward consequence of the following two results:

Lemma 3.7 Let $K = \langle L, D \rangle$ be a background context, and D' be a non-empty subset of D. Then, if $r \to s$ stands for the quasi-conjunction $C(D')$ of D', $r \mathrel{\vdash\!\!\!\sim}_K s$.

Lemma 3.8 Let $K = \langle L, D \rangle$ and $K' = \langle L, D' \rangle$ be two background contexts with the same set L of sentences. If $p \to \neg q$ clashes with $r \to s$ in K' and $r \mathrel{\vdash\!\!\!\sim}_K s$, then $p \mathrel{\vdash\!\!\!\sim}_K q$.

Thus, the core is complete with respect to entailment in *consistent* background contexts. The consistency condition is required because the semantic accounts legitimize any sentence when K is inconsistent, while the core does so only in certain contexts. For example, from an inconsistent background context K containing two defaults $p \to q$ and $p \to \neg q$, the core will not derive $E \mathrel{\vdash\!\!\!\sim}_K$ **false**, unless it can previously derive $E \mathrel{\vdash\!\!\!\sim}_K p$.

There are actually various ways in which the consistency requirement can be dropped from the completeness theorem. One is to legitimize arbitrary derivations when K is inconsistent. This can be accomplished by means of an additional rule which permits the special atom **false** to be derived when an inconsistency in K is detected [Ada75]. A second, more appealing option consists of relaxing the admissibility requirements on structures and probability distributions. This approach was used in [KLM90], and amounts to dropping the requirement that every default be verified in some world. In terms of probabilities, this amounts to taking into considerations non-proper probability distributions, for which $P_K(q \mid p)$ is set to one when $P_K(p)$ is equal to zero (see [Ada66]). We have chosen the more stringent admissibility condition, because they provide a simpler and more insightful correspondence between the probabilistic and model-theoretic accounts of defaults. Furthermore, the resulting consistency conditions impose a reasonable integrity constraint on defaults: pairs of defaults such as "birds fly" and "birds do not fly," for instance, are ruled out as inconsistent. Last but not least, these consistency conditions, expressed in terms of default rankings, are essential for the extensions of the core that we explore below.

3.7 Extensions

The picture is now complete: ϵ-entailment, l-entailment and p-entailment are equivalent, and the core provides a sound and complete axiomatization of them all. Yet, as mentioned earlier, the interpretation of defaults that results from these entailment relations is too conservative. For example, it does not sanction that a *red* bird flies, given that birds fly, as this involves an unstated assumption about independence: that 'redness' does not affect 'flying'. In Chapter 2, we addressed this problem by extending the core. In this section we will extend instead the entailment relations considered. The two approaches will be compared in Chapter 4.

The straightforward way of extending l-entailment and p-entailment is by considering a single, in a sense, *canonical admissible structure,* as opposed to all of them. The resulting entailment relation will be stronger, although it will still be consistent with the core. The choice of such canonical structures is obvious once we notice the following proposition:

Proposition 3.1 For every consistent background $K = \langle L, D \rangle$ there is unique *minimal* admissible default ranking σ^*, such that for any default $p \rightarrow q$ in D and any admissible default ranking σ, $\sigma^*(p \rightarrow q) \leq \sigma(p \rightarrow q)$.

This property is a consequence of the fact that if σ_1 and σ_2 are two admissible default ranking functions, then $\sigma_3(x) = \min\{\sigma_1(x), \sigma_2(x)\}$ will be an admissible default ranking function as well.

As noted in Section 3.5, we can map an admissible default ranking function into an admissible world ranking function, and vice versa, and hence we can obtain a unique admissible layered structure $\langle \mathcal{W}_L, \kappa^* \rangle$ from σ^*, by setting $\mathcal{W}_L$ to the set of worlds which satisfy L, and $\kappa^*(W)$ to zero if W violates no default, and to one plus the rank of the highest ranked default violated by W otherwise. This suggests the following new entailment relation:

Definition 3.11 A default theory $T = \langle K, E \rangle$ l*-entails a proposition p if p holds in the preferred worlds of E in the canonical layered structure $\langle \mathcal{W}_L, \sigma^* \rangle$.

l*-entailment is thus a proper extension of l-entailment, hence of the core. For example, given a background containing a single default $\mathtt{a} \rightarrow \mathtt{b}$ and a body of evidence $E = \{\mathtt{a}, \mathtt{e}\}$, l*-entailment, unlike l-entailment, correctly sanctions $\mathtt{b}$. The same can be said about default transitivity and contraposition. l*-entailment corresponds, in fact, to the extension of the core devised by Pearl [Pea90], called 1-entailment, which in turn is equivalent to Lehmann's [Leh89] rational closure.

These two entailment relations, although superior to p-entailment and ϵ-entailment suffer from a number of problems. For example, from a background with two defaults a $\rightarrow$ b and c $\rightarrow$ d, 1*-entailment fails to conclude d from a, c, and $\neg$b. Intuitively, this is not correct as there is nothing to suggest that the second default should not be applicable when the first default is not; yet, the semantics of 1*-entailment is such that a world that violates one default receives the same 'penalty' as a world that violates several defaults of equal rank.

This anomaly does not require us to do away with the canonical default ranking function σ^*. Instead we can use it to define a different order among interpretations in which preferred models will be guaranteed to be *minimal* in the set of defaults they violate. Like prioritized circumscription, we can define a canonical *preferential* structure $\langle \mathcal{I}_L, <^* \rangle$ where $\mathcal{I}_L$ stands for the set of interpretations that satisfy the sentences in L, and '$<^*$' represents a strict partial order such that $M <^* M'$ holds if the rank of the highest ranked default which is violated by M *but not* by M' is lower than the rank of the highest ranked default which is violated by M' *but not* by M. We will show later that the resulting structure is preferential and admissible and that the entailment relation it defines constitutes an extension of the core. We will call the resulting entailment relation p*-entailment.

Definition 3.12 A default theory $T = \langle K, E \rangle$ p*-entails a proposition p if p holds in the preferred models of E in the canonical preferential structure $\langle \mathcal{I}_L, <^* \rangle$.

p*-entailment solves some of the problems of 1*-entailment but not all. For example, two defaults p$\wedge$s $\rightarrow$ q and r $\rightarrow$ $\neg$q, together with a body of evidence $E = \{\mathtt{p}, \mathtt{s}, \mathtt{r}\}$, leave the status of the proposition q ambiguous. However, if a new default p $\rightarrow$ $\neg$q supporting the *negation* of q is added, the ambiguity is resolved *in favor* of q. This is because the addition of p $\rightarrow$ $\neg$q raises the ranking of p$\wedge$s $\rightarrow$ q, which hence gets 'stronger' than the conflicting default r $\rightarrow$ $\neg$q.

The source of this strange behavior lies with the commitment to a unique layered order among defaults. Indeed, we want p $\wedge$ s $\rightarrow$ q to be stronger than p $\rightarrow$ $\neg$q but *not* than r $\rightarrow$ $\neg$q. One approach to solve this problem is to appeal to *multiple* ranking functions; the other, more natural, is to give up ranking functions completely, and consider instead *partial orders.* In the next chapter we will develop a semantics which accommodates both features: namely, *multiple orders* among defaults which may also be *partial*. We will also analyze why this is needed, and how we can compute with the resulting account.

3.8   Related Work

The soundness and completeness of Rules 1–5 relative to ϵ-entailment, were informally sketched in [GP87], and can be traced back to [Ada66, Ada75]. Preferential structures and layered structures, correspond, in essence, to structures advanced in [LM88, Mak89, KLM90]. Lehmann and Magidor also noted the connection between accounts based on high probabilities and model-preference, a connection which Adams himself explored in [Ada78]. The notion of default rankings is due to Pearl [Pea90]. l*-entailment is equivalent to Pearl's 1-entailment and Lehmann's [Leh89] rational closure. In the next chapter we will develop the model and proof-theory of conditional entailment, which is a refinement of both l*-entailment and p*-entailment. Below we discuss some issues relevant to the inference rules that make up the core.

Our discussion in Section 2.5 made clear that Rules 1–5 and the semantic accounts which render them sound and complete, do not provide a satisfactory characterization of default reasoning. In particular, they fail to sanction inference patterns involving independence assumptions. What is not so clear, however, is whether these rules should be regarded as a *minimal* core to be satisfied by any reasonable account of defeasible inference. In this regard, *augmentation* and *reduction*, also known as *cumulative monotony* and *cumulative transitivity* [Mak89], have attracted most of the attention. These two rules establish that two contexts $T = \langle K, E \rangle$ and $T' = \langle K, E + \{p\} \rangle$ should be equivalent, when p is a consequence of T. Gabbay [Gab85] argued on proof-theoretic grounds that, together with a weak form *deduction*, these rules define minimal requirements on any reasonable non-monotonic consequence relation. Such a position has been lately echoed on semantic grounds by Kraus *et al.* [KLM90] and Pearl [Pea89a]. Our position is that while these rules are reasonable, they are not 'inescapable'. Indeed, both the probabilistic and model-theoretic accounts which validate cumulativity, contain questionable assumptions. The probabilistic interpretation, for example, regards defaults as having arbitrarily high conditional probabilities. This abstraction yields a qualitative account of defaults but it is not entirely reasonable. The model-theoretic account, likewise, regards the preference relation on models to be an exclusive function of the background context. Again, it is not obvious why preference relations have to be restricted in this manner. In Chapter 5 we will look at examples whose intended behavior demands preferences to depend on *both* background and evidence. However, once the space of admissible structures is so determined, the cumulative behavior is no longer guaranteed.

Lehmann and Magidor [LM88] discuss a rule called *rational monotony*, which holds in what we have called layered structures but does not hold in preferential structures. Rational monotony is a strong form of augmentation, which permits us to carry a conclusion q from a context $T = \langle K, E \rangle$ to a context $T' = \langle K, E + \{p\} \rangle$, as long as the *negation* of p is *not* a consequence of T. Rational monotony holds in l-entailment (and l*-entailment) but not in p-entailment (or p*-entailment).

We believe that the question of whether rational monotony is a reasonable property of default reasoning is mainly empirical and can be illuminated by considering concrete examples. For instance, a consequence relation obeying rational monotony will force us to conclude $\neg p'$ from p, and $\neg p$ from p', given any unresolved conflicting pair of defaults $p \rightarrow q$ and $p' \rightarrow \neg q$. Such behavior, however, may be too adventurous, as when p is connected to p' via a 'diamond' structure (e.g., $p \rightarrow r \rightarrow p'$ and $p \rightarrow s \rightarrow \neg p'$). For even though there are no grounds to conclude q over $\neg q$ given p and p', there are no grounds to conclude $\neg p'$ from p either. Still, a consequence relation obeying cumulativity and rational monotony has to draw one conclusion or the other.

4 Priorities, Minimality and Irrelevance

4.1 Introduction

In the last two chapters we discussed in detail two conditional interpretations of defaults, one based on probabilities, and the other on models.[1] The probabilistic interpretation regards a default $p \rightarrow q$ as asserting that the probability of q is high, given that p *represents all the available evidence.* The preferential interpretation regards $p \rightarrow q$ as asserting that q is true in *all preferred models of* p. In both cases something is asserted about a particular context, and implicitly, other contexts are constrained as well as a result of the axioms of probability theory and of the postulates on the preference relation on models respectively. The core, Rules 1–5, is the logic of such constraints.

Most work in non-monotonic logics has neglected this conditional dimension of defaults. Non-monotonic logics do not view a default $p \rightarrow q$ as an assertion q bound to a particular context p, but as a *prima facie reason* to assert q in *all* the contexts in which p holds. This has created the need to account for preferences among defaults by other means, ranging from *specificity* considerations (e.g., [Poo85, Nut88b, Lou87a]) to devices such as *priorities* [McC86, Lif88a] or *non-normal defaults* [ER83] to be employed by the user.

There is nevertheless a feature in the non-monotonic reading of defaults which the conditional interpretations fail to capture. This has to do with the assumptions about independence (cf. Chapters 2 and 3). For example, none of the standard non-monotonic logics has any trouble in concluding that a 'red bird' flies given a default 'birds fly'. Yet the same inference is not sanctioned by ϵ-entailment or preferential entailment. The problem is that the contexts "Tim is a bird" and "Tim is a *red* bird" are distinct, and while one is constrained by the default 'birds fly' the other one is not.

We discussed this limitation in Section 2.5 where we developed an extension of the core based on *irrelevance* considerations. The idea was to strengthen the inferential import of defaults $p \rightarrow q$ by asserting the

[1] This chapter contains excerpts from the paper "Conditional entailment: Bridging two approaches to default reasoning" by H. Geffner and J. Pearl that appeared in the journal Artificial Intelligence. They are reprinted here by permission of the publisher, North Holland/Elsevier, Amsterdam.

material conditional $p \Rightarrow q$ in contexts which do not provide evidence for p and $\neg q$. Unfortunately, the irrelevance account raises as many questions as it solves. First of all it is not clear under what conditions the 'closure' of the core under the irrelevance rule is consistent. Even if it is, we would like to know whether the account presented is adequate, and whether it can be justified on independent grounds, just as the core can be justified in terms of high probabilities and preferential structures.

A more principled method for extending the core was then explored in Section 3.7 where we considered extensions of p-entailment and l-entailment which depend on a single, suitably chosen admissible structure. These extensions, called l*-entailment and p*-entailment, are better motivated than the irrelevance account and automatically enforce consistency. On the other hand, their behavior is not as intuitive, and it is not clear how they can be computed when enumerating all models is not possible.

In this chapter we will show that the two methods for extending the core — one based on irrelevance, the other, on default rankings and canonical structures — are two sides of the same coin. More precisely, we will develop a second extension of preferential entailment which avoids the problems of p*-entailment while rendering the irrelevance account in Chapter 2 sound. The new extension of preferential entailment will be defined in terms of the class of admissible preferential structures induced by a suitably class of *priorities* on defaults. These priorities, in turn, are like ranking functions, except that they represent *partial* orders as opposed to *layered* ones.

The resulting account, called *conditional entailment,* sheds also some light on the relation between conditional interpretations of defaults like ϵ-entailment and p-entailment, and standard non-monotonic formalisms such as prioritized circumscription [McC86, Lif85]. Conditional entailment is roughly equivalent to prioritized circumscription, except that priorities are not supplied by the 'user' but are extracted automatically from the knowledge base.

We will also develop a *proof-theory* which will permit us to compute conditional entailment without having to enumerate models. The proof-theory is based on the notion of *arguments* introduced in Chapter 2. Roughly, arguments of different strength compete and propositions supported by the 'strongest' arguments are accepted. The proof-theory, unlike Rules 1–6, is both sound and complete relative to conditional entailment. An architecture which implements a fragment of the proof-theory in terms of an assumption-based truth-maintenance system [dK86] is also presented.

4.2 Defaults and Minimal Models

Conditional entailment is more easily understood if we take a closer look at the difference between a *conditional* interpretation of defaults such as p-entailment, and a *extensional* interpretation of defaults such as minimal models. Let us therefore assume that a default theory $T = \langle K, D \rangle$, with background $K = \langle L, D \rangle$, is interpreted by considering the models of T which are *minimal* in the set of defaults they violate,[2] and let us compare the resulting entailment relation, *minimal entailment,* with p-entailment.

Minimal entailment, unlike p-entailment, captures the 'independencies' that characterize extensional non-monotonic formalisms. Namely, given a default "birds fly" we would not only be able to conclude that a bird flies, but also that a *red* bird flies. Like the other extensional formalisms, however, minimal entailment misses patterns, such as specificity preferences which p-entailment does capture.

By now, however, we have established that the patterns of inference sanctioned by p-entailment (and ϵ-entailment) can be completely captured by the following rules (Theorem 3.5, page 53):

Rule 1 (Defaults) $p \mathrel{|\!\!\!\sim_K} q$ if $p \rightarrow q \ \in D$

Rule 2 (Deduction) If $E, L \vdash p$ then $E \mathrel{|\!\!\!\sim_K} p$

Rule 3 (Augmentation) If $E \mathrel{|\!\!\!\sim_K} p$ and $E \mathrel{|\!\!\!\sim_K} q$ then $E, p \mathrel{|\!\!\!\sim_K} q$

Rule 4 (Reduction) If $E \mathrel{|\!\!\!\sim_K} p$ and $E, p \mathrel{|\!\!\!\sim_K} q$ then $E \mathrel{|\!\!\!\sim_K} q$

Rule 5 (Disjunction) If $E, p \mathrel{|\!\!\!\sim_K} r$ and $E, q \mathrel{|\!\!\!\sim_K} r$ then $E, p \vee q \mathrel{|\!\!\!\sim_K} r$

It thus makes sense to ask *which* of these rules is not valid under minimal entailment. Clearly not all the rules can be valid, otherwise minimal entailment would capture all the inferences that p-entailment does.

[2] A model M violates a default $p \rightarrow q$ when M satisfies p but does not satisfy q.

It turns out that the only rule violated by minimal entailment is Rule 1. Namely, the minimization of default violations renders a semantics that complies with all rules in the core except Rule 1. Rule 1, however, is crucial; in fact, it is the only rule in the core that looks at the defaults in the knowledge base. Rule 1 permits us to derive the consequent q of a default $p \rightarrow q$, provided its antecedent p represents all the available evidence.

The reason minimal entailment does not satisfy Rule 1 can be illustrated in the 'birds fly, penguins don't fly' example. Given that Tim is a penguin, two classes of minimal models arise: one which violates the default `bird(tim)` $\rightarrow$ `fly(tim)`; and one which violates the default `penguin(tim)` $\rightarrow$ $\neg$`fly(tim)`. As a result, $\neg$`fly(tim)` , although derivable by Rule 1, is not true in all minimal models, and thus is not minimally entailed.

Since we would like to capture the patterns of inference that are sanctioned by both p-entailment and minimal entailment, it would be wise to develop an account which combines the features of both. There are two ways in which this can be done. One is by means of a sixth inference rule which would permit us to adopt the defaults which hold in all minimal models; the other is by modifying the minimal model semantics in such a way that Rule 1 becomes valid.

A refinement of the first approach was pursued in Chapter 2. In fact, if a default $p \rightarrow q$ holds in all minimal models of a default theory $T = \langle K, E \rangle$, then the body of evidence E will be irrelevant to $p \rightarrow q$, and thus the material conditional $p \Rightarrow q$ will be derivable from Rule 6.

The second approach was explored in Section 3.7. There we used an admissible default ranking function for defining a preferential structure with two properties: first, the structure is *admissible*, and second, the preferred models are minimal. As a result, p*-entailment extends both p-entailment and the minimal models semantics.

The two approaches, however, are intimately related. In this chapter we develop a refinement of p*-entailment, called *conditional entailment*, which makes both the core *and* the irrelevance rule sound. Conditional entailment also fixes the 'glitches' in p*-entailment (cf. Section 3.7), by relying on *priorities*, i.e., strict partial orders, as opposed to default ranking functions.

4.3 Priorities

The role of priorities in conditional entailment will be similar to the role of default ranking functions in p*-entailment: priorities on defaults are extracted from the background K, and are used to determine a preference relation on interpretations. As usual, the propositions entailed by a theory $T = \langle K, E \rangle$ will be the propositions that hold in the preferred models of E.

Priority relations are binary relations that are irreflexive and transitive. We usually denote them by symbols like '$\prec$' and '$\prec'$', and write $p \rightarrow q \prec p' \rightarrow q'$ to say that the default $p' \rightarrow q'$ has higher priority than the default $p \rightarrow q$.

As for default rankings, not every priority ordering will do. *Admissible* priority orderings will have to reflect the preferences implicit in the background context. These preferences originate from regarding defaults as conditionals (cf. Section 3.5). That is, since given the evidence $E = \{p\}$, we can apply a default $p \rightarrow q$ *even in the presence of sets of defaults* D *in conflict with* $p \rightarrow q$ (Rule 1), we will assume that each such set D contains a default $p' \rightarrow q'$ with priority lower than $p \rightarrow q$:[3]

Definition 4.1 A priority ordering '$\prec$' over a background $K = \langle L, D \rangle$ is *admissible* if every set of defaults $\mathsf{D} \subseteq D$ in conflict with a default $p \rightarrow q$ in D contains a default $p' \rightarrow q'$ such that $p' \rightarrow q' \prec p \rightarrow q$.

This definition can be compared with the analogous definition for default ranking functions (Definition 3.9, page 50). Indeed, if σ is a default ranking function admissible with K, then the priority ordering $\prec_\sigma$ defined as $p' \rightarrow q' \prec_\sigma p \rightarrow q$ iff $\sigma(p' \rightarrow q') < \sigma(p \rightarrow q)$ will be admissible as well. On the other hand, there are admissible priority orderings with no corresponding ranking functions. If $p_i \rightarrow q_i$, $i = 1, 2, 3$ are three defaults, and σ is an admissible ranking function such that $\sigma(p_1 \rightarrow q_1) < \sigma(p_2 \rightarrow q_2)$, then, due to the total order on integers, we must have either $\sigma(p_1 \rightarrow q_1) < \sigma(p_3 \rightarrow q_3)$ or $\sigma(p_3 \rightarrow q_3) < \sigma(p_2 \rightarrow q_2)$. On the other hand, no such constraint exists on priorities which provide a *partial* order on defaults only.

[3] Recall that a set of defaults $D' \subseteq D$ is in conflict with a default $p \rightarrow q \in D$ in a background $K = \langle L, D \rangle$ when D' supports the negation of q in the context $\{p\}_K$. This is equivalent to saying that $\neg q$ is a logical consequence of L, p and D', provided that each default $p_i \rightarrow q_i$ is replaced by the material conditional $p_i \Rightarrow q_i$.

For example, if K contains two defaults $\mathtt{p} \rightarrow \mathtt{q}$ and $\mathtt{p} \wedge \mathtt{r} \rightarrow \neg\mathtt{q}$, then the priority ordering '$\prec$' will be admissible only if $\mathtt{p} \rightarrow \mathtt{q} \prec \mathtt{p} \wedge \mathtt{r} \rightarrow \neg\mathtt{q}$ (i.e., the more 'specific' defaults gets higher priority). If K also contains the default $\mathtt{q} \rightarrow \neg\mathtt{p}$, then '$\prec$' will also have to satisfy $\mathtt{q} \rightarrow \neg\mathtt{p} \prec \mathtt{p} \rightarrow \mathtt{q}$, and by transitivity, $\mathtt{q} \rightarrow \neg\mathtt{p} \prec \mathtt{p} \wedge \mathtt{r} \rightarrow \neg\mathtt{q}$.

4.4 Conditional Entailment

Priorities we will be used to define a particular class of preferential structures called *prioritized structures.* These structures have two main properties: first, models which violate defaults of lower priority are preferred to models which violate defaults of higher priority, and second, models which violate smaller sets of defaults are preferred to models which violated larger sets of defaults.

We will refer to the collection of defaults violated by a model M as the *gap* of the model and denote it by $D[M]$. We will also assume that all defaults are drawn from a predefined set $\mathcal{D}$. Prioritized structures are then defined as follows:

Definition 4.2 A *prioritized structure* is a quadruple $\langle \mathcal{I}_{\mathcal{L}}, <, \mathcal{D}, \prec \rangle$, where $\mathcal{I}_{\mathcal{L}}$ stands for the set of interpretations over the underlying language $\mathcal{L}$, $\mathcal{D}$ stands for the universe of defaults, '$\prec$' stands for an irreflexive and transitive priority relation over $\mathcal{D}$, and '$<$' is a binary relation over $\mathcal{I}_{\mathcal{L}}$, such that for two interpretations M and M', $M < M'$ holds iff $D[M] \neq D[M']$ and for every default $d \in \mathcal{D}$ in $D[M] - D[M']$ there is a default $d' \in \mathcal{D}$ in $D[M'] - D[M]$ such that $d \prec d'$.

We also require that priority orderings do not contain infinite ascending chains $d_1 \prec d_2 \prec d_3 \prec \cdots$. This will guarantee that the order on interpretations induced by any priority ordering will be both strict and partial:

Lemma 4.1 If the quadruple $\langle \mathcal{I}_{\mathcal{L}}, <, \mathcal{D}, \prec \rangle$ is a prioritized structure, then the pair $\langle \mathcal{I}_{\mathcal{L}}, < \rangle$ is a preferential structure.

This order on interpretations regards the relation $d \prec d'$ as a preference to sustain the default d' over the default d in cases of conflict. A similar mapping from priorities to preferences occurs in Przymusinski's characterization of the perfect model semantics of logic programs [Prz87] and in McCarthy's prioritized circumscription [McC86, Lif85].

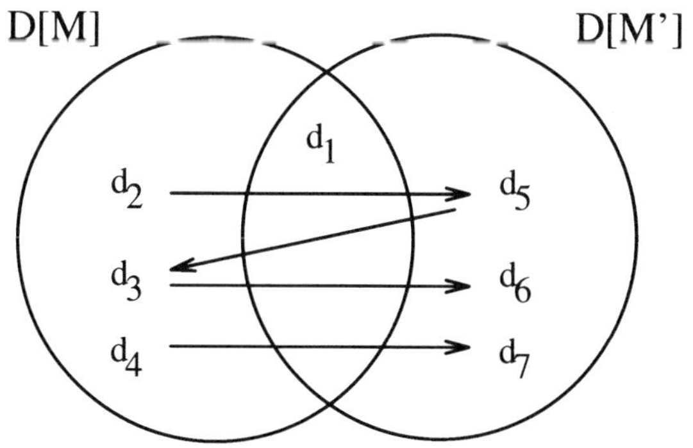

Figure 4.1
Preferences in prioritized structures

Figure 4.1 illustrates the preference on two interpretations M and M' determined by an arbitrary priority ordering on defaults depicted by arrows. An arrow connecting a default d_i to a default d_j expresses that d_i has lower priority than d_j, i.e., $d_i \prec d_j$. To check whether M is preferred to M', it is sufficient to check that each default d in $D[M] - D[M']$ is linked by an arrow to a default d' in $D[M'] - D[M]$ (since $D[M] \neq D[M']$). Note that defaults violated by both M and M' (e.g., d_1) play no role in determining the preferences between M and M'.

An important feature of the preference on models determined by any prioritization is that preferred models M are guaranteed to be *minimal* in the set $D[M]$ of defaults that they violate:

Lemma 4.2 In any prioritized structure, if M is a preferred model of a theory T, then M is *minimal* in $D[M]$, i.e., there is no model M' of T such that $D[M'] \subset D[M]$.

Also, models M and M' with identical gaps will not be distinguished: if M is a preferred model of T, for example, so will M' be if $D[M'] = D[M]$, and vice versa. For this reason, we will often talk about *classes of models*, where a class $\mathcal{C}$ is a non-empty collection of models M with a common gap. We will say that a class $\mathcal{C}_1$ is preferred to a class $\mathcal{C}_2$ if any one model in $\mathcal{C}_1$ is preferred to any one model in $\mathcal{C}_2$. Since the preference on interpretations depends on the gaps of the interpretations only, this will guarantee that any *other* model in $\mathcal{C}_1$ will be preferred to any *other* model in $\mathcal{C}_2$ as well.

Classes made up of models which are minimal will be called *minimal classes.* Since preferred models are minimal, preferred classes of models will be guaranteed to be minimal as well. It is simple to show then that a proposition p holds in a *minimal* class $\mathcal{C}$ — i.e., in every model in the class — if there is an argument for p validated by $\mathcal{C}$. Recall from Section 2.5 that an argument for p is a set of defaults $p_i \rightarrow q_i$ such that T augmented with the material conditionals $p_i \Rightarrow q_i$ is logically consistent and logically entails p.

If the minimality of preferred models provides conditional entailment with the 'extensional' features of non-monotonic logics, the focus on the class of *admissible* priority orderings which reflect the structure of K (page 63) endows conditional entailment with the features of p-entailment and ϵ-entailment:

Definition 4.3 A prioritized structure $\langle \mathcal{I}_{\mathcal{L}}, <, \mathcal{D}, \prec \rangle$ is *admissible* with a background $K = \langle L, D \rangle$ iff the universe of defaults $\mathcal{D}$ is equal to D and the priority ordering '$\prec$' is admissible with K.

Definition 4.4 A proposition q is *conditionally entailed* by a default theory $T = \langle K, E \rangle$, iff q holds in all the preferred models of T of every prioritized structure admissible with K.

Conditional entailment combines the two target notions: minimality and conditionality. In fact, if the underlying language $\mathcal{L}$ and the theories $T = \langle K, E \rangle$ are such that they give rise to a *finite* number of worlds (e.g., $\mathcal{L}$ may be a finite propositional language, or the theories may be universal, and contain a finite number of constants and no function symbols) the following result can be shown:[4]

Theorem 4.1 If T preferentially entails p, then T also conditionally entails p.

Since preferential entailment and ϵ-entailment coincide under those assumptions, the same subsumption relation applies to ϵ-entailment. For the subsumption relation to be meaningful though, we need to show

[4]The restrictions on this theorem are needed because the preferential structures $\langle \mathcal{I}_{\mathcal{L}}, < \rangle$ embedded in the prioritized structures $\langle \mathcal{I}_{\mathcal{L}}, <, \mathcal{D}, \prec \rangle$ are not necessarily well-founded in the sense defined in Chapter 3.

that T does not conditionally entail everything. Let us thus say that a background K is *conditionally consistent* when it accepts an admissible prioritized structure $\langle \mathcal{I}_{\mathcal{L}}, <, \mathcal{D}, \prec \rangle$. Then we immediately obtain the following result:

Theorem 4.2 A background K is *preferentially consistent* only if it is *conditionally consistent.*

Since the presence of admissible prioritized structures implies that a theory $T = \langle K, D \rangle$ will not conditionally entail both a proposition and its negation if T is logically consistent, this means that conditional entailment will be well-behaved as long as preferential entailment is well-behaved. This result is a consequence of the mapping of admissible default rankings into admissible priority orderings discussed in Section 4.2. Another way to look at this result is that conditional entailment will not sanction a contradiction if Rules 1–5 do not sanction one.

4.5 Examples

In this section we will illustrate how conditional entailment works in a number of examples. For each of the examples, we will first determine the admissible priorities by looking at the defaults in K, and then consider the preferred classes of models for different contexts $T = \langle K, E \rangle$ of interest. The determination of priorities can thus be understood as a 'compile-time' operation whose results are good for any particular set of observations.

Some abbreviations will be useful. We will write $E, D \vdash_K p$ when a set D of defaults supports a proposition p in the context $T = \langle K, E \rangle$. Recall that a set of defaults $p_i \rightarrow q_i$ in D supports p if p is a logical consequence of L, E and the material conditionals $p_i \Rightarrow q_i$. Also, we will write $D \prec d$ to express that there is a default $d' \in D$ such that $d' \prec d$ holds. These two abbreviations we will permit us to say that a priority ordering '$\prec$' is admissible when $D \prec p \rightarrow q$ holds for every set of defaults $D \subseteq D$ D in conflict with a default $p \rightarrow q$ in D, i.e., $p, D \vdash_K \neg q$. Note that this admissibility test needs to be applied to *minimal* D's only. When D is in conflict with a default d, we will also say that d *dominates* D (cf. Section 2.5).

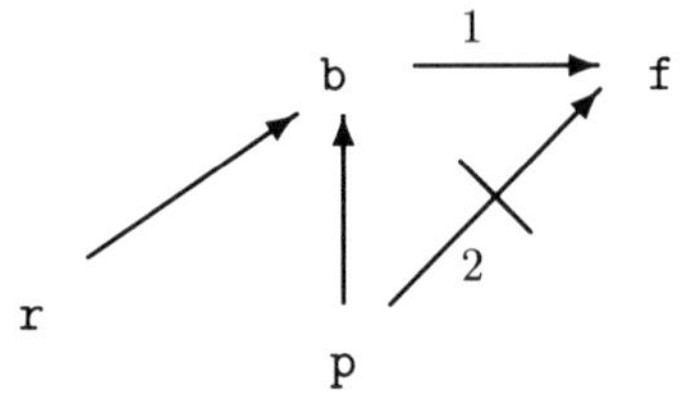

Figure 4.2
Strict specificity

Example 4.1 Consider a background $K = \langle L, D \rangle$ containing the rules:[5]

$$d_1(x) : \mathtt{b}(x) \rightarrow \mathtt{f}(x) \qquad \mathtt{p}(x) \Rightarrow \mathtt{b}(x)$$
$$d_2(x) : \mathtt{p}(x) \rightarrow \neg\mathtt{f}(x) \qquad \mathtt{r}(x) \Rightarrow \mathtt{b}(x)$$

The symbols $\mathtt{b}$, $\mathtt{f}$, $\mathtt{p}$, and $\mathtt{r}$, can be understood as standing for the predicates 'bird,' 'fly,' 'penguin,' and 'red-bird,' respectively. The symbols $d_i(x)$, on the other hand, will be used to refer to defaults. For instance, $d_2(a)$ will refer to the default $\mathtt{p}(a) \rightarrow \neg\mathtt{f}(a)$.

From Definition 4.1, a priority ordering '$\prec$' will be admissible with K if the relation $D \prec d_i(a)$ holds for any minimal set of defaults D dominated by the default $d_i(a)$, where a is any ground term and i is either 1 or 2. First note that there is no set of defaults D in conflict with instances of the default $\mathtt{b}(x) \rightarrow \mathtt{f}(x)$, as for any ground term a there are interpretations which satisfy K and $\mathtt{b}(a)$ and that violate no default. As a result, instances of $d_1(x)$ do not dominate any set of defaults and thus impose no constraint on the admissible priority orderings.

Defaults of the form $\mathtt{p}(a) \rightarrow \neg\mathtt{f}(a)$, on the other hand, dominate a single minimal set of defaults $D = \{\mathtt{b}(a) \rightarrow \mathtt{f}(a)\}$, as D is in conflict with $\mathtt{p}(a) \rightarrow \neg\mathtt{f}(a)$, i.e. $\mathtt{p}(a), D \vdash_K \mathtt{f}(a)$. Therefore, a priority ordering '$\prec$' will be admissible with K iff the relation $\mathtt{b}(a) \rightarrow \mathtt{f}(a) \prec \mathtt{p}(a) \rightarrow \neg\mathtt{f}(a)$ is satisfied for every ground term a in the language. We also write in these cases $\mathtt{b}(x) \rightarrow \mathtt{f}(x) \prec \mathtt{p}(x) \rightarrow \neg\mathtt{f}(x)$.

Provided with this characterization of the admissible prioritized structures, we can now turn to the propositions which are conditionally entailed in the different contexts of interest. For example, for an individual

[5] Free variables in wffs are assumed to be universally quantified.

Tim ($\mathtt{t}$), the preferred models of $\mathtt{b(t)}$ in K are the models which violate no default. As a result, both defaults $\mathtt{b(t)} \rightarrow \mathtt{f(t)}$ and $\mathtt{p(t)} \rightarrow \neg\mathtt{f(t)}$ will hold in the context $T = \langle K, \{\mathtt{b(t)}\}\rangle$ and both $\mathtt{f(t)}$ and $\neg\mathtt{p(t)}$ will be conditionally entailed (i.e., Tim is presumed to be a normal flying bird, and therefore, not a penguin).

A different scenario arises if we consider the evidence $\mathtt{p(t)}$ instead of $\mathtt{b(t)}$. In this case, every interpretation satisfying the evidence and the sentences in the background is forced to violate one of the two defaults $\mathtt{b(t)} \rightarrow \mathtt{f(t)}$ or $\mathtt{p(t)} \rightarrow \neg\mathtt{f(t)}$. Thus, two classes of minimal models will arise, one comprised of models which violate the first default, and another comprised of models which violate the second default. However, since the second default has higher priority than the first default, models M_1 in the first class will be preferred to models M_2 in the second one; indeed, we have

$$D[M_2] - D[M_1] = \{\mathtt{p(t)} \rightarrow \neg\mathtt{f(t)}\}$$
$$D[M_1] - D[M_2] = \{\mathtt{b(t)} \rightarrow \mathtt{f(t)}\}$$

and $\mathtt{b(t)} \rightarrow \mathtt{f(t)} \prec \mathtt{p(t)} \rightarrow \neg\mathtt{f(t)}$. Thus, from Definition 4.2, we get $M_1 < M_2$. This means that the 'more specific' default $\mathtt{p(t)} \rightarrow \neg\mathtt{f(t)}$ holds in $T' = \langle K, \{\mathtt{p(t)}\}\rangle$, and therefore, $\neg\mathtt{f(t)}$ is conditionally entailed. Similar conclusions are legitimized by preferential entailment and ϵ-entailment.

Finally, consider the scenario in which the target context is enhanced with the information that Tim is a red bird, i.e. $T'' = \langle K, E''\rangle$, with $E'' = \{\mathtt{p(t)}, \mathtt{r(t)}\}$. In this case, neither ϵ-entailment nor p-entailment constrain the preferred models of T''. Conditional entailment, on the other hand, guarantees that the preferred models of T'' are minimal, and thus, that they violate the default $\mathtt{b(t)} \rightarrow \mathtt{f(t)}$ or $\mathtt{p(t)} \rightarrow \neg\mathtt{f(t)}$. Remember, however, that models which violate the first default are preferred to models which violate the second one. As a result, the default $\mathtt{p(t)} \rightarrow \neg\mathtt{f(t)}$ still holds in the context T'' and the proposition $\neg\mathtt{f(t)}$ is conditionally entailed. This conclusion is not legitimized by either ϵ-entailment or p-entailment, nor by minimality considerations alone.

The example above illustrates different contexts built on top of a background which forces every admissible priority ordering '$\prec$' to satisfy the relation $d_1(a) \prec d_2(a)$ for all ground terms a in the language. This means that every admissible priority *relation* '$\prec$' must include all tuples of the form $\langle d_1(a), d_2(a)\rangle$; other tuples may also be included, e.g., $\langle d_1(a), d_2(b)\rangle$, but they are not necessary for the relations to be admissible. We will say that an admissible priority relation is *minimal* when no set of tuples can be deleted without violating the admissibility constraints. For instance, in the example above, there is a *single* minimal admissible ordering which includes all and only the tuples of the form $\langle d_1(a), d_2(a)\rangle$. We may ask then whether conditional entailment can be computed by restricting attention to *minimal* admissible priority orderings only. The answer is yes. Indeed, if we can obtain an admissible priority ordering '$\prec$' by deleting certain tuples from an admissible priority ordering '$\prec'$', the preferred models in the structure $\langle \mathcal{I}_\mathcal{L}, <', \mathcal{D}, \prec'\rangle$ will be a subset of the preferred models of the structure $\langle \mathcal{I}_\mathcal{L}, <, \mathcal{D}, \prec\rangle$. Thus, if we say that an admissible prioritized structure $\langle \mathcal{I}_\mathcal{L}, <, \mathcal{D}, \prec\rangle$ is *minimal* if the relation '$\prec$' is a minimal admissible priority ordering, the following alternative characterization of conditional entailment results:

Lemma 4.3 A proposition q is *conditionally entailed* by a default theory $T = \langle K, E\rangle$ iff q holds in all the preferred models of T of every *minimal* prioritized structure admissible with K.

The second question is whether this minimal structure is unique; if it is, we could compute conditional entailment like 1*-entailment and p*-entailment (cf. Section 3.7), by considering a single structure. In the example above, the structure $\langle \mathcal{I}_\mathcal{L}, <, \mathcal{D}, \prec\rangle$, where $d \prec d'$ holds iff $d = d_1(a)$ and $d' = d_2(a)$, is the only minimal admissible structure. However, this is not true in general. Often theories give rise to multiple minimal admissible structures all of which need to be considered for determining what is conditionally entailed (see Example 4.4 below).

Example 4.2 (Cycles) In this example we illustrate the interpretation of the cyclic network depicted in Fig. 4.3, represented by the background $K = \langle L, D\rangle$:

$$d_1(x) : \mathsf{c}(x) \rightarrow \mathsf{u}(x)$$

$$d_2(x) : \mathsf{u}(x) \rightarrow \mathsf{a}(x)$$

$$d_3(x) : \mathsf{a}(x) \rightarrow \neg\mathsf{u}(x)$$

These defaults can be read as stating that "most people sitting in the class are university students," "most university students are adults," and "most adults are not university students."

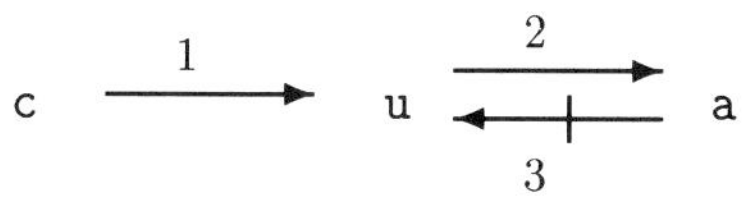

Figure 4.3
Cyclic inheritance hierarchy

In order to determine the space of admissible prioritized structures, we need to look first at the dominance patterns. There are two such patterns in this background. First, for any ground term a, the default $d_2(a)$ dominates the default set $D = \{d_3(a)\}$, as D is in conflict with $d_2(a)$, i.e. $\mathtt{u}(a), D \vdash_K \neg \mathtt{a}(a)$. This implies that any admissible priority ordering '$\prec$' must be such that $d_3(a) \prec d_2(a)$ holds. Secondly, the default $d_1(a)$ dominates the default set $D' = \{d_2(a), d_3(a)\}$, as $\mathtt{c}(a), D' \vdash_K \neg \mathtt{u}(a)$. As a result every admissible priority ordering must also satisfy either $d_2(a) \prec d_1(a)$ or $d_3 \prec d_1(a)$, a disjunction which we abbreviate as $\{d_2(a), d_3(a)\} \prec d_1(a)$.

Note that if the priority order is such that $d_2(a) \prec d_1(a)$ holds, by transitivity, it must also be the case that $d_3(a) \prec d_1(a)$ holds. Moreover, since either $d_2(a)$ or $d_3(a)$ *must* have a lower priority than $d_1(a)$, the relation $d_3(a) \prec d_1(a)$ must hold even if the relation $d_2(a) \prec d_1(a)$ does not hold. Therefore, there is a single *minimal* priority ordering '$\prec$' admissible with K which only satisfies $d_3(a) \prec d_1(a)$ and $d_3(a) \prec d_2(a)$ for ground terms a in the language.

The behavior of conditional entailment under such a prioritization can be illustrated by considering a context $T = \langle K, E \rangle$ where the evidence is $E = \{\mathtt{c}(\mathtt{k}), \mathtt{a}(\mathtt{k})\}$. That is, we know that an adult, say Ken, is sitting in the class; we want to know whether he is likely to be a university student, $\mathtt{u}(\mathtt{k})$. First, the context T has two minimal classes of models: a class $\mathcal{C}_1$ of models which violate the default $d_1(\mathtt{k})$ ('Ken is in the class, then he is a university student'), and a class $\mathcal{C}_3$ of models which violate the default $d_3(\mathtt{k})$ ('Ken is an adult, then he is not a university student'). However, the latter class is preferred to the former one, as for any models $M_1 \in \mathcal{C}_1$ and $M_3 \in \mathcal{C}_3$,

$$D[M_1] - D[M_3] = \{d_1(\mathtt{k})\}$$

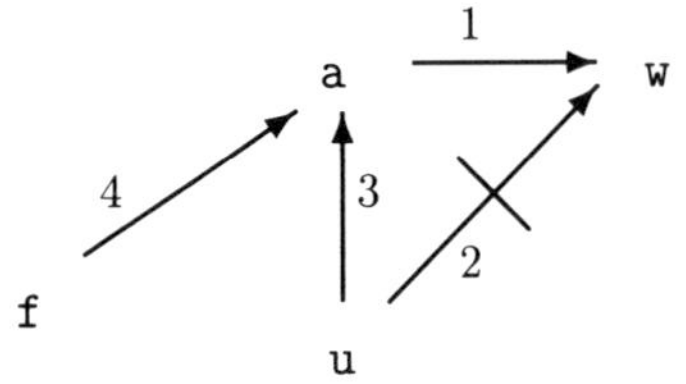

Figure 4.4
Default specificity

$$D[M_3] - D[M_1] = \{d_3(\mathtt{k})\}$$

and $d_3(\mathtt{k}) \prec d_1(\mathtt{k})$. Then, since $d_3(\mathtt{k})$ is the only default violated in the preferred class $\mathcal{C}_3$, the default $d_1(\mathtt{k})$ must hold in T and, therefore, the proposition $\mathtt{u}(\mathtt{k})$ is conditionally entailed. The same result follows from p-entailment and ϵ-entailment. However, neither p-entailment or ϵ-entailment would be able to sanction the same conclusion in the presence of irrelevant information such as 'Ken is blond'.

Example 4.3 Consider now a slightly different background K comprising the defaults

$$d_1 : \mathtt{a} \Rightarrow \mathtt{w}$$
$$d_2 : \mathtt{u} \Rightarrow \neg\mathtt{w}$$
$$d_3 : \mathtt{u} \Rightarrow \mathtt{a}$$
$$d_4 : \mathtt{f} \Rightarrow \mathtt{a}$$

The defaults may express that "adults work," "university students do not work," "university students are adults," and "Frank Sinatra fans are adults." The background has the same structure as the background in Example 4.1 (Fig. 4.2), except that all rules are now defeasible.

There are two relevant dominance relations in this background. First, the default d_2 dominates the set $D = \{d_1, d_3\}$ as D is in conflict with d_2, i.e., $\mathtt{u}, D \vdash_{\overline{K}} \mathtt{w}$. Likewise, d_3 dominates the set $\{d_1, d_2\}$. Thus, any priority ordering '$\prec$' admissible with K must be such that both relations $\{d_1, d_3\} \prec d_2$ and $\{d_1, d_2\} \prec d_3$ must hold. Moreover, due to the asymmetric and transitive character of priority orderings, such constraints imply $d_1 \prec d_2$ and $d_1 \prec d_3$. To show that this is the case, let us first assume that $d_2 \prec d_3$ holds. Then, by asymmetry we must have $d_3 \not\prec d_2$, and therefore, from the constraints above, $d_1 \prec d_2$. Now assume $d_2 \not\prec d_3$. If $d_1 \prec d_2$ didn't hold, the constraints above would imply $d_1 \prec d_3$ and $d_3 \prec d_2$ in contradiction with the transitivity of '$\prec$'. Thus, in either case the relation $d_1 \prec d_2$ must hold. By similar arguments we can conclude that $d_1 \prec d_3$ must hold as well.[6]

With this space of admissible priority orderings, let us first consider a context $T = \langle K, E \rangle$, with $E = \{\mathtt{f}\}$. Since there is an interpretation that satisfies T and every default, the single preferred class in every admissible prioritized structure is the class of models which violate no default. In particular, the defaults d_1 and d_4 hold, and thus the propositions $\mathtt{a}$ and $\mathtt{w}$ which they support are conditionally entailed. Note that these inferences involve default chaining, a pattern which is not sanctioned by either ϵ-entailment or by p-entailment.

A different situation arises when the proposition $\mathtt{u}$ is observed. The context $T' = \langle K, E' \rangle$, with $E' = \{\mathtt{f}, \mathtt{u}\}$, gives rise to three classes of minimal models: a class $\mathcal{C}_1$ of models which violate d_1, a class $\mathcal{C}_2$ of models which violate d_2, and a class $\mathcal{C}_3$ of models which violate both d_3 and d_4. However, since $d_1 \prec d_2$ and $d_1 \prec d_3$, any model M in $\mathcal{C}_1$ will be preferred to any model M' in $\mathcal{C}_2$ and any model M'' in $\mathcal{C}_3$. Hence $\mathcal{C}_1$ represents the class of preferred models of T', and therefore, all defaults other than d_1 hold in T', and thus both $\mathtt{a}$ and $\neg\mathtt{w}$ are conditionally entailed.

Example 4.4 Let K represent the hierarchy depicted in Fig. 4.5:

$d_1 : \mathsf{a} \rightarrow \mathsf{b}$

$d_2 : \mathsf{a} \rightarrow \mathsf{d}$

$d_3 : \mathsf{b} \rightarrow \mathsf{c}$

$d_4 : \mathsf{c} \rightarrow \neg\mathsf{d}$

In order to determine the admissible priorities, we have to identify first the relevant dominance patterns. There are two such patterns: the default d_1 dominates the set $\mathsf{D} = \{d_2, d_3, d_4\}$, and the default d_2 dominates the set $\mathsf{D}' = \{d_1, d_3, d_4\}$. Both relations are a result of the support relations $\mathsf{a}, \mathsf{D} \vdash_K \neg\mathsf{b}$ and $\mathsf{a}, \mathsf{D}' \vdash_K \neg\mathsf{d}$. Thus, every admissible priority ordering must be such that both $\{d_2, d_3, d_4\} \prec d_1$ and $\{d_1, d_3, d_4\} \prec d_2$

[6] Note that on 'specificity' grounds the priority of d_3 over d_1 does not appear justified. However, without $d_1 \prec d_3$ we would not be able to conclude $\mathtt{a}$ from $\mathtt{u}$.

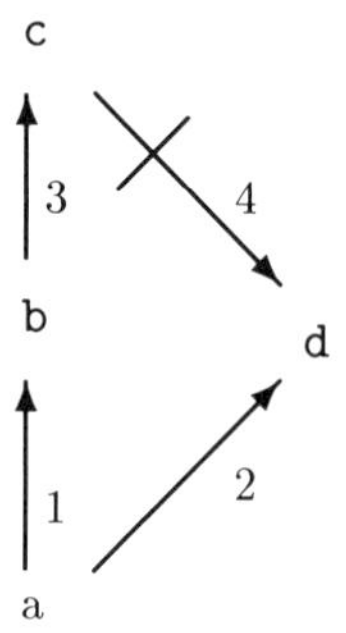

Figure 4.5
Disjunctive constraints

hold. Moreover, based on these two constraints and the fact that priority orderings are asymmetric and transitive, it is possible to show as above that every admissible ordering must also comply with the simplified constraints $\{d_3, d_4\} \prec d_1$ and $\{d_3, d_4\} \prec d_2$. These last constraints, however, cannot be simplified further, and thus we will need to deal with *four* structures which are both admissible and minimal.

Let us consider now the evidence $E = \{\mathsf{a}\}$. The theory $T = \langle K, E\rangle$ has four minimal classes $\mathcal{C}_i$ each comprising the models which violate the default d_i, $i = 1, \ldots, 4$. We show first that the preferred models of T in any prioritized structure $\tau = \langle \mathcal{I}_\mathcal{L}, <, \mathcal{D}, \prec\rangle$ admissible with K must belong to either $\mathcal{C}_3$ and $\mathcal{C}_4$. Let M_i be a model in $\mathcal{C}_i$, for $i = 1, \ldots, 4$ and assume that $d_3 \prec d_1$ holds. Then, since

$$D[M_3] - D[M_1] = \{d_3\}$$
$$D[M_1] - D[M_3] = \{d_1\}$$

M_3 must be preferred to M_1 in τ; therefore, M_1 is not a preferred model of T in τ. Assume now the opposite, viz. that $d_3 \prec d_1$ does not hold. Then given the constraint $\{d_3, d_4\} \prec d_1$ above, the relation $d_4 \prec d_1$ must be true. By similar arguments, it follows that M_4 is preferred to M_1 in τ and therefore, that M_1, again, is not a preferred model of T in τ. Replacing M_1 by M_2, we obtain similarly that M_2 is not a preferred model of T either. Furthermore, since d_3 does not have priority higher than d_4, nor vice versa, neither $\mathcal{C}_3$ and $\mathcal{C}_4$ is preferred over the other, and thus, both turn out to be the preferred classes of T. As a result, the defaults d_1 and d_2 hold in T, and thus, the propositions b and d are conditionally entailed.

It is worth noticing that conditional entailment does not subsume inheritance reasoning. For instance, in this example, most inheritance accounts would derive c from a. Yet conditional entailment fails to sanction c because the *intended* class of models M_4, in which the default d_4 is violated, is not preferred to the class of models M_3 in which the default d_3 is violated. We could, in principle, modify the way priorities are selected to capture these inferences; however, the value of conditional entailment as an account of default reasoning is to show what a combination of minimality and conditional considerations can and cannot account for. Examples as the last one show that default reasoning involves aspects other than minimality and conditionality. We will return to this topic in Chapter 5.

4.6 Proof Theory

Conditional entailment provides a characterization of the propositions entailed by a given default theory but does not provide effective methods for computing them. In this section we will focus on such methods. We will develop a number of *syntactic* criteria for testing conditional entailment some of which are amenable to implementation in ATMS-type of systems (Section 4.8).

As the proof-theory of classical deduction is structured around the notion of *proofs*, the proof-theory of conditional entailment is structured around the notion of *arguments* [Lou87a, Pol87]. Arguments, as defined in Section 2.5, are sets of defaults which are consistent with the underlying theory (recall that we treat defaults as material conditionals). An argument *for* a proposition p in a context $T = \langle K, E\rangle$ with background $K = \langle L, D\rangle$ is a collection of defaults which is consistent with T and which together with L and E logically entails p. We also say in that case that D supports p in the context T. An argument *against* p is an argument for the negation of p. Likewise, if D_1 and D_2 are two arguments but their union $D_1 + D_2$ is not an argument, i.e., $D_1 + D_2$ is inconsistent, we will say that D_1 and D_2 are in *conflict* and that their union constitutes a *conflict set.*

For the results below we will assume that the underlying theory $T = \langle K, E \rangle$ is such that there are only a *finite* number of (minimal) conflict sets. This will guarantee that the theory T will be well-founded relative to any structure $\langle \mathcal{I}_{\mathcal{L}}, <, \mathcal{D}, \prec \rangle$; i.e., for any non-preferred model M' of T there will be a *preferred* model M of T such that $M < M'$. Other restrictions could be used for this purpose but this one is sufficiently general for practical purposes.

We will develop the proof-theory of conditional entailment step by step. We start with the conditions under which a default $d \in D$ can be applied in the context T. The first condition is a simple consequence of the minimality of preferred models within the class of prioritized structures:

Lemma 4.4 A default $d \in D$ is conditionally entailed if there are no arguments against it.

Since we treat defaults as material conditionals, arguments against a default $p \rightarrow q$ are arguments against the material conditional $p \Rightarrow q$, and to say that a default $p \rightarrow q$ is conditionally entailed is to say that the material conditional $p \Rightarrow q$ is conditionally entailed.

Lemma 4.4 is a simplification of the irrelevance condition developed in Chapter 2. Later on we will show that the irrelevance condition is in turn a simplification of the conditions under which a default is conditionally entailed.

The lemma above permits us to identify the defaults that hold in every *minimal* model but not the defaults that hold in every *preferred* model. In fact, a default may face counterarguments and still be entailed. The "birds fly–penguins don't" example provides one such case. If Tim is a penguin, the default "Tim does not fly, because he is a normal penguin" faces the counterargument "Tim flies, because he is a normal bird"; yet the first default is conditionally entailed and the second one is not.

In order to capture these conclusions by proof-theoretic means, we need to consider the priority orderings determined by K. If the default $\mathtt{p(t)} \rightarrow \neg\mathtt{f(t)}$ is sanctioned in spite of the conflict with the default $\mathtt{b(t)} \rightarrow \neg\mathtt{f(t)}$ it is because its priority is higher. The assertability conditions below take these priorities into account. Recall that we write $D \prec d$ as an abbreviation of the expression "$\exists d' \in D$ such that $d' \prec d$."

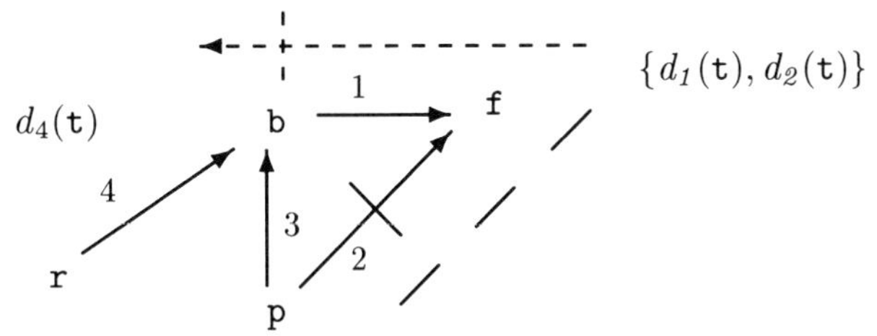

Figure 4.6
Defeat among arguments

Lemma 4.5 A default d is conditionally entailed if for every argument D against d and every admissible priority ordering '$\prec$', the relation $D \prec d$ holds.

Note that it is sufficient to consider only the *minimal* arguments D against d; if $D \prec d$ holds, so will $D' \prec d$ for any superset D' of D.

The condition introduced by Lemma 4.5 permits us to handle examples such as the one above. Indeed, given the evidence $E = \{\mathtt{p(t)}\}$ ('Tim is a penguin'), $D = \{\mathtt{b(t)} \rightarrow \mathtt{f(t)}\}$ is the only (minimal) argument against the default $\mathtt{p(t)} \rightarrow \neg\mathtt{f(t)}$, and since the latter default has a higher priority than the former, Lemma 4.5 permits us to apply $\mathtt{p(t)} \rightarrow \neg\mathtt{f(t)}$ and thus derive 'Tim does not fly'.

Lemma 4.5, however, is not yet complete relative to conditional entailment. This can be illustrated by converting the *strict* 'links' in Example 4.1 into *default* 'links', yielding a structure analogous to that of Example 4.3 which is depicted in Fig. 4.6. By arguments similar to those used in Example 4.3 we can show that the default $\mathtt{r(t)} \rightarrow \mathtt{b(t)}$ is conditionally entailed by the theory $T' = \langle K', E \rangle$, with $E = \{\mathtt{p(t)}, \mathtt{r(t)}\}$; yet, Lemma 4.5 does not sanction it: $D = \{\mathtt{b(t)} \rightarrow \mathtt{f(t)}, \mathtt{p(t)} \rightarrow \neg\mathtt{f(t)}\}$ is an argument against $\mathtt{r(t)} \rightarrow \mathtt{b(t)}$ in T' but $D \prec \mathtt{r(t)} \rightarrow \mathtt{b(t)}$ does not hold.

Intuitively, the default $\mathtt{r(t)} \rightarrow \mathtt{b(t)}$ is applicable in T' despite the counterargument D because D contains a default $\mathtt{b(t)} \rightarrow \mathtt{f(t)}$ which is *defeated*. That is to say, $\mathtt{b(t)} \rightarrow \mathtt{f(t)}$ is in conflict with with two 'stronger' defaults $\mathtt{p(t)} \rightarrow \mathtt{b(t)}$ and $\mathtt{p(t)} \rightarrow \neg\mathtt{f(t)}$ which knock out the argument D, leaving the default $\mathtt{r(t)} \rightarrow \mathtt{b(t)}$ unchallenged.

In order to account for these interactions, we will need to consider multiple conflicts at the same time. Some definitions will be necessary. We will write below $D' \prec D$ as an abbreviation of the expression "for every d in D, there is a d' in D' such that $d' \prec d$."

Definition 4.5 Given a priority ordering '$\prec$', an argument D *defeats* an argument D' if the two arguments are in conflict and the relation $D' \prec D$ holds. We say in this case that D is a *defeater* of D'.

Definition 4.6 An argument D is *protected* from a conflicting argument D' iff for every priority ordering admissible with K, D contains a defeater of D'.

Intuitively, when an argument D is protected from a conflicting argument D' it means that D is *stronger* than D'. For example, for the background K' depicted in Fig. 4.6, both defaults $d_2(\mathtt{t})$ and $d_3(\mathtt{t})$ have higher priority than $d_1(\mathtt{t})$. Hence in the context $T' = \langle K', E \rangle$ with $E = \{\mathtt{p}(\mathtt{t}), \mathtt{r}(\mathtt{t})\}$, in which the argument $D_1 = \{d_2(\mathtt{t}), d_3(\mathtt{t})\}$ is in conflict with the argument $D_2 = \{d_1(\mathtt{t})\}$, D_1 *defeats* D_2. Thus, any argument which includes D_1, like the argument $D_0 = D_1 + \{d_4(\mathtt{t})\}$ will be *protected* from D_2.

When an argument is protected from every conflicting argument, we will say the argument is *stable:*

Definition 4.7 An argument is *stable* iff it is protected from every conflicting argument.

As suggested above, a stable argument is better than *any* of its competitors, and propositions supported by stable arguments are conditionally entailed:

Lemma 4.6 A proposition is conditionally entailed if it is supported by a stable argument.

For example, the arguments D_1 and D_0 above are stable, as the only arguments D' in conflict with either of them must contain the default $d_1(\mathtt{t})$ which is defeated by the subargument $\{d_2(\mathtt{t}), d_3(\mathtt{t})\}$ of both D_1 and D_0. Thus, according to Lemma 4.6, the defaults $d_2(\mathtt{t})$, $d_3(\mathtt{t})$ and $d_4(\mathtt{t})$ and all the propositions that they support will be conditionally entailed.

The notion of stable arguments is very powerful and accounts for most of the natural inferences authorized by conditional entailment. Nonetheless, Lemma 4.6 is still not complete. For example, let us assume that we have a theory with three defaults d_1, d_2 and d_3 such that every pair of defaults is inconsistent, and both d_1 and d_2 have higher priority than d_3. Let us also assume that both d_1 and d_2 support p. Then p will be conditionally entailed although p will not be supported by a stable argument (neither $D_1 = \{d_1\}$ or $D_2 = \{d_2\}$ are stable since they are in conflict and neither one is protected from the other).

To account for such conclusions we need to consider *disjunctive* arguments. We will accommodate disjunctive arguments by considering the assertability conditions of collections of arguments which we call *covers.* For instance, the *cover* $C = \{D_1, D_2\}$ in the example above will be *stable,* legitimizing any proposition, like p, which is supported by *all* the arguments in the cover.

We will make the notion of *stable covers* precise by refining first the conditions under which an argument is protected:

Definition 4.8 An argument D is *strongly protected* from a conflicting argument D' if for every subargument D'_i of D' in conflict with D there exists a subargument D_i of D in conflict with D' such that $D'_i \prec D_i$.

Note that if an argument D is protected from a conflicting argument D'_i but is not protected from a conflicting argument D'_i, D will *not* be strongly protected from the union $D'_i + D'_i$ even though D will be protected from it. The distinction between the two notions is irrelevant for stable arguments, which are *both* protected and strongly protected from every conflicting argument, but it is needed for *disjunctive* arguments.

The notions of *conflict* and *protection* can be generalized from *arguments* to *covers* as follows:

Definition 4.9 An argument D is *in conflict with a cover* if D is in conflict with every argument in the cover.

Definition 4.10 *A cover is protected* from a conflicting argument D if the cover contains an argument D' which is *strongly protected* from D.

The conditions under which a *cover* C is stable can then be obtained as a generalization of the conditions under which an *argument* is stable. The only difference is that, for the purpose of completeness, we only consider arguments D in conflict with C that have as many defaults from C as possible. We call such conflicting arguments *definite* as they either include or rebut each of the defaults which occur in C.

Definition 4.11 A *cover* is *stable* iff it is protected from every definite conflicting argument D.[7]

As expected, the conditions of Lemma 4.6 can be strengthened by replacing stable arguments by stable covers. Furthermore, if we say that a proposition p is supported by a *cover* when it is supported by every argument in the cover, the following *complete* characterization of conditional entailment results:

Theorem 4.3 (Main) A proposition p is conditionally entailed if and only if p is supported by a stable cover.

We have thus arrived at a complete syntactic characterization of conditional entailment, which can now be computed by manipulating either models or arguments. An undesirable feature of both approaches though is that they rely on the identification of the set of admissible priority orderings for testing whether relations of the form $D' \prec D$ are satisfied. This, however, is a non-trivial task. Fortunately, it is possible to replace such a test by a corresponding *syntactic* test on K.

Let us first generalize the definition of dominance from Section 2.5 and say that a *set D of defaults dominates a set D'* of defaults if every default d in D dominates the union $D + D'$.[8] Then, due to the asymmetry and transitivity of priority orderings, the following result can be obtained:

Theorem 4.4 (Dominance) For two sets of defaults D and D', the relation $D' \prec D$ holds in every priority ordering '$\prec$' admissible with a *consistent background* $K = \langle L, D \rangle$ if and only if D is part of a set D'' that *dominates* D' in K.[9]

Theorems 4.3 and 4.4 permit us to determine by purely syntactic means whether a given proposition is conditionally entailed. For that, we need to look for stable covers and corresponding dominance relations.

[7] A consequence of this definition is that the stability of a cover C cannot be computed by considering the *minimal* arguments in conflict with C only. Rather, such arguments have to be made 'definite' by extending them with as many defaults from C as possible, which can lead to a proliferation of arguments if C is large.

[8] A default $p \rightarrow q$ dominates a set D' of defaults when D is conflict with $p \rightarrow q$, i.e., $p, D' \vdash_K \neg q$ (page 34).

[9] A background K is consistent when there exists a priority ordering admissible with K. See Section 4.4.

We can now make sense of the irrelevance rule in Chapter 2. The irrelevance rule (Rule 6) permits us to assert the material conditional $p \Rightarrow q$ when all the arguments against a default $p \rightarrow q$ are *preempted* (see page 36). However, since $p \rightarrow q$ preempts an argument D' only when $p \rightarrow q$ belongs to a set D that *dominates* D', by Theorem 4.4 it follows that E is irrelevant to $p \rightarrow q$ when all the arguments D' against $p \rightarrow q$ in the context $T = \langle K, E \rangle$ are such that $D' \prec p \rightarrow q$ holds, for any admissible priority ordering '$\prec$'. This in turn means that the argument $\{p \rightarrow q\}$ is *stable* in T, and therefore, that the material conditional $p \Rightarrow q$ is conditionally entailed:

Theorem 4.5 (Irrelevance) If E is irrelevant to a default $p \rightarrow q$ in D given a background $K = \langle L, D \rangle$, then $p \Rightarrow q$ is conditionally entailed by $T = \langle K, E \rangle$.

Given the soundness of the core for finite propositional languages, the following result is an straightforward consequence of the soundness of the irrelevance rule:

Theorem 4.6 For finite propositional languages, *all* the rules of **P** are *sound* rules of conditional entailment.

Rules 1–6, however, are not *complete* relative to conditional entailment. The irrelevance rule as defined in Chapter 2 is an incomplete approximation of Lemma 4.6, which permits us to accept propositions supported by stable arguments. Indeed, the irrelevance rule permits us to assert a default $p \rightarrow q$ in K in the context $T = \langle K, E \rangle$ *only* if the singleton argument $\{p \rightarrow q\}$ is stable. Yet, the default $p \rightarrow q$ may *belong* to a stable argument even if it is not stable by itself. For example, given the three rules:

$$\mathtt{b}(x) \rightarrow \mathtt{f}(x) \qquad \mathtt{p}(x) \rightarrow \neg\mathtt{f}(x) \qquad \mathtt{p}(x) \Rightarrow \mathtt{b}(x)$$

and their 'mirror' rules

$$\mathtt{b}'(x) \rightarrow \mathtt{f}(x) \qquad \mathtt{p}'(x) \rightarrow \neg\mathtt{f}(x) \qquad \mathtt{p}'(x) \Rightarrow \mathtt{b}'(x)$$

together with the evidence $E = \{\mathtt{p}(a), \mathtt{p}'(a)\}$, conditional entailment sanctions the literal $\neg\mathtt{f(a)}$ but Rules 1–6 do not. This is because, although the pair of defaults $\mathtt{p}(a) \rightarrow \neg\mathtt{f}(a)$ and $\mathtt{p}'(a) \rightarrow \neg\mathtt{f}(a)$ constitutes a stable argument, neither default is stable by itself (the first default is not protected from the rebuttal $\Delta_1' = \{\mathtt{b}'(a) \rightarrow \mathtt{f}(a)\}$, and the second default is not protected from the rebuttal $\Delta_2' = \{\mathtt{b}(a) \rightarrow \mathtt{f}(a)\}$).

4.7 Defaults and Assumptions

In the introduction of this chapter we said that conditional entailment is like prioritized circumscription except that priorities are not provided by the user but are automatically extracted from the knowledge base. Yet so far our representation of defaults shows little relation to the representation of defaults used in circumscription. In circumscription, defaults $p(x) \rightarrow q(x)$ are encoded as sentences $p(x) \wedge \neg \mathsf{ab}_i(x) \rightarrow q(x)$, where ab_i's are 'abnormality' predicates whose extensions are expected to be minimal [McC86]. The resulting default theory is thus a 'flat' classical theory, possibly augmented by priorities, and the role of circumscription is to minimize 'abnormality' in accordance with these priorities (see Section 1.5). In our framework, default theories are more structured — sentences are separated between those in the background and those in the evidence set — and defaults are part of the meta-theory and not of the object-theory. In this section we will show that we can obtain a representation of defaults which is closer to the one used in circumscription, and which is advantageous in many ways. The implementation of conditional entailment we will pursue in the next section uses one of these encodings.

First, let us consider the theory $T' = \langle K', E \rangle$ with a background $K' = \langle L', D' \rangle$ that results from a theory $T = \langle K, E \rangle$ with background $K = \langle L, D \rangle$ by replacing each default $p_i(x) \rightarrow q_i(x)$ in D by a new default $p_i(x) \rightarrow \delta_i(x)$ and the sentence $p_i(x) \wedge \delta_i(x) \Rightarrow q_i(x)$,[10] where δ_i is a predicate unique to each default which does not occur in T.

The encoding of defaults in T' is closer to circumscription, with δ_i's playing the role of 'normality' predicates. Likewise, the theories T and T' are closely related. In fact, for every model M of T (i.e., $M \models L + E$) there is a model M' of T' such that M violates a default $p_i(a) \rightarrow q_i(a)$ iff M' violates the default $p_i(a) \rightarrow \delta_i(a)$, and vice versa.[11] Furthermore, if '$\prec$' is a priority ordering admissible with K, the priority ordering '$\prec'$' defined as

$$p_i(a) \rightarrow \delta_i(a) \prec p_j(b) \rightarrow \delta_j(b) \text{ iff } p_i(a) \rightarrow q_i(a) \prec p_j(b) \rightarrow q_j(b)$$

---

[10] Free variables in wffs are assumed to be universally quantified.

[11] If M is a model of T, we can build the model M' by preserving from M the domain and the interpretation of symbols other than the δ_i's, and by setting $\delta_i(o)$ to false, if o is an *unnamed* object in the domain, and to the value of $p(o) \Rightarrow q(o)$ otherwise.

will be admissible with K', and vice versa. Thus, there is a correspondence between the defaults violated in the preferred models of both T and T' and between the way defaults in T and T' are ordered. The result, not surprisingly, is that the propositions conditionally entailed by T and T' which do not involve the predicates δ_i are the same.

We can go a step further. Consider the theory T'' obtained from T' by replacing each default schema $p_i(x) \rightarrow \delta_i(x)$ by a default $\mathbf{true} \rightarrow \delta_i(x)$, where **true** is an special atom satisfied in every model. References to defaults in T'' can therefore be replaced by reference to atoms; viz., a default $\mathbf{true} \rightarrow \delta_i(a)$ will hold if the atom $\delta_i(a)$ holds, and vice versa. Likewise, priorities among defaults in T'' can be understood as priorities over the atoms $\delta_i(a)$, and T'' can be interpreted like prioritized circumscription by simply minimizing these atoms in accordance with these priorities. That is to say, a model M will be preferred to a model M' if for every atom $\delta_i(a)$ violated by M there is an atom $\delta_j(b)$ of higher priority than $\delta_i(a)$ which is violated by M'. If T'' is interpreted in this manner, and the priorities among the atoms $\delta_i(a)$ are obtained from T rather than from T'', (i.e., $\delta_i(a) \prec \delta_j(b)$ iff $p_i(a) \rightarrow q_i(a) \prec p_j(b) \rightarrow q_j(b)$), the conclusions sanctioned by T'' would be identical to the conclusions sanctioned by the original theory T, except for propositions involving δ_i's. In addition, the defaults in T'' can be discarded and the sentences in the background $K'' = \langle L'', D'' \rangle$ and in the evidence set E can be merged. The result is thus a *flat* theory which captures the conclusion of the original default theory T and in which, like in circumscription, certain predicates are minimized in accordance with certain priorities.

Besides permitting a closer comparison with circumscription, the encoding of defaults by means of auxiliary predicates δ_i has some practical benefits. For example, to express that a default $p_i(x) \rightarrow q_i(x)$ is not applicable when a condition $s(x)$ holds, we can just write $s(x) \Rightarrow \neg\delta_i(x)$ without having to justify $\neg q_i(x)$. In [Gef90b] we have actually used the encoding of defaults corresponding to T' above to present the ideas discussed in this chapter. In such a encoding, all references to defaults can also be replaced by reference to atoms. Indeed, we referred to theories such as T' as *assumption-based default theories* as the atoms $\delta_i(a)$ play the role of *assumptions*, i.e, atoms which we expect to be true. In this chapter we have followed the more general encoding of defaults for the sake of uniformity. However, for presenting the architecture below we will find it convenient to assume that defaults have been encoded in terms of assumptions like in T'' above, and that the priorities among these assumptions are given.

4.8 Architecture

Computing conditional entailment within either the model-theoretic or proof-theoretic framework, is a formidable task. From a practical point of view, it is probably best to construct a sound but incomplete account which, by capturing most patterns of interest, can be both useful and understandable.

An obvious target for approximating conditional entailment are the propositions supported by stable arguments. Theorem 4.3 guarantees that such propositions are conditionally entailed and that incompleteness results from the exclusion of disjunctive arguments (covers) only. If we further commit ourselves to a single minimal admissible priority ordering, we will find that testing whether a given set of default constitutes a stable argument can be accomplished in terms of the computations performed by assumption-based truth-maintenance systems (ATMS's). Recall that the two basic tasks of an ATMS are the computation of the minimal sets of assumptions inconsistent with the underlying theory (conflict sets) and the minimal consistent sets of assumptions supporting a given atom [dK86].

We will assume that defaults have been encoded in terms of *assumptions,* as in theory T'' above, and that the priorities among these assumptions are given. All references to defaults can thus be replaced by references to assumptions. Thus adopting a default **true** $\rightarrow \delta_i$ is adopting the assumption δ_i, an argument becomes a collection Δ of *assumptions* δ logically consistent with the underlying context, and so on.

First we need to incorporate the information about priorities in the conflict sets computed by the ATMS. However, since priorities only play a role in determining defeat relations among arguments, this information can be accommodated by partitioning each conflict set C_i, $i = 1, \ldots, n$ into two sets C_i^0 and C_i^1, such that $C_i^0 \prec C_i^1$ and C_i^1 is maximal (such partition is unique and can be easily computed by setting C_i^0 to the set of assumptions δ in C_i which are *minimal* relative to the ordering

'$\prec$').[12] If C_i^1 is non-empty, we will call the pairs $\langle C_i^0, C_i^1 \rangle$ *basic defeat pairs*, since C_i^1 defeats C_i^0 and all other relevant defeat information can be inferred from such pairs. We can check whether an argument is stable as follows:

Theorem 4.7 An argument Δ is *stable* if and only if for every conflict set C_i, $C_i \cap \Delta \neq \emptyset$, there is a *basic defeat pair* $\langle C_j^0, C_j^1 \rangle$ such that $C_j^0 + C_j^1 \subseteq C_i + \Delta$ and $C_j^0 \subseteq C_i - \Delta$.

Indeed, if Δ' is a minimal argument in conflict with Δ, then there will be a conflict set C_i such that $\Delta' = C_i - \Delta$ and $C_i \cap \Delta$ is non-empty. Also if Δ is stable, Δ will contain a defeater of Δ', namely, a subargument Δ_j in conflict with Δ' such that $\Delta' \prec \Delta_j$. In particular, there must a minimal Δ_j in Δ, and for such Δ_j, the set $\Delta_j + \Delta'$ will be a minimal conflict set (recall that we are assuming that Δ' is a minimal argument in conflict with Δ). Such a conflict set, call it C_j, can thus be partitioned into two sets $C_j^0 = \Delta'$ and $C_j^1 = \Delta_j$ such that $C_j^0 \prec C_j^1$. The pair $\langle C_j^0, C_j^1 \rangle$ is not necessarily a basic defeat pair since the set C_j^1 is not necessarily maximal. Yet a basic defeat pair can be constructed from it by moving assumptions from C_j^0 to C_j^1. For the resulting pair, both $C_j^0 \subseteq \Delta'$ and $C_j^1 \subseteq \Delta + \Delta'$ hold, as in the theorem.

Provided with the conflict sets computed by an ATMS, we can obtain the basic defeat pairs and test whether an argument is stable or not. This provides the basic module for testing whether there is a stable argument that supports a given proposition p of interest. To achieve this goal, we will construct stable arguments incrementally: i.e., we will adopt a set of assumptions Δ_0 that supports p and try to prove it stable. If it Δ_0 is not stable, we will incrementally extend it with a set Δ_1 of assumptions that defeats the counterarguments of Δ_0, and show that $\Delta_0 + \Delta_1$ is stable, and so on.

To make this method precise, let (supports-of p) be a function that returns the minimal arguments Δ_i supporting a given atom p, and (defeaters-of Δ') be a function which returns the minimal arguments Δ_j which defeat a given argument Δ'. The function supports-of is part of the normal ATMS task, while the function defeaters-of can be computed from the basic defeat pairs $\langle C_j^0, C_j^1 \rangle$ for which $C_j^0 \subseteq \Delta'$ by setting

[12]Like for defaults, $\Delta' \prec \Delta$ means that for each assumption δ in Δ there is an assumption δ' in Δ' such that $\delta' \prec \delta$.

Δ_j to $C_j^1 - \Delta'$. Also, let

$$\textsf{(choose } x_i \textsf{ among } List \textsf{ until } p(x_i))$$

be an iterative procedure which binds x_i successively to the elements of *List* until $p(x_i)$ evaluates to **true**, in which case the procedure returns **true**, or until the list has been exhausted, in which case the procedure returns **false**. Finally, let

$$\textsf{(for-a-rebuttal } \Delta' \textsf{ of } \Delta \textsf{ do } p(\Delta'))$$

be a function which finds a rebuttal Δ' of Δ, and evaluates to $p(\Delta')$ if one is found, and to **true** otherwise. Δ' is a rebuttal of Δ if both are in conflict but Δ does not contain a defeater of Δ'.

Testing then whether a proposition p is supported by a stable argument can be achieved by invoking the procedure (provable? p) below:

$$\begin{aligned}\textsf{(provable? } p) \quad \stackrel{\textbf{def}}{=} \quad & \textsf{(choose } \Delta_i \textsf{ among (supports-of } p) \\ & \quad \textsf{until (proven-support } \Delta_i))\end{aligned}$$

where:

$$\begin{aligned}\textsf{(proven-support } \Delta_i) \quad \stackrel{\textbf{def}}{=} \quad & \textsf{(for-a-rebuttal } \Delta' \textsf{ of } \Delta_i \textsf{ do} \\ & \quad \textsf{(choose } \Delta_D \textsf{ among (defeaters-of } \Delta') \\ & \quad\quad \textsf{until (proven-support } \Delta_i + \Delta_D)))\end{aligned}$$

This method for testing whether a proposition p is supported by a stable argument is not aimed at being efficient but clear: we build arguments supporting p, search for rebuttals of those arguments, and try to defeat those rebuttals. For finite languages, the procedure terminates and will be both correct and complete. For practical purposes, however, additional refinements would be needed (e.g., caching results, evaluating certain expressions on need, etc.).

4.9 Related Work

Conditional entailment provides the formal justification for the extension of the core developed in Chapter 2 based on irrelevance considerations. We have been revising our definition of irrelevance for a while, in view of examples that were not handled correctly (e.g., [GP87, Gef88]). Now, we have come to the conclusion that conditional entailment provides a correct specification of the behavior that can be expected from defaults when only conditional and minimality considerations are taken into account. This obviously does not solve the 'problem of default reasoning' — as defaults involve other types of considerations as well, see Chapter 5 — yet it seems a step in the right direction which can be built upon.

An idea similar to irrelevance appears in a recent proposal by Poole [Poo90]. Poole starts with a logical argument system, in which a proposition is accepted if it is supported by a (disjunctive) argument which is not rebutted. He then introduces a dominance-like criterion which allow some of the rebuttals to be ignored. Poole's proposal has some of the problems of the irrelevance account (e.g., its lack of formal justification), plus a few others (e.g., the resulting system, unlike the one he starts with, is not deductively closed). A comparison with conditional entailment brings out another pair of problems. For instance, consider our example involving penguins, birds and red-birds (Example 4.1), plus the default 'if it looks like a penguin, it is a penguin'. Poole's basic proposal, while able to conclude that something that looks like a penguin is a penguin and a bird, cannot maintain the first conclusion when the second one is *confirmed* (i.e., it violates cumulativity, see Section 3.8). The problem here is that Poole's proposal does not capture the transitivity of default preferences, which in conditional entailment is enforced by means of priorities. The 'iterated' account which Poole introduces later compensates for this deficiency in certain cases (like in the example above), but not in others (e.g., if 'penguins are birds' is expressed as a default).

The second problem in Poole's proposal stems from not distinguishing the notions which we have called *protection* and *defeat*. To illustrate this problem, consider an additional default 'if it looks like a red-bird, then it is a red-bird' in the example above, and a scenario in which we know that Tim is a penguin and looks like a red-bird. Intuitively, we would expect to derive that Tim is a red-bird. However, Poole can conclude that Tim is a bird, that Tim does not fly, but *not* that Tim is a red-bird. In our terminology, this is because none of the arguments supporting 'Tim is a red bird' *defeats* all its counterarguments; yet, what really matters is that some of those argument are *protected* from their counterarguments, and thus are stable. Both problems point to the advantage of deriving an argument-system from model-theoretic considerations where we are forced to make sure that no legitimate patterns of inference are left out.

Horty *et al.* [HTT87], Nute [Nut88a], and Simari and Loui [SL90] also propose systems based on arguments which enforce 'specificity' preferences among defaults. The main difference between these systems and ours is that they regard defaults as rules of inference which do not contrapose nor allow reasoning by cases. Nute's system in particular implicitly embeds an interesting, although not unusual assumption (our irrelevance account embeds a similar assumption, see page 81): it permits us to derive the consequent q of a default $p \rightarrow q$ only when all defaults $p' \rightarrow \neg q$ with supported antecedents p' are less 'specific' than $p \rightarrow q$. Regardless of how this specificity criterion is determined, such a rule is limited to derive defaults *which can be established one at a time.* This can be seen if we consider the three rules

$$\mathtt{b}(x) \rightarrow \mathtt{f}(x) \qquad \mathtt{p}(x) \rightarrow \neg\mathtt{f}(x) \qquad \mathtt{p}(x) \Rightarrow \mathtt{b}(x)$$

together with their 'mirror' rules

$$\mathtt{b}'(x) \rightarrow \mathtt{f}(x) \qquad \mathtt{p}'(x) \rightarrow \neg\mathtt{f}(x) \qquad \mathtt{p}'(x) \Rightarrow \mathtt{b}'(x)$$

Given then the atoms $\mathtt{p}(a)$ and $\mathtt{p}'(a)$, we would expect these rules to yield $\neg\mathtt{f(a)}$. Yet, the rule $\mathtt{b(a)} \rightarrow \mathtt{f(a)}$ is no less specific than the conflicting default $\mathtt{p'(a)} \rightarrow \neg\mathtt{f(a)}$, and the rule $\mathtt{b'(a)} \rightarrow \mathtt{f(a)}$ is no less specific than the conflicting default $\mathtt{p(a)} \rightarrow \neg\mathtt{f(a)}$. Thus, the conclusion $\neg\mathtt{f(a)}$ is not sanctioned by the above criterion. Conditional entailment produces the desired conclusion because, even though neither of the two 'more specific' defaults supporting the conclusion $\neg\mathtt{f(a)}$ is stable by itself, *their union* is stable. In [Gef91], we referred to stable arguments D which can be written as a list $\{d_1, \ldots, d_n\}$ of defaults such that each prefix $D_i = \{d_1, \ldots, d_i\}$, $1 \leq i \leq n$, is stable, as *linear stable arguments* (see also Section 5.7). The computation of linear stable arguments is more efficient than the computation of non-linear stable arguments, as the former can be built and proved one default at a time. On the other hand, as this example shows, a restriction to compute *only* linear stable arguments, implies that certain reasonable conclusions will not be derived.

Conditional entailment is closest to two recent extensions of preferential entailment developed independently by Pearl and Lehmann [Pea90, Leh89] (both extensions are also equivalent to 1*-entailment, discussed in Section 3.7). Like conditional entailment, Pearl and (implicitly) Lehmann rank defaults according to a dominance-like criterion, and use those rankings to infer a preference relation on models. However, Pearl and Lehmann deal with integer rankings as opposed to strict partial orders; they define the rank of a model as the rank of the highest ranked default violated by the model; and they only consider *one* (minimal) prioritized structure, as opposed to many. The consequences of these choices are that preferred models are not always minimal, and that conflicts among defaults that should remain unresolved are sometimes resolved anomalously.

Two examples illustrate these problems. Given two defaults $\mathtt{p} \rightarrow \mathtt{q}$ and $\mathtt{p} \rightarrow \neg\mathtt{r}$, Pearl's and Lehmann's accounts fail to authorize the conclusion $\mathtt{q}$ given $\mathtt{p} \wedge \mathtt{r}$, because in the resulting world ranking the violation of a single default "costs" as much as the violation of many defaults of equal rank. This renders exceptional subclasses (e.g., penguins) unable to inherit properties from their superclasses (e.g., birds). The second problem in these two proposals stems from their commitment to a unique integer ranking on worlds. Consider for example two defaults $\mathtt{p} \wedge \mathtt{s} \rightarrow \mathtt{q}$ and $\mathtt{r} \rightarrow \neg\mathtt{q}$ which render the status of $\mathtt{q}$ ambiguous in the presence of $\mathtt{p} \wedge \mathtt{s} \wedge \mathtt{r}$. In Pearl's and Lehmann's approaches, this ambiguity is anomalously resolved *in favor* of $\mathtt{q}$ when a new default $\mathtt{p} \rightarrow \neg\mathtt{q}$ is added. The reason is that the introduction of $\mathtt{p} \rightarrow \neg\mathtt{q}$ automatically raises the ranking of the more specific default $\mathtt{p} \wedge \mathtt{s} \rightarrow \mathtt{q}$ which thus becomes preferred to $\mathtt{r} \rightarrow \neg\mathtt{q}$. The extension of ϵ-semantics based on the principle of maximum-entropy [GMP90] remains committed to a unique integer ranking on worlds and thus confronts similar problems.

Another difference between conditional entailment and Pearl's and Lehmann's accounts is that the latter validate a stronger version of the augmentation rule, called *rational-monotony* [LM88], by which conclusions of a theory $T = \langle K, E \rangle$ are also conclusions of the theory $T' = \langle K, E + \{p\} \rangle$, whenever the negation of p is not a consequence of T. Rational monotony does not hold in conditional entailment, and whether it is a reasonable property of defeasible inference is an open issue. Yet, a weaker form of rational monotony does hold in conditional entailment. Let us say that a proposition q is *arguable* in T if there is an argument D for q such that T does not sanction $\neg\mathsf{D}$. Then, in conditional entailment, conclusions of the theory $T = \langle K, E \rangle$ will be conclusions of the theory $T' = \langle K, E + \{p\} \rangle$ when $\neg p$ is not *arguable* in T. This is because the effect of assimilating propositions like p is to exclude *some* but not *all* models from each of the preferred classes of T.

When default theories are encoded in terms of *assumptions* (see Section 4.7 and [Gef90b]), conditional entailment is closely related to prioritized circumscription. Prioritized circumscription is a refinement of parallel circumscription, originally proposed by McCarthy [McC86] and later developed by Lifschitz [Lif85, Lif88a]. Roughly, the effect of prioritized circumscription is to induce a preference for models that assign smaller extensions to predicates of higher priority. In the propositional case, the only difference between conditional entailment and prioritized circumscription is the source of the priorities: prioritized circumscription relies on the user, while conditional entailment extracts the priorities from the knowledge base itself.

Two other technical differences arise in the first order case. First, the priorities in prioritized circumscription are on *predicates* as opposed to *atoms*. Such a difference often produces a different behavior. For instance, in the "birds fly, penguins don't" example, the conclusion $\neg$`flies(tim)` is conditionally entailed by `penguin(tim)` by virtue of the priority of the assumption δ_2(`tim`) ('if Tim is a penguin, Tim does not fly') over the assumption δ_1(`tim`) ('if Tim is a bird, Tim flies'). The same behavior would normally be accommodated in prioritized circumscription by *assigning* a higher priority to the *predicate* $\mathtt{ab}_2 = \neg\delta_2$ than to the *predicate* $\mathtt{ab}_1 = \neg\delta_1$. However, such an encoding produces an unexpected behavior which does not arise in conditional entailment: given that either Tim is a flying penguin or that Tweety is a non-flying bird, prioritized circumscription is forced to conclude that Tweety is a non-flying bird.[13]

The second difference between conditional entailment and prioritized circumscription is the notion of *minimality* employed. In conditional entailment, the minimality of models is understood *syntactically*: a model is minimal if it violates a minimal set of assumptions $\delta_i(a)$, where each assumption is a ground atom. In circumscription, on the other hand, the minimality of models is understood *semantically:* a model is minimal if the *extension* of the predicates δ_i is minimal. Both criteria would be equivalent if every individual was guaranteed to have a distinct name

[13]The proposal in [Lif88a] permits a finer grained specification of priorities which avoids this problem.

in the language. However, this is usually false, and thus the behavior sanctioned by the two criteria will sometimes diverge. For example, given a default 'birds fly', i.e., $\forall x.\, \texttt{bird}(x) \wedge \delta_1(x) \Rightarrow \texttt{flies}(x)$, circumscription will conclude that *no* bird flies, while conditional entailment will abstain. On the other hand, given $\texttt{bird(tweety)}$, $\texttt{bird(tim)}$ and $\neg\texttt{flies(tweety)}$, conditional entailment will conclude $\texttt{flies(tim)}$ while circumscription will abstain.

In light of the relation between the model theory of prioritized circumscription and conditional entailment, it is not surprising to find their respective proof-theories related as well. An elegant proof-theory for prioritized circumscription has recently been developed by Baker and Ginsberg [BG89]. Baker and Ginsberg address the case in which predicates are *linearly* ordered; namely, circumscribed predicates are drawn from sets P_1, P_2, ..., P_n such that the priority of a predicate in a set P_i is higher than the priority of a predicate in a set P_j, if $j < i$. While differing in technical detail, the proof-theory they present has the same *dialectical* flavor as the proof-theory developed in Section 4.5, and both are closely related to systems of defeasible inference based on the evaluation of arguments [Lou87a, Pol87]. The differences are mainly in the treatment of disjunctions, which in our case are pushed completely into what we called *covers,* and our commitment to priority orderings which may be *partial* as opposed to *linear.* In this regard, the results in Sections 4.5 and 4.7 are relevant to prioritized circumscription, as they relax some of the assumptions on which the proof-theory of Baker and Ginsberg is based.

Other systems which rely on priorities among assumptions or defaults are Brewka's [Bre89] and Zadrozny [Zad87]. For a discussion of a number of subtle issues involving priorities, see Grosof's [Gro91].

5 Causality: Evidence vs. Explanation

Conditional entailment integrates the *conditional* interpretations of defaults based on probabilities and preferential structures, and the *extensional* interpretations based on standard non-monotonic logics. This is accomplished by means of a priority ordering on defaults extracted from the background context which captures both 'specificity' preferences and independence assumptions. Many default theories, however, are not interpreted correctly by conditional entailment. In those theories, *unintended* models slip into the set of *preferred* models and the resulting behavior is too weak. In this chapter, we will argue that this problem stems from ignoring the *causal* aspects of defaults. We then elaborate a new interpretation of defaults, called *causal entailment,* in which those aspects are addressed.

For this new interpretation of defaults to be useful three prerequisites will have to be met: first, the resulting language must permit defeasible knowledge to be encoded naturally; second, the semantics must capture what the user has in mind; and third, the authorized conclusions must be computable in a reasonable fashion. We will consider each these aspects in turn: we will first introduce the language and semantics of *causal theories,* then we will illustrate how these theories can be used for representing and reasoning with defaults, and finally, we will develop a proof-theory and show how a significant fragment of it can be efficiently implemented.

5.1 Introduction

A natural place to start our discussion is the famous "Yale shooting problem" (YSP) [HM86]. The problem describes a simple scenario where a gun loaded at a certain time is shot at a person (Fred) at a later time. The task is to predict the fate of Fred after the shooting. The scenario was devised to show that some of the best-known non-monotonic formalisms — circumscription [McC80, McC86], default logic [Rei80], McDermott's and Doyle's non-monotonic logic [MD80] — produced a behavior that was weaker than expected, in which the fate of Fred is undecided. Below we present a simplified description of the scenario which gives rise to the same problems pointed out by Hanks and McDermott.

Example 5.1 (Yale Shooting Problem) A gun loaded at time t is shot at a later time t' at a person alive at t. The task is to predict the

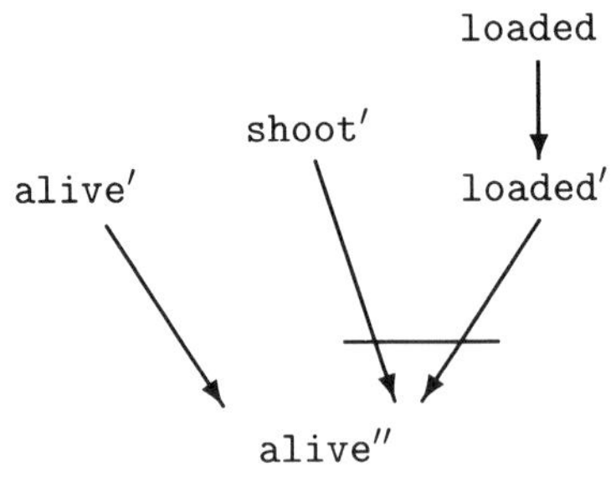

Figure 5.1
The Yale shooting problem

fate of the person after the shooting. We encode the relevant relations in a background $K = \langle L, D \rangle$ (Fig. 5.1):

$$\texttt{loaded} \rightarrow \texttt{loaded}'$$

$$\texttt{alive}' \rightarrow \texttt{alive}''$$

$$\texttt{shoot}' \wedge \texttt{loaded}' \Rightarrow \neg\texttt{alive}''$$

The evidence is given by the set $E = \{\texttt{loaded},\texttt{alive}',\texttt{shoot}'\}$. In the resulting context $T = \langle K, E \rangle$ the conflict between the defaults $\texttt{loaded} \rightarrow \texttt{loaded}'$ and $\texttt{alive}' \rightarrow \texttt{alive}''$ produce two classes of minimal models: the expected class $\mathcal{C}_2$, in which the first default holds and the second one is violated, and the spurious class $\mathcal{C}_1$, in which the second default holds, and the first one is violated. The class $\mathcal{C}_2$ would be preferred to $\mathcal{C}_1$ if the first default had higher priority than the second default; however, since we can apply the default $\texttt{loaded} \rightarrow \texttt{loaded}'$ without violating the default $\texttt{alive}' \rightarrow \texttt{alive}''$, and vice versa, no default receives a higher priority (cf. Section 4.3), and as a result, as in the frameworks analyzed by Hanks and McDermott, neither $\neg\texttt{alive}''$ nor $\texttt{loaded}'$ are conditionally entailed.

The lack of priorities between the conflicting defaults $\texttt{alive}' \rightarrow \texttt{alive}''$ and $\texttt{loaded} \rightarrow \texttt{loaded}'$ is not unreasonable; after all their status is normally independent: the persistence of `loaded` does not normally presume the clipping of `alive` nor does the persistence of `alive` normally presume the clipping of `loaded`. It is only in the particular context of a shooting at a particular person that the status of one default becomes relevant to the status of the other. Indeed, only in such context it makes sense to regard one default as preferred to the other.

Not surprisingly those preferences cannot be captured within the framework of conditional entailment in a natural way; for while the space of priority orderings admissible with a given default theory $T = \langle K, E \rangle$ *depends* on the background K it is *independent* of the evidence E. In particular, since in the absence of a shooting the 'fluents' `loaded` and `alive` are unrelated, they remain unrelated even when a shooting is known to occur.

Nonetheless, even if we could determine the priorities by looking at both the background and the evidence, there would be an additional problem to solve, viz. the logical symmetry between the defaults $\texttt{loaded} \rightarrow \texttt{loaded}'$ and $\texttt{alive}' \rightarrow \texttt{alive}''$. Indeed, if we could derive that the priority of $\texttt{loaded} \rightarrow \texttt{loaded}'$ should be higher than the priority of $\texttt{alive}' \rightarrow \texttt{alive}''$ by just looking at the formulas in T, then we should switch to the opposite priorities once the shooting rule is rewritten as the logically equivalent rule $\texttt{shoot} \wedge \texttt{alive}'' \Rightarrow \neg\texttt{loaded}'$. The problem here is that the *logical symmetry* between the two defaults hides an important *causal asymmetry:* the conjunction of $\texttt{shoot}'$ and $\texttt{loaded}'$ *explains* $\neg\texttt{alive}''$, yet the conjunction of $\texttt{shoot}'$ and $\neg\texttt{alive}''$ is evidence for but does not explain $\neg\texttt{loaded}'$. As argued elsewhere by Pearl [Pea88a], the need for distinguishing *explanatory* from *evidential* relations is not particular to the Yale shooting problem but to many scenarios involving both causal relations and defaults. Two more examples will illustrate this point.

Example 5.2 We get up in the morning and want to drive to work. When we get to the car, however, we notice that we left the lights on the previous night. At that point we want to assess the chances that the car will start upon turning the ignition key. The assumptions are that the car will normally start when the ignition key is turned, but that the car will not start if the battery is dead. Moreover, the battery is likely to be dead after having left the lights on the previous night (Fig. 5.2):

$$d_1 : \texttt{turn\_key} \rightarrow \texttt{starts}$$

$$d_2 : \texttt{turn\_key} \wedge \texttt{battery\_dead} \rightarrow \neg\texttt{starts}$$

$$d_3 : \texttt{lights\_were\_on} \rightarrow \texttt{battery\_dead}$$

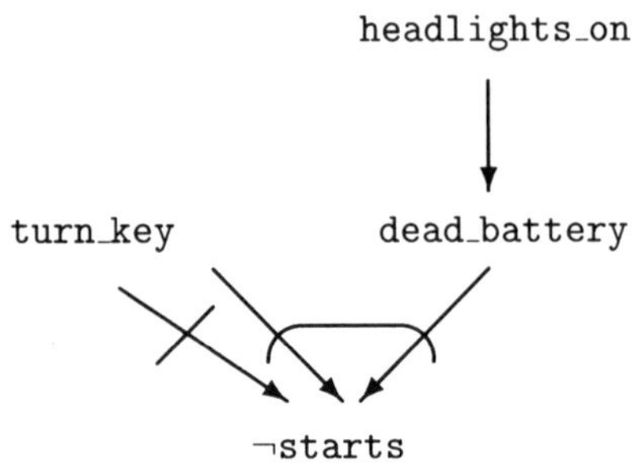

Figure 5.2
The battery problem

The context $T = \langle K, E \rangle$ with $E = \{\texttt{lights\_were\_on}, \texttt{turn\_key}\}$ gives rise to three minimal classes: $\mathcal{C}_1$, $\mathcal{C}_2$, and $\mathcal{C}_3$, where $\mathcal{C}_i$ stands for the class of models that violate the default d_i only. Models in the class $\mathcal{C}_1$ are preferred to models in the class $\mathcal{C}_2$, since d_2 has higher priority than d_1. No such preference exists, however, between the defaults d_1 and d_3, and thus, models in $\mathcal{C}_1$ and $\mathcal{C}_3$ are equally preferred. As a result, conditional entailment sanctions the disjunction $\neg\texttt{starts} \vee \neg\texttt{battery\_dead}$ but not the stronger, expected conclusion $\neg\texttt{starts}$.

Note again that while we *can explain* the car not starting by predicting a dead battery, we *cannot explain* the battery not dying by predicting that the car will start. Like in the Yale shooting problem, the *logical symmetry* between a pair of conflicting defaults hides a *causal asymmetry* that needs to be uncovered if the correct behavior is to be captured.

Example 5.3 As a last example, consider a scenario in which Mary is organizing a party. We know that most of her friends are expected to go, but that a person x will not go if x cannot stand y and y goes:

$$\texttt{friend}(x) \rightarrow \texttt{go}(x)$$

$$\texttt{cant\_stand}(x, y) \wedge \texttt{go}(y) \Rightarrow \neg\texttt{go}(x)$$

Furthermore, Olga and Tom are Mary's friends (i.e., $\texttt{friend}(\texttt{o})$ and $\texttt{friend}(\texttt{t})$) and Olga cannot not stand Tom (i.e., $\texttt{cant\_stand}(\texttt{o}, \texttt{t})$).

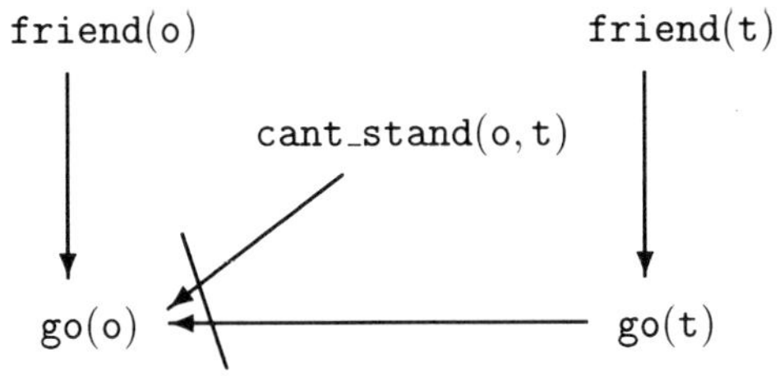

Figure 5.3
The party problem

Provided with this information, it is reasonable to expect that Tom will go to the party but Olga will not.[1] Yet, neither conclusion is sanctioned by conditional entailment. In this case, like in the YSP above, the problem does not lie exclusively with conditional entailment but with the formulation of the problem. Indeed, the logical equivalence between the formulas $\texttt{cant\_stand}(x, y) \wedge \texttt{go}(y) \Rightarrow \neg\texttt{go}(x)$ and $\texttt{cant\_stand}(x, y) \wedge \texttt{go}(x) \Rightarrow \neg\texttt{go}(y)$ fails to reflect the distinction between the *causal* statement "Olga will not go if Tom goes" and the fact "either Olga or Tom will not go." Yet, this distinction is crucial for handling this example correctly.

The three examples above illustrate the two aspects of default reasoning that are central to the framework we develop in this chapter. First, *explanatory* statements play a different role than *evidential* statements; e.g., Tom going to the party *explains* that Olga doesn't go, but Olga's going to the party is only *evidence* that Tom is not going. Similarly, the gun staying loaded *explains* Fred dying, but the Fred staying alive only provides *evidence* that the gun was unloaded. Second, the *intended* classes of models correspond to the classes that are more *coherent*; e.g., where Olga does not go *because* Tom is going, where Fred dies *because* he was shot with a loaded gun, and so on. On the other hand, the

[1] It may be argued that Mary, knowing that Olga will not go the party if Tom does, may decide not to invite Tom or ask Tom not to show up. Similar arguments have been advanced in relation to the YSP; e.g., perhaps, a long time (e.g., years) passed before the shooting, everything may have been a bad joke, etc. These arguments, however, miss the basic convention in non-monotonic reasoning by which relevant information is supposed to be made explicit; otherwise, we could not even jump to the conclusion that a bird flies, because the bird may happen to be a penguin.

*un*intended classes are classes in which defaults are violated without *explanation*; e.g., the gun gets mysteriously unloaded, Tom does not show up at the party, the battery happens not to die, etc.

In the proposal below, we will distinguish explanatory from evidential relations by introducing a 'causal' operator C in the language such that formulas of the form Cp will be read as "p is explained." We will thus be able to test whether an abnormality $\mathtt{ab}_i(a)$ is *explained* in a class of models by checking whether the formula $C\mathtt{ab}_i(a)$ holds. The default theories augmented with the operator C will be called *causal default theories*, or simply, *causal theories*.

5.2 Causal Theories

Causal theories are classical first order theories augmented with the causal operator 'C'. Formulas which do not involve the operator 'C' will be called *plain* formulas, while formulas which involve the operator 'C' will be called *causal* formulas. The operator 'C' will only take plain formulas as arguments and will be used to distinguish propositions which are *true* from propositions which are *explained.*

In the context of causal theories, defaults $p_i(x) \rightarrow q_i(x)$ will be encoded as sentences $p_i(x) \wedge \neg\mathtt{ab}_i(x) \Rightarrow q_i(x)$, with unique 'abnormality' predicates $\mathtt{ab}_i$ [McC86]. Literals of the form $\neg\mathtt{ab}_i(a)$ will be treated in a special way as they encode 'normality' *assumptions*; i.e., literals which are expected to be true. As discussed in Section 4.7, these assumptions will sometimes be ordered according to certain priorities, although we will ignore these priorities for the time being.

Formulas in the background K will still be distinguished from formulas in the evidence set E. As usual, the former stand for generic, defeasible or undefeasible knowledge, and the latter, for the specific facts that characterize the situation at hand.

The operator C will normally be used for encoding causal or explanatory rules as sentences of the form $a \Rightarrow Cb$. A rule such as 'rain causes the grass to be wet' will thus be expressed as a sentence $\mathtt{rain} \Rightarrow C\mathtt{grass\_wet}$, which can then be read as saying that if `rain` is true, `grass_wet` is explained.

We will assume that if a proposition α is explained (i.e., $C\alpha$ holds), then α must be true. This will be enforced by extending causal theories with the postulate $C\alpha \Rightarrow \alpha$ on the operator C for any plain formula α. Two additional postulates were considered in [Gef90a], but they will not be needed here.[2]

5.3 Semantics

Causal theories are interpreted by grouping models into classes and by ordering classes of models according to the explained and unexplained abnormalities that they sanction. For example, given the defaults

$$\texttt{bird}(x) \wedge \neg\texttt{ab}_1(x) \Rightarrow \text{C}\texttt{flies}(x)$$

$$\texttt{injured}(x) \wedge \neg\texttt{ab}_2(x) \Rightarrow \text{C}\texttt{ab}_1(x)$$

and the facts $\texttt{bird(tim)}$ and $\texttt{injured(tim)}$, the assumptions $\neg\texttt{ab}_1(\texttt{tim})$ and $\texttt{ab}_2(\texttt{tim})$ are inconsistent, producing two minimal classes of models: a class that sanctions the abnormality $\texttt{ab}_1(\texttt{tim})$, and a class that sanctions the abnormality $\texttt{ab}_2(\texttt{tim})$. In the first class, the assumption $\neg\texttt{ab}_2(\texttt{tim})$ holds and explains $\texttt{ab}_1(\texttt{tim})$ because it entails $\text{C}\texttt{ab}_1(\texttt{tim})$. In the second class, the assumption $\neg\texttt{ab}_1(\texttt{tim})$ holds but does not explain $\texttt{ab}_2(\texttt{tim})$ because $\text{C}\texttt{ab}_2(\texttt{tim})$ does not follow from $\neg\texttt{ab}_1(\texttt{tim})$. As a result, the first class of models is more 'coherent' than the second class, and will be preferred. So the assumption $\neg\texttt{ab}_2(\texttt{tim})$ will be entailed, but the assumption $\neg\texttt{ab}_1(\texttt{tim})$ will not.

We will make these ideas precise by means of some definitions. First, we will say that an interpretation M is a *model* of a causal theory $T = \langle K, E\rangle$ if M satisfies all the sentences in T as well as the postulate $C\alpha \Rightarrow \alpha$. Moreover, like with defaults, we will refer to the set of *abnormalities* sanctioned by an interpretation M as the *gap* of the interpretation, expressed as $A[M]$. Since the preference relation on models will be an exclusive function of these gaps we will group models into *classes of models* as follows.

Definition 5.1 A *class* $\mathcal{C}$ of default theory T *with a gap* $A[\mathcal{C}]$ stands for the non-empty collection of models M of T with a gap $A[M] \subseteq A[\mathcal{C}]$.

Since the negation of abnormalities are *assumptions* which are expected to hold, a class $\mathcal{C}$ with a gap $A[\mathcal{C}]$ can also be thought as the non-empty

[2] The two additional postulates were $C(\alpha \Rightarrow \beta) \Rightarrow (C\alpha \Rightarrow C\beta)$ and 'if $\vdash_K \alpha$ then $C\alpha$'. These postulates or equivalent ones would be needed to conclude, for example, Cp from Cq, given the background information $q \Rightarrow p$.

collection of models of T that satisfy all the assumptions $\neg\mathtt{ab}_i(a)$ for $\mathtt{ab}_i(a) \notin A[\mathcal{C}]$. We will also say that a proposition p *holds* in a class $\mathcal{C}$ when p holds in every model in the class, and that p is *explained* in $\mathcal{C}$ when $\mathrm{C}p$ holds in every model in $\mathcal{C}$. Proof-theoretically this is equivalent to p (resp. $\mathrm{C}p$) being derivable from T and a set of assumptions $\neg\mathtt{ab}_i(a)$ that hold in $\mathcal{C}$. Every explanation in a class $\mathcal{C}$ of T is thus *grounded* on T and the assumptions legitimized by $\mathcal{C}$.[3]

Classes of models are ordered according to the *explained* and *unexplained* abnormalities that they sanction. If we denote the set of explained abnormalities in a class $\mathcal{C}$ by $A^c[\mathcal{C}]$, then the preference relation on classes of a theory T can be defined as follows:

Definition 5.2 A class $\mathcal{C}$ is *at least as preferred as* a class $\mathcal{C}'$, written $\mathcal{C} \leq \mathcal{C}'$, iff $A[\mathcal{C}] - A^c[\mathcal{C}] \subseteq A[\mathcal{C}']$. Similarly, a class $\mathcal{C}$ is *preferred to* a class $\mathcal{C}'$, written $\mathcal{C} < \mathcal{C}'$, iff $\mathcal{C} \leq \mathcal{C}'$ and $\mathcal{C}' \not\leq \mathcal{C}$.

In other words, $\mathcal{C}$ is preferred to $\mathcal{C}'$ when every abnormality in $\mathcal{C}$ but not in $\mathcal{C}'$ has an explanation but not vice versa. The reason for ordering classes according to Definition 5.2 instead of simply minimizing the *unexplained gaps* $A[\mathcal{C}] - A^c[\mathcal{C}]$ is because the latter criterion, although simpler, introduces an *abductive bias* which is not adequate for default reasoning. For example, if $\neg\alpha_1$ and $\neg\alpha_2$ are two assumptions such that $\neg\alpha_1$ explains α_2 and $\neg\alpha_2$ explains α_1, and an abnormality α_3 is observed that $\neg\alpha_1$ explains but $\neg\alpha_2$ doesn't, the minimization of 'unexplained gaps' would select the assumption $\neg\alpha_1$ over the competing assumption $\neg\alpha_2$. The criterion that corresponds to Definition 5.2, on the other hand, remains uncommitted. It will then be the task of abduction to choose $\neg\alpha_1$ over $\neg\alpha_2$ in this case, if α_3 is worth explaining. Moreover, since abductive reasoning is computationally harder than default reasoning, establishing a clear separation between the two tasks will be beneficial for developing reasoning architectures (see Section 5.7).[4]

The preference relation on classes captured by Definition 5.2 is not

[3] This would have been not true if we had chosen the condition $A[M] = A[\mathcal{C}]$ instead of $A[M] \subseteq A[\mathcal{C}]$ in the definition of classes. In a theory like $T = \{\mathtt{a} \Rightarrow \mathrm{C}\mathtt{b}\}$, the former condition would render $\mathtt{b}$ explained in the class $\mathcal{C}$ with gap $A[\mathcal{C}] = \{\mathtt{a}\}$, even though $\mathrm{C}\mathtt{b}$ does not follow from T and any consistent set of assumptions. The two conditions though are equivalent for classes $\mathcal{C}$ with minimal gaps (i.e., minimal classes).

[4] The benefits of this separation can be seen in [DP91], where Dechter and Pearl compare the difficulty of *predictive* reasoning as opposed to *diagnostic* reasoning.

transitive. It is therefore possible to obtain three classes of models such that $\mathcal{C}_1$ is preferred to $\mathcal{C}_2$, $\mathcal{C}_2$ is preferred to $\mathcal{C}_3$, and yet $\mathcal{C}_1$ is *not* preferred to $\mathcal{C}_3$. Indeed, $\mathcal{C}_3$ may even be preferred to $\mathcal{C}_1$, resulting in a "preference loop" $\mathcal{C}_1 < \mathcal{C}_2 < \mathcal{C}_3 < \mathcal{C}_1 < \cdots$.[5] Thus, special care is required for defining what the overall preferred classes of a causal theory are, if these scenarios are not to be ruled out as inconsistent.

The key in the definition of 'preferred classes' will be the notion of *basis.* Intuitively, a *basis* is a collection of classes which is guaranteed to contain all the 'best' classes. We will use the term *minimal classes* to refer to classes $\mathcal{C}$ with minimal gaps $A[\mathcal{C}]$.[6]

Definition 5.3 A basis $\mathcal{B}$ for a causal theory T is a collection of classes of T which obeys two conditions. First, no *minimal* class $\mathcal{C}'$ *outside* $\mathcal{B}$ is as preferred as a class $\mathcal{C}$ *inside* $\mathcal{B}$.[7] Second, for every class $\mathcal{C}'$ *outside* $\mathcal{B}$ there is a class $\mathcal{C}$ *inside* $\mathcal{B}$ such that $\mathcal{C}$ is at least as preferred as $\mathcal{C}'$.

A consequence of this definition is that every logically consistent causal theory will have a basis and thus will be *causally* consistent. If we further say that a basis $\mathcal{B}$ *supports* a proposition p when p holds in every class in $\mathcal{B}$, then the entailment relation associated with default causal theories can be defined as follows:

Definition 5.4 A theory T (causally) entails a proposition p if there is a basis for T which supports p.

Let us consider again the example at the beginning of this section. Since the assumptions $\neg\mathtt{ab_1(tim)}$ and $\neg\mathtt{ab_2(tim)}$ are in conflict, there are two minimal classes of models: a class $\mathcal{C}_1$ in which $\mathtt{ab_1(tim)}$ holds, i.e., $A[\mathcal{C}_1] = \{\mathtt{ab_1(tim)}\}$, and a class $\mathcal{C}_2$ in which $\mathtt{ab_2(tim)}$ holds, i.e., $A[\mathcal{C}_2] = \{\mathtt{ab_2(tim)}\}$. Moreover, since the assumption $\neg\mathtt{ab_2(tim)}$ holds in $\mathcal{C}_1$, and $\neg\mathtt{ab_2(tim)}$ implies $\mathtt{Cab_1(tim)}$, $\mathtt{ab_1(tim)}$ is explained in $\mathcal{C}_1$, i.e., $A^c[\mathcal{C}_1] = \{\mathtt{ab_1(tim)}\}$, but $\mathtt{ab_2(tim)}$ is not explained in $\mathcal{C}_2$, i.e., $A^c[\mathcal{C}_2] = \emptyset$. As a result, $\mathcal{C}_1$ is at least as preferred as $\mathcal{C}_2$, i.e., $\mathcal{C}_1 \leq \mathcal{C}_2$, but $\mathcal{C}_2$ is not at least as preferred as $\mathcal{C}_1$. Therefore, since $\mathcal{C}_1$ and $\mathcal{C}_2$ are

[5] A theory which gives rises to this 'loop' is: $\neg\mathtt{ab_1} \Rightarrow \mathtt{Cab_2}$, $\neg\mathtt{ab_2} \Rightarrow \mathtt{Cab_3}$ and $\neg\mathtt{ab_3} \Rightarrow \mathtt{Cab_1}$.

[6] Bases are similar to spheres in Lewis' semantics for counterfactuals [Lew73]. The main difference is that the preference relation on classes, unlike Lewis' similarity relation on worlds, is not transitive.

[7] The minimality condition allows us to exclude from a basis any class which is not minimal.

the only two minimal classes of T, $\mathcal{B} = \{\mathcal{C}_1\}$ is a a basis for T, and the propositions that hold in $\mathcal{C}_1$ are (causally) entailed.

Bases can always be constructed by considering only the classes of models which are minimal. Indeed, the collection of all minimal classes is always a basis, and if a basis $\mathcal{B}$ contains a non-minimal class $\mathcal{C}$, the class $\mathcal{C}$ can be removed, and the collection of classes that is left will be a basis as well. The collection of all minimal classes, however, is often not the *smallest* basis. In the theory above, for example, $\mathcal{C}_1$ and $\mathcal{C}_2$ are the two minimal classes and thus form a basis $\mathcal{B}'$. Yet since $\mathcal{C}_1$ is preferred to $\mathcal{C}_2$, $\mathcal{C}_2$ can be dropped from $\mathcal{B}'$, and the collection of classes left, $\mathcal{B} = \{\mathcal{C}_1\}$ is a basis that is smaller than $\mathcal{B}'$.

Since for determining causal entailment we are interested in the *smallest* bases, we will normally focus on the classes that are minimal relative to the '$<$'-ordering (recall that we write $\mathcal{C}_1 < \mathcal{C}_2$ when $\mathcal{C}_1$ is strictly preferred to $\mathcal{C}_2$). Since every class that is $<$-minimal must belong to every basis,[8] if the collection $\mathcal{B}_0$ of $<$-minimal classes is a basis, it will be the smallest one:

Lemma 5.1 If the collection $\mathcal{B}_0$ of $<$-minimal classes is a basis, it is the smallest one; i.e., every basis is a superset of $\mathcal{B}_0$.

One way $\mathcal{B}_0$ can be shown to be a basis is by proving that for every minimal class $\mathcal{C}$ which is *not* $<$-minimal, there is $<$-minimal class $\mathcal{C}'$ preferred to $\mathcal{C}$. For example, $\mathcal{C}_1$ and $\mathcal{C}_2$ above are the only minimal classes, and since $\mathcal{C}_1$ is preferred to $\mathcal{C}_2$ and $\mathcal{C}_1$ is a $<$-minimal class, $\mathcal{B} = \{\mathcal{C}_1\}$ is guaranteed to be the smallest basis.

When $\mathcal{B}_0$ is a basis, we will refer to the classes in $\mathcal{B}_0$ as the *preferred classes*, since a proposition p will be causally entailed when p holds in all such classes.

That $\mathcal{B}_0$ is not always a basis can be illustrated with the causal theory $T_1 = \{\neg \mathsf{a} \Rightarrow C\mathsf{b}, \neg \mathsf{b} \Rightarrow C\mathsf{c}, \neg \mathsf{c} \Rightarrow \mathsf{a}\}$, where a, b and c are abnormalities. If $\mathcal{C}_1$ and $\mathcal{C}_2$ stand for the classes of models that sanction $\neg\mathsf{a}$ and $\neg\mathsf{c}$ respectively, $\mathcal{C}_1$ is the only $<$-minimal class of T_1, and yet $\mathcal{C}_1$ is not as preferred as $\mathcal{C}_2$. So $\mathcal{B}_0 = \{\mathcal{C}_1\}$ cannot be a basis.

$\mathcal{B}_0$ can in fact be empty even for theories that are logically consistent. For example, if the rule $\neg\mathsf{c} \Rightarrow \mathsf{a}$ in T_1 is replaced by the causal rule $\neg\mathsf{c} \Rightarrow C\mathsf{a}$, we will get $\mathcal{C}_1 < \mathcal{C}_2 < \mathcal{C}_3 < \mathcal{C}_1$, and therefore, that none of

[8] A class $\mathcal{C}$ is $<$-minimal if there is no class $\mathcal{C}'$ such that $\mathcal{C}' < \mathcal{C}$.

the classes is $<$-minimal. The advantage of defining entailment in terms of bases is that since the intersection of two bases cannot be empty, a causal theory T will be consistent as long as T is *logically* consistent.[9]

5.4 Implicit Explanations

We will illustrate the use of causal theories for representing and reasoning with defaults with a causal encoding of Yale shooting problem discussed in Example 5.1 above.

Example 5.4 A possible formulation of the YSP as a causal theory is given by the background K:

$$\texttt{loaded} \wedge \neg \texttt{ab}_1 \Rightarrow \mathrm{C}\texttt{loaded}'$$

$$\texttt{alive}' \wedge \neg \texttt{ab}_2 \Rightarrow \mathrm{C}\texttt{alive}''$$

$$\texttt{shoot}' \wedge \texttt{loaded}' \Rightarrow \mathrm{C}\neg\texttt{alive}''$$

$$\texttt{shoot}' \wedge \texttt{loaded}' \Rightarrow \mathrm{C}\texttt{ab}_2$$

The differences between this and the earlier formulation are essentially three: 1) defaults are encoded at the object-level by means of 'abnormality' predicates, 2) all rules are now causal or explanatory, and 3) a cancellation axiom, which is present in the formulation of Hanks and McDermott, has been added (more about this below).

In the target context $T = \langle K, E \rangle$ with $E = \{\texttt{loaded}, \texttt{alive}', \texttt{shoot}'\}$, we obtain again two minimal classes: a class $\mathcal{C}_1$, where the assumption $\neg\texttt{ab}_2$ holds and the assumption $\neg\texttt{ab}_1$ is violated; and a class $\mathcal{C}_2$, where the assumption $\neg\texttt{ab}_1$ holds and the assumption $\neg\texttt{ab}_2$ is violated.

[9] In [Gef91] we claimed wrongly that the intersection of two bases is always a basis. This is not correct, as noticed by Ramiro Guerreiro. As a result, causal theories may possess more than one "smallest" basis and for such theories causal entailment may fail to be deductively closed. An example of such a theory (due to Ramiro) is $\neg\texttt{ab}_1 \Rightarrow \mathrm{C}\texttt{ab}_2 \wedge \mathrm{C}\texttt{ab}_3$, $\neg\texttt{ab}_2 \vee \neg\texttt{ab}_3 \Rightarrow \mathrm{C}\texttt{ab}_4$, $\texttt{ab}_1 \vee \texttt{ab}_4$ and $\texttt{ab}_2 \vee \texttt{ab}_3$. This theory accepts two minimal bases: $\mathcal{B}_1 = \{\mathcal{C}_1, \mathcal{C}_2\}$ and $\mathcal{B}_2 = \{\mathcal{C}_1, \mathcal{C}_3\}$, where $\mathcal{C}_i$ stands for the class of models in which the assumption $\neg\texttt{ab}_i$ holds. Since $\neg\texttt{ab}_1 \vee \neg\texttt{ab}_2$ holds in $\mathcal{B}_1$ and $\neg\texttt{ab}_1 \vee \neg\texttt{ab}_3$ holds in $\mathcal{B}_2$, both formulas are entailed even though their conjunction is not.

An account which is deductively closed and which preserves consistency can be obtained by using the preference relation '$\leq$' to *prune* classes as opposed to *select* them. For example, we could label a class $\mathcal{C}$ as *admissible* if every class $\mathcal{C}'$ preferred to $\mathcal{C}$ is such that $A[\mathcal{C}'] \not\subset A[\mathcal{C}]$, and define the *preferred* classes as the admissible classes with minimal gaps. Although we haven't yet investigated this account in detail, most of the results in this chapter would be applicable because the basic preference relation on classes remains the same.

The classes $\mathcal{C}_1$ and $\mathcal{C}_2$, however, are no longer symmetrical. Indeed, while the assumption $\neg\mathtt{ab}_1$ *explains* the abnormality $\mathtt{ab}_2$ in $\mathcal{C}_2$, i.e., $E, K, \neg\mathtt{ab}_1 \vdash \mathrm{C}\mathtt{ab}_2$, no set of assumptions in $\mathcal{C}_1$ explains $\mathtt{ab}_1$. Thus, $A[\mathcal{C}_2] = A^c[\mathcal{C}_2] = \{\mathtt{ab}_2\}$, while $A[\mathcal{C}_1] = \{\mathtt{ab}_1\}$ and $A^c[\mathcal{C}_1] = \emptyset$. As a result, the minimal class $\mathcal{C}_2$ is preferred to the only other minimal class $\mathcal{C}_1$, and therefore, $\mathcal{B} = \{\mathcal{C}_2\}$ is a basis for T ($\mathcal{B} = \{\mathcal{C}_2\}$ is the smallest basis of T). Hence the propositions that hold in $\mathcal{C}_2$, e.g., $\mathtt{loaded}'$ and $\neg\mathtt{alive}''$, are causally entailed.

The example illustrates how causal theories capture the correct intuition underlying the YSP.[10] Yet, in order to show that causal theories provide a *general* framework for representing and reasoning with defaults, we need to show that causal theories permit knowledge to be encoded in a natural way. From this perspective though, the formulation above is not completely satisfying because it depends on the presence of the cancellation axiom $\mathtt{shoot}' \wedge \mathtt{loaded}' \Rightarrow \mathrm{C}\mathtt{ab}_2$.[11] Had we removed this axiom or even the C from its consequent, the correct behavior would not have been captured (removing the C's from the consequent of the other rules wouldn't have any effect though).

The justification for this axiom, however, is not difficult to come by: as far the constraints which we have imposed on the operator 'C' go, practically the only way in which an abnormality $\mathtt{ab}_i$ can be explained is if there is an axiom of the form $p \Rightarrow \mathrm{C}\mathtt{ab}_i$ in the database. Yet this is not entirely reasonable. Indeed, if $p_i \wedge \neg\mathtt{ab}_i \Rightarrow q_i$ is a default, and certain conditions explain why q_i is not true, then those conditions should also be taken as an explanation for why $\neg\mathtt{ab}_i$ is not true. In other words, explanations for the negation of q_i should also count as explanations for the assumption that predicts q_i.

In the YSP, the assumption $\neg\mathtt{ab}_2$ predicts $\mathtt{alive}''$, while the conjunction $\mathtt{shoot}' \wedge \mathtt{loaded}'$ explains the negation of $\mathtt{alive}''$. According to our reasoning, the conjunction $\mathtt{shoot}' \wedge \mathtt{loaded}'$ should also explain the abnormality $\mathtt{ab}_2$. That is what the cancellation axiom captures.

Yet, if cancellation axioms can be justified by appealing to other rules in the database, why do we need them in the first place? Can't we

[10] Other solutions to the Yale shooting problem which rest on the same intuition of minimizing, or even banning unexplained abnormality, are [Lif87, Hau87, MS88a].

[11] By cancellation axioms we mean axioms of the form $A \Rightarrow \mathrm{C}\alpha$, where α is an abnormality.

achieve the same effect without having to make cancellation axioms explicit? The benefits of doing without explicit cancellation axioms would be similar to the benefits of extracting priorities automatically from the knowledge base: the user would be exclusively concerned with describing the relevant aspects of the domain and the system would take care of the interactions.

The effect of explicit cancellation axioms can be captured by automatically adding formulas of the form

$$p_i(x) \wedge \mathrm{C}\neg q_i(x) \Rightarrow \mathrm{C}\mathsf{ab}_i(x)$$

for each default $p_i(x) \wedge \neg\mathsf{ab}_i(x) \Rightarrow \mathrm{C}q_i(x)$ in the theory, making indeed every explanation for $\neg q_i(a)$ into an explanation for $\mathsf{ab}_i(a)$ (provided $p_i(a)$ holds).[12] However, since there are usually only a few ways in which the causal literal $\mathrm{C}\neg q_i(x)$ can be established, we would find it more convenient to replace $\mathrm{C}\neg q_i(x)$ by the *plain* literals that can make $\mathrm{C}\neg q_i(x)$ true. The theory that will result from adding the new formulas to the original theory T will be referred to as the *closure* of T. By assuming that a user means the *closure* of T when she writes down T, we will save her from having to provide the cancellation axioms explicitly.

Closing a Causal Theory

The closure of a causal theory is a compilation-time operation (i.e., it depends only on the background information) and its role is to make explicit the ways in which abnormalities $\mathsf{ab}_i(a)$ are explained. Roughly, the explanations for $\mathsf{ab}_i(a)$, for a default $p_i(x) \wedge \neg\mathsf{ab}_i(x) \Rightarrow q_i(x)$ will be given by the explanations for propositions $q_i'(a)$ incompatible with $q_i(a)$.

In order to guarantee certain desirable properties on the closure of a causal theory T, we will make a few assumptions about the form of T. First of all, we will assume that the abnormality predicates ab_i occur only positively; i.e., they only occur in positive literals of the form $\mathsf{ab}_i(x)$ when the formulas in the theory are expressed in clausal form. Similarly, we will assume that the operator C appears only in strict or defeasible rules of the form $p_i(x) \Rightarrow \mathrm{C}q_i(x)$ or $p_i(x) \wedge \neg\mathsf{ab}_i(x) \Rightarrow \mathrm{C}q_i(x)$,[13] where $q_i(x)$ is an atom and $p_i(x)$ is an arbitrary formula. Likewise, we will

[12] A related encoding of defaults in autoepistemic logic can be found in [Gel89a] and [KM89]. We will discuss the relation between causal and autoepistemic theories in Section 5.8.

[13] As usual, free variables are assumed to be universally quantified.

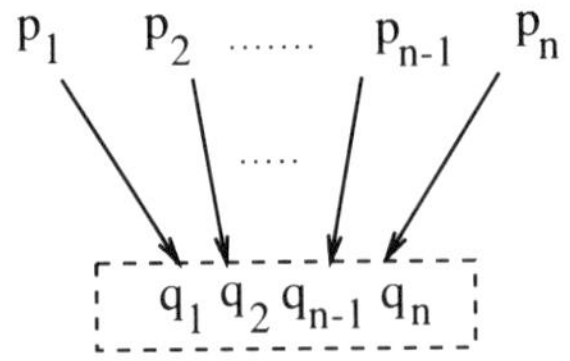

Figure 5.4
Rules in head-to-head conflict

assume that the formulas $q_i(x)$ and $p_i(x)$ have a single free variable x or no free variables at all.

The restriction on the use of the predicates $\texttt{ab}_i$ does not have practical significance because the abnormalities $\texttt{ab}_i$ appear normally either positively in the consequent of rules or negatively in their antecedents. The same applies to the use of the operator C, as formulas involving C normally fall into one of the two categories above. The restriction on the free variables in $p_i(x)$ and $q_i(x)$, on the other hand, is for the sake of simplicity only, and we will sometimes appeal to a generalization of this condition, although we will skip over the details.

We will write causal rules as $p_i(x) \wedge \alpha_i(x) \Rightarrow \mathrm{C}q_i(x)$, and let $\alpha_i(x)$ stand for $\neg\texttt{ab}_i(x)$ if the rule is defeasible, and for **true**, if the the rule is strict. The explanations for abnormalities $\texttt{ab}_i(a)$, for defaults r_i : $p_i(x) \wedge \neg\texttt{ab}_i(x) \Rightarrow \mathrm{C}q_i(x)$ will then be given by the rules r_j : $p_j(x) \wedge \alpha_i(x) \Rightarrow \mathrm{C}q_j(x)$ whose *heads* $\mathrm{C}q_j(x)$ are incompatible with $q_i(x)$.

To make this precise, let us refer to the formulas in a background K which do not involve either abnormality predicates or the operator C as *constraints* (e.g., $\texttt{dead}(x) \equiv \neg\texttt{alive}(x)$ and $\texttt{clear}(x) \equiv \neg\exists y.\, \texttt{on}(y, x)$ are constraints). Then if we denote the collection of such constraints by K_S, we will say that a collection of causal rules is in *head-to-head conflict* when the following holds:

Definition 5.5 The rules $p_i(x) \wedge \alpha_i(x) \Rightarrow \mathrm{C}q_i(x)$ in K, $i = 1, \ldots, n$, are in *head-to-head conflict* iff they are a minimal collection of causal rules for which $K_S \vdash \forall x. \neg(q_1(x) \wedge \cdots \wedge q_n(x))$ holds.

Thus, causal rules are in head-to-head conflict when the heads of the rules are incompatible relative to the generic constraints in the background context (this incompatibility is represented by a box in Fig. 5.4). For example, in the context of inheritance hierarchies, the head-to-head conflicts correspond to the pairs of conflicting links $p_1 \rightarrow q$ and $p_2 \not\rightarrow q$.

Similarly, in reasoning about change, head-to-head conflicts arise between rules like

$$\texttt{alive}(t) \wedge \texttt{ab}_1(t) \Rightarrow \texttt{Calive}(t+1)$$

$$\texttt{shoot}(t) \wedge \texttt{loaded}(t) \Rightarrow \texttt{Cdead}(t+1)$$

which describe the persistence of a fluent and how the fluent may change.

In general, head-to-head conflicts may involve more than two defaults, and as the last example shows, the 'heads' do not have to be tautologically incompatible (like p and $\neg p$). Likewise, not every collection of *conflicting* rules is in *head-to-head* conflict. For example, if the gun was loaded at time $t = 1$ but was found unloaded at time $t = 3$, then the defaults

$$\texttt{loaded}(1) \wedge \neg\texttt{ab}_1(1) \Rightarrow \texttt{Cloaded}(2)$$

$$\texttt{loaded}(2) \wedge \neg\texttt{ab}_1(2) \Rightarrow \texttt{Cloaded}(3)$$

will be in *conflict* but they will not in *head-to-head* conflict. This is because the facts $\texttt{loaded}(1)$ and $\neg\texttt{loaded}(3)$ that make the two defaults inconsistent are *evidential* and not *background* information.

This last scenario also illustrates an important feature that distinguishes head-to-head conflicts from other types of conflicts among defaults: *head-to-head conflicts do not arise due to observations but to the inherent incompatibility of defaults.* In particular, if the causal rules $p_i(x) \wedge \alpha_i(x) \Rightarrow \mathrm{C}q_i(x)$, $i = 1, \ldots, n$, are in head-to-head conflict, and $\mathcal{C}$ is a class of models in which each of the antecedents $p_i(a)$ holds, then, *regardless of the observations gathered,* some abnormality $\texttt{ab}_i(a)$, for $\alpha_i(a) = \neg\texttt{ab}_i(a)$, will have to hold in $\mathcal{C}$. Our assumption in 'closing' causal theories will be that if $\texttt{ab}_i(a)$ is the *only* such abnormality in $\mathcal{C}$, then $\texttt{ab}_i(a)$ should be explained. The intuition is that *unexplained abnormalities should be the result of observations and not of conflicts among rules which are inherently incompatible.* The closure of a causal theory T is hence defined as follows:

Definition 5.6 (Closure) The *closure* of a causal theory $T = \langle K, E\rangle$ is the causal theory $T^\circ = \langle K', E\rangle$ that results from adding to T the 'justifications':

$$\bigwedge_{j\in[1,n]} p_j(x) \quad \bigwedge_{\substack{k\in[1,n]\\ \alpha_k\neq\alpha_i}} \alpha_k(x) \;\Rightarrow\; \mathrm{C}\texttt{ab}_i(x)$$

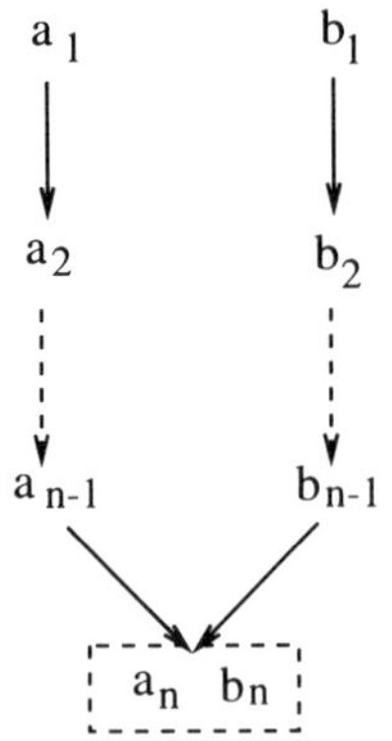

Figure 5.5
Forward reasoning in causal theories

for each collection of rules $p_i(x) \wedge \alpha_i(x) \Rightarrow Cq_i(x)$, $i = 1, \ldots, n$ in head-to-head conflict in T and each assumption $\alpha_i(x) = \neg \mathsf{ab}_i(x)$.

When a user writes a causal theory T, we will assume that he or she means the closure T° of T unless otherwise specified. Since we are assuming that abnormalities only occur positively in T (i.e., either negated in the "body" or unnegated in the "head"), the effect of the 'justifications' added to T — which except for the C's, are logical consequences of the rules which explicitly appear in T — will be simply to explain the abnormalities that result from head-to-head conflicts. These justifications, however, do not affect the classes of models that the original theory T gives rise to, and thus, can be ignored, except for testing whether an abnormality is explained.[14]

The effect of the closure operation on the *behavior* of causal theories can be illustrated by the theory T depicted in Figure 5.5, where the rules $p_i \rightarrow p_{i+1}$, for $p = \mathsf{a}$ or $p = \mathsf{b}$, stand for the causal formulas $p_i \wedge \neg \mathsf{ab}_i^p \Rightarrow Cp_{i+1}$, and the last two rules

$$\mathsf{a}_{n-1} \wedge \neg \mathsf{ab}^{\mathsf{a}}_{n-1} \Rightarrow C\mathsf{a}_n$$

$$\mathsf{b}_{n-1} \wedge \neg \mathsf{ab}^{\mathsf{b}}_{n-1} \Rightarrow C\mathsf{b}_n$$

are in head-to-head conflict.

[14]Note that this would not have been true if we had excluded $p_i(x)$ from the conjunction $\bigwedge_{j \in [1,n]} p_j(x)$ in the definition of the closure of T.

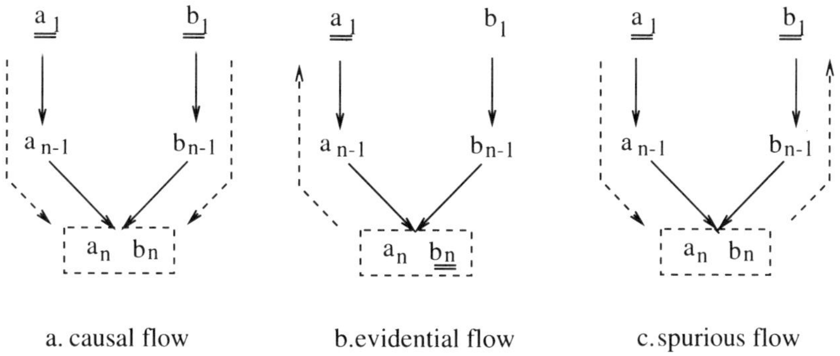

Figure 5.6
Flow of information in causal theories

Given $\mathtt{a_1}$ and $\mathtt{b_1}$, any class of T has to violate one of the rules $p_j \rightarrow p_{j+1}$ for some j, $1 \leq j \leq n-1$ (i.e., it must sanction one abnormality $\mathtt{ab}_j^p$). The closure of T makes the classes that violate one of the *last* rules $p_{n-1} \rightarrow p_n$ preferred over the classes that violate one of the *preceding* rules $p_{j-1} \rightarrow p_j$, for $j \neq n$. This is because the justifications in the closure of T permit us to explain the abnormalities associated with the last rules, which are in head-to-head conflict, but none of the other abnormalities. The result is that we can conclude each of the atoms p_j, for $1 \leq j < n$ and $p = \mathtt{a}$ or $p = \mathtt{b}$, but none of the atoms p_n.

If we were given $\mathtt{a_1}$ and $\mathtt{b_n}$ instead, the classes of T would have to violate one of the rules $p_j \rightarrow p_{j+1}$ for some j, $1 \leq j \leq n-1$, and $p = \mathtt{a}$. But since we can no longer establish $\mathtt{b_{n-1}}$, we can no longer explain the violation of any of these rules, and thus, all the minimal classes would be equally preferred and no atom $\mathtt{a}_j$ would follow.

The flow of information in causal theories resembles the flow of information in Bayesian Networks [Pea88b]. In both frameworks, when given $\mathtt{a_1}$ and $\mathtt{b_1}$, the information flows forward only (along the direction of the rules; Fig. 5.6a), in spite of the logically acceptable arguments for the propositions p_j, $j < n$, which rely on the contraposition of the rules (Fig. 5.6c). This is because arguments involving defaults in head-to-head conflict are weaker in causal theories (because such arguments can be explained), while paths involving head-to-head rules carry no information in Bayesian Networks (because of assumptions about causality and independence). When given $\mathtt{a_1}$ and $\mathtt{b_n}$, the information flows both forward and backward, because the path $\mathtt{a_1} \rightarrow \ldots \rightarrow \mathtt{a_n}$, whose origin

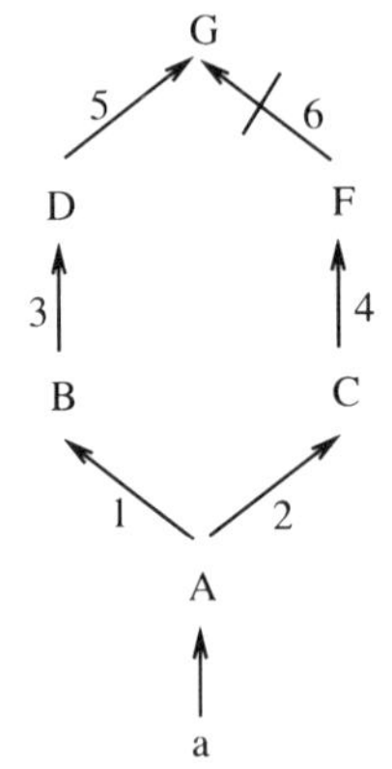

Figure 5.7
Extended diamonds

$\mathtt{a_1}$ is confirmed and whose end $\mathtt{a_n}$ is negated, doesn't involve rules which are in head-to-head conflict. (Fig. 5.6b).

It is worth mentioning that if causal rules were interpreted according to chronological minimization [Sho88],[15] reasoning would always proceed forward only, and thus we would conclude $\mathtt{a}_j$, $1 \leq j < n-1$, *both* when given $\mathtt{a_1}$ and $\mathtt{b_1}$ and when given $\mathtt{a_1}$ and $\mathtt{b_n}$. On the other hand, if causal rules are interpreted according to minimal models (e.g., [McC86]), reasoning will always proceed both backward and forward, and thus would *not* conclude $\mathtt{a}_j$, $1 \leq j < n-1$, either when $\mathtt{a_1}$ and $\mathtt{b_1}$ are given, or when $\mathtt{a_1}$ and $\mathtt{b_n}$ are.

Example 5.5 (Extended Diamonds) To illustrate the use of causal theories on a concrete example, we will consider the inheritance network depicted in Fig. 5.7. The theory $T = \langle K, E \rangle$ will be defined from mapping each link $U \xrightarrow{i} V$ into the formula $U(x) \wedge \neg \mathtt{ab}_i(x) \Rightarrow [\neg]\mathrm{C}V(x)$ in K, and each link $a \rightarrow U$ into the literal $[\neg]U(a)$ in E (negations are to be used when the links are negated). The network in the figure corresponds to what has been called 'extended diamonds' as they extend the classical 'Nixon diamond' with additional links. Extended and regular diamonds are different in more than the number of links though, because while regular diamonds do not require any sort of priorities, extended diamonds cannot do without them [Hau88].

[15] Assuming the rules are extended with the relevant temporal information.

For example, the theory T defined above has six minimal classes $\mathcal{C}_i$, where $\mathcal{C}_i$ represents the class that violates the link labeled i. Without any prioritization, not only we would not be able to conclude whether a is a G, which is reasonable, but whether a is a D or F, which is not (since the paths a $\rightarrow$ A $\rightarrow$ B $\rightarrow$ D and a $\rightarrow$ A $\rightarrow$ C $\rightarrow$ F are not contradicted).

Causal entailment provides such a prioritization as it picks up the classes that violate the abnormalities $\mathtt{ab}_5(\mathtt{a})$ and $\mathtt{ab}_6(\mathtt{a})$ as the 'preferred' classes, and sanctions both D(a) and F(a). This is because the defaults

$$\mathtt{D}(x) \wedge \neg \mathtt{ab}_5(x) \Rightarrow \mathrm{C}\mathtt{G}(x)$$
$$\mathtt{F}(x) \wedge \neg \mathtt{ab}_6(x) \Rightarrow \mathrm{C}\neg\mathtt{G}(x)$$

are in head-to-head conflict, and thus the closure of T contains the justifications:

$$\mathtt{D}(x) \wedge \mathtt{F}(x) \wedge \neg \mathtt{ab}_5(x) \Rightarrow \mathrm{C}\mathtt{ab}_6(x)$$
$$\mathtt{D}(x) \wedge \mathtt{F}(x) \wedge \neg \mathtt{ab}_6(x) \Rightarrow \mathrm{C}\mathtt{ab}_5(x)$$

These justifications explain the abnormalities $\mathtt{ab}_5(\mathtt{a})$ and $\mathtt{ab}_6(\mathtt{a})$ in the classes $\mathcal{C}_5$ and $\mathcal{C}_6$ respectively, making both classes preferred to each of the classes $\mathcal{C}_i$, with $i = 1, \ldots, 4$.

Example 5.6 (Party Problem) Let us look again at Example 5.3. We know that most of Mary's friends are expected to attend her party but that a person x will not go, if x cannot stand y and y attends. Olga and Tom are Mary's friends and Olga cannot stand Tom, i.e. $T = \langle K, E \rangle$, with $E = \{\mathtt{friend(o)}, \mathtt{friend(o)}, \mathtt{cant\_stand(o,t)}\}$.

The use of the operator C breaks up the equivalence between the statements 'Olga will not go if Tom goes' and 'either Olga or Tom will not go'. Indeed, while Olga's not going to the party can be explained, Tom's not going cannot. This is because of the head-to-head conflict between the two rules

$$\mathtt{friend}(x) \wedge \neg \mathtt{ab}_1(x) \Rightarrow \mathrm{C}\mathtt{go}(x)$$
$$\mathtt{cant\_stand}(x, y) \wedge \mathtt{go}(y) \Rightarrow \mathrm{C}\neg\mathtt{go}(x)$$

in the background K of the theory, make the closure of T contain the justification:

$$\mathtt{friend}(x) \wedge \mathtt{cant\_stand}(x, y) \wedge \mathtt{go}(y) \Rightarrow \mathrm{C}\mathtt{ab}_1(x)$$

Hence, among the two minimal classes $\mathcal{C}_1$ and $\mathcal{C}_2$ of T, where $\mathcal{C}_1$ sanctions $\texttt{ab}_1\texttt{(o)}$ and $\mathcal{C}_2$ sanctions $\texttt{ab}_1\texttt{(t)}$, $\mathcal{C}_1$ is preferred, sanctioning the expected conclusions $\texttt{go(t)}$ and $\neg\texttt{go(o)}$.

A similar analysis applies to the formulation of the YSP in Example 5.4, without the need to make the cancellation axiom explicit.

5.5 Priorities and Explanations

So far, we have encoded default $p(x) \rightarrow q(x)$ as sentences of the form $p(x) \wedge \neg\texttt{ab}_i(x) \Rightarrow q(x)$, where $\texttt{ab}_i(a)$'s are abnormality literals expected to be false. Yet we know that by collapsing defaults like $p(x) \rightarrow q(x)$ and **true** $\rightarrow p(x) \Rightarrow q(x)$ whose encodings are logically equivalent, information about the *conditional* preferences among the defaults — captured by ϵ-entailment and p-entailment — may be lost. To recover those preferences it is necessary to order the assumptions $\neg\texttt{ab}_i(a)$ by means of priorities (cf. Section 4.7).

If both *causal* and *conditional* preferences among defaults are to captured, we thus need a way for incorporating *priorities* into causal theories. We will do that by modifying the way causal theories are closed (recall from the previous section, that the closure of a causal theory T refers to the theory that results by making explicit a number of justifications which we assume implicit in T).

Definition 5.7 (Closure w/ Priorities) The closure of a causal theory $T = \langle K, E\rangle$ augmented with priorities is given by the causal theory $T^\bullet = \langle K', E\rangle$ that results from adding to T the 'justifications':

$$\bigwedge_{j\in[1,n]} p_j(x) \bigwedge_{\substack{k\in[1,n] \\ \alpha_k\neq\alpha_i}} \alpha_k(x) \Rightarrow \mathrm{C}\texttt{ab}_i(x)$$

for each collection of rules $p_i(x) \wedge \alpha_i(x) \Rightarrow \mathrm{C}q_i(x)$, $i = 1, \ldots, n$ in head-to-head conflict in T, and each assumption $\alpha_i(x) = \neg\texttt{ab}_i(x)$ *whose priority is not higher than the priority of some* $\neg\texttt{ab}_j(x)$, $1 \leq j \leq n$.

The only difference with the plain closure of a causal theory is that 'justifications' for an abnormality $\texttt{ab}_i(a)$ which rely on assumptions with lower priority than $\neg\texttt{ab}_i(a)$ are excluded. This prevents explaining a 'flying penguin', for example, on the grounds that penguins are birds and birds fly.

As before we will assume that when a user expresses a causal theory T augmented with priorities he or she really means the closure $T^\bullet$ of T unless otherwise specified. Under the assumptions above, the 'extra' justifications in $T^\bullet$ need only be consulted for testing whether an abnormality is explained in T but not for determining what the classes of T are.

Example 5.7 As an illustration of the use of priorities in causal theories, let us consider again Example 5.2 discussed in Section 5.1. The background of the theory $T = \langle K, E \rangle$ consists of the following three defaults:

$$\texttt{turn\_key} \wedge \neg\texttt{ab}_1 \Rightarrow C\texttt{starts}$$

$$\texttt{turn\_key} \wedge \texttt{battery\_dead} \wedge \neg\texttt{ab}_2 \Rightarrow C\neg\texttt{starts}$$

$$\texttt{lights\_were\_on} \wedge \neg\texttt{ab}_3 \Rightarrow C\texttt{battery\_dead}$$

where we assume $\neg\texttt{ab}_2$ to have priority over $\neg\texttt{ab}_1$, as it follows from either conditional or specificity considerations.[16] The closure of this background includes also the justification:

$$\texttt{turn\_key} \wedge \texttt{battery\_dead} \wedge \neg\texttt{ab}_2 \Rightarrow C\texttt{ab}_1$$

that results from the head-to-head conflict between the first two rules. The justification:

$$\texttt{turn\_key} \wedge \texttt{battery\_dead} \wedge \neg\texttt{ab}_1 \Rightarrow C\texttt{ab}_2$$

does not make it into the closure because the priority of the assumption $\neg\texttt{ab}_2$ is higher than the priority of the assumption $\neg\texttt{ab}_1$.

With these rules, the evidence $E = \{\texttt{lights\_were\_on}, \texttt{turn\_key}\}$ gives rise to three minimal classes: $\mathcal{C}_1$, $\mathcal{C}_2$, and $\mathcal{C}_3$, where $\mathcal{C}_i$ stands for the class of models that sanction the abnormality $\texttt{ab}_i$. However, while the abnormality $\texttt{ab}_1$ is explained in $\mathcal{C}_1$, due to the justification for $\texttt{ab}_1$ in the closure of the theory, neither $\texttt{ab}_2$ or $\texttt{ab}_3$ are explained in $\mathcal{C}_2$ or $\mathcal{C}_3$. As a result, $\mathcal{C}_1$ is preferred to both $\mathcal{C}_2$ and $\mathcal{C}_3$, $\mathcal{B} = \{\mathcal{C}_1\}$ is the smallest basis of the theory, and the propositions that hold in $\mathcal{C}_1$, including $\texttt{dead\_battery}$ and $\neg\texttt{start}$, are (causally) entailed.

[16]For determining priorities in accordance with conditional entailment, we would need, in addition to the sentences $p \wedge \neg\texttt{ab}_i \Rightarrow q$ in K, the defaults $p \rightarrow \neg\texttt{ab}_i$. Then the priorities on the assumptions $\neg\texttt{ab}_i$ can be obtained from the priorities on the defaults $p \rightarrow \neg\texttt{ab}_i$. See Section 4.7 for details.

Example 5.8 The expressive power that results from the incorporation of priorities into causal theories can be further illustrated by considering an alternative formulation of the Yale shooting problem. We will use *two* types of abnormality predicates ($\texttt{cp}_i$ and $\texttt{pv}_i$) instead of a single *one* ($\texttt{ab}_i$). The new abnormality predicates serve to distinguish defaults which describe changes from defaults which describe persistences, and to give the former defaults precedence over the latter ones. More precisely, assumptions of the form $\neg\texttt{pv}_i(x)$ ('the action is not prevented') will have priority over assumptions of the form $\neg\texttt{cp}_j(x)$ ('the fluent is not clipped'). The background of the YSP can then be described as:

$$\texttt{loaded}(t) \wedge \neg\texttt{cp}_1(t) \Rightarrow \texttt{Cloaded}(t+1)$$

$$\texttt{alive}(t) \wedge \neg\texttt{cp}_2(t) \Rightarrow \texttt{Calive}(t+1)$$

$$\texttt{shoot}(t) \wedge \texttt{loaded}(t) \wedge \neg\texttt{pv}_1(t) \Rightarrow \texttt{Cdead}(t+1)$$

$$\texttt{alive}(t) \equiv \neg\texttt{dead}(t)$$

The closure of this background contains the justification:

$$\texttt{shoot}(t) \wedge \texttt{loaded}(t) \wedge \texttt{alive}(t) \wedge \neg\texttt{pv}_1(t) \Rightarrow \texttt{Ccp}_2(t)$$

that results from the head-to-head conflict between the shooting rule and the persistence rule for `alive`, but does not contain the justification

$$\texttt{shoot}(t) \wedge \texttt{loaded}(t) \wedge \texttt{alive}(t) \wedge \neg\texttt{cp}_2(t) \Rightarrow \texttt{Cpv}_1(t)$$

since $\neg\texttt{cp}_2(t)$ has lower priority than $\neg\texttt{pv}_1(t)$.

Given the evidence $E = \{\texttt{loaded(0)}, \texttt{alive(1)}, \texttt{shoot(1)}\}$, we obtain again three classes of minimal models: the class $\mathcal{C}_1$ which sanctions $\texttt{cp}_1\texttt{(0)}$, the class $\mathcal{C}_2$ which sanctions $\texttt{cp}_2\texttt{(1)}$, and the class $\mathcal{C}_3$ which sanctions $\texttt{pv}_1\texttt{(1)}$. However, $\mathcal{C}_2$ is the only class which explains the abnormality that it sanctions, and thus it is preferred to both $\mathcal{C}_1$ and $\mathcal{C}_3$. As a result, $\mathcal{B} = \{\mathcal{C}_2\}$ is the single minimal basis of $T = \langle K, E\rangle$, and all assumptions other than $\neg\texttt{cp}_2\texttt{(1)}$, as well as the propositions `loaded(1)` and `dead(2)`, are entailed.

Local vs. Global Priorities

The last example showed the convenience of accommodating priorities in causal theories: encoding knowledge becomes simpler and the same behavior is retained. Yet priorities in causal theories are not interpreted in the same way as in conditional entailment or prioritized circumscription. While priorities in the latter two frameworks play a role in *any* conflict among assumptions, priorities in causal theories play a role only among assumptions which are in *head-to-head* conflict. In this sense, priorities in causal theories have a *local* scope, while priorities in the standard frameworks have a *global* scope. The result is that causal theories augmented with priorities may fail to sanction conclusions which could be captured by the priorities alone.

For example, consider the defaults: 'if Peter says x, x is true' and 'if Tom says y, y is true'. Moreover, let us assume that the second default has priority over the first one (i.e., Tom is more reliable than Peter) and that Peter tells us that he heard from Tom that the Mets won. We know, however, that the Mets lost; we want to know who is lying. According to the priorities, we should believe Tom over Peter and thus assume that Peter is lying. However, in the causal formulation, since the defaults are not in head-to-head conflict, the priorities play no role and no conclusion is drawn.

The local scope of priorities in causal theories is not necessarily a limitation though. For example, in the formulation of the Yale shooting problem above we assumed that defaults about change had priority over defaults about persistences This assumption would be wrong if priorities were not limited to act on defaults which are in head-to-head conflict. Otherwise, if the person shot at time $t = 1$ was wearing a metal vest at time $t = 0$, we would anomalously conclude that the person was no longer wearing the vest at time $t = 1$ in order for the shooting rule to succeed. The interpretations of priorities in causal theories avoids this problem.

The benefits and shortcomings of global vs. local priorities suggest that it should be possible to combine the best of both into a single framework. We will not attempt this here.

5.6 Proof-Theory

The semantics of causal theories, like the semantics of conditional entailment, provides a precise specification of the conclusions that follow from a default theory but does not provide efficient methods for computing them. In this section and in the next we will focus on such methods.

First we will present a sound and complete proof-theory for causal entailment that characterizes the valid conclusions in terms of *arguments* rather than models. Then, based on this proof theory, we will develop a sound architecture for reasoning with causal theories which trades completeness for efficiency (Section 5.7). We will be assuming that all the justifications in the closure of T have been made explicit (this is not necessary from an implementation point of view, see page 129).

The proof-theory of causal theories is structured around the notion of *arguments*. An argument Δ is a collection of assumptions which is consistent with the underlying theory (see also Section 4.6).[17] Moreover, Δ is an argument *for* a proposition p, if $T + \Delta$ logically entails p. The proposition p, in this case, is also said to be supported by Δ. When a set of assumptions Δ is *not* consistent with T, it is called a *conflict set*. Two arguments are *in conflict* when their union is a conflict set. In such a case we also say that one argument *refutes* the other.

For instance, in a theory T consisting of the expressions $\neg \mathtt{ab}_1 \Rightarrow \mathrm{C}\mathtt{ab}_2$ and $\neg \mathtt{ab}_3 \Rightarrow \mathrm{C}\mathtt{q}$, the arguments $\Delta_1 = \{\neg \mathtt{ab}_1\}$ and $\Delta_2 = \{\neg \mathtt{ab}_2\}$ are in conflict, but no argument is in conflict with $\Delta_3 = \{\neg \mathtt{ab}_3\}$.

From the minimality of 'preferred' classes it easily follows that propositions supported by unrefuted arguments are causally entailed. Thus, we can safely conclude, for example, that $\mathrm{C}\mathtt{q}$ and $\mathtt{q}$ above are entailed, as both are supported by the unrefuted argument Δ_3.

Arguments which are refuted, however, may also provide legitimate support. For example, $\mathtt{ab}_2$ above is causally entailed by T in spite of having a single supporting argument $\Delta_1 = \{\neg \mathtt{ab}_1\}$ which is refuted by $\Delta_2 = \{\neg \mathtt{ab}_2\}$. This is because although Δ_2 refutes $\{\neg \mathtt{ab}_1\}$, Δ_2 does not *explain* $\mathtt{ab}_1$; Δ_1, on the other hand, refutes $\{\neg \mathtt{ab}_2\}$ and explains $\mathtt{ab}_2$. In these cases, we will say that Δ_1 is *protected* from Δ_2. As we will see, propositions supported by protected arguments may also be entailed.

Formally, let us say that an argument Δ *explains* a proposition p when Δ is an argument for $\mathrm{C}p$. Then the notion of *protection* can be defined as follows:

Definition 5.8 An argument Δ is *protected* from a conflicting argument Δ' iff there is a set of assumptions $\Delta'' \subseteq \Delta'$ such that $\Delta + \Delta''$ is not

[17] The notions of consistency, derivation and entailment are to be understood relative to the classical modal logic that results from the operator C and the postulate $\mathrm{C}\alpha \Rightarrow \alpha$.

a conflict set, and every abnormality $\mathtt{ab}_i(a)$ for $\neg\mathtt{ab}_i(a) \in \Delta' - \Delta''$, is explained by $\Delta + \Delta''$.

In the example above, Δ_1 is *protected* from the conflicting argument Δ_2, but Δ_2 is not protected from Δ_1. When an argument Δ is protected from all counterarguments and no counterargument is protected from Δ, we will say that Δ is *stable.* As in conditional entailment, being supported by a stable argument is a sufficient condition for being (causally) entailed:

Theorem 5.1 If p is supported by a *stable* argument, then p is causally entailed.

In the formulation of the Yale shooting problem above, for example, the argument $\Delta = \{\neg\mathtt{cp_1(0)}, \neg\mathtt{pv_1(1)}\}$ which supports the conclusion $\mathtt{dead}(2)$ is stable, as $\Delta' = \{\neg\mathtt{cp_2(1)}\}$ is the only minimal argument in conflict with Δ, and while Δ explains $\mathtt{cp_2(1)}$, no set of assumptions explains either $\mathtt{cp_1(0)}$ or $\mathtt{pv_1(1)}$.

Stable arguments, however, provide sufficient but not *necessary* conditions for causal entailment. For instance, the proposition $\mathtt{ab_3}$ is causally entailed by the theory comprised of the formulas $\mathtt{ab_1} \vee \mathtt{ab_2}$ and $\neg\mathtt{ab_1} \vee \neg\mathtt{ab_2} \Rightarrow C\mathtt{ab_3}$, and yet $\mathtt{ab_3}$ is not supported by any stable argument (neither $\{\neg\mathtt{ab_1}\}$ nor $\{\neg\mathtt{ab_2}\}$ is stable because both arguments are in conflict and neither one is protected from the other).

A simple extension of the definition above takes care of such cases. As in Section 4.6, let us refer to a (disjunctive) collection of arguments as a *cover,* and let us say that a cover *supports* a proposition p if every argument in the cover supports p. Let us also say that an argument Δ is in *conflict* with a cover $C = \{\Delta_1, \ldots, \Delta_n\}$ when Δ is in conflict with every argument Δ_i in the cover; that Δ is protected from the cover C when Δ is protected from some Δ_i in C; and that the cover C is protected from Δ when some Δ_j in C is protected from Δ. Let us also say that a cover C is *stable* when C is protected from every conflicting argument but no conflicting argument is protected from C. Then the following sound and complete characterization of causal entailment results:

Theorem 5.2 (Main) A proposition p is causally entailed if and only if p is supported by a stable *cover.*

For the theory comprised of the sentences $\neg\mathtt{ab_1} \vee \neg\mathtt{ab_2} \Rightarrow C\mathtt{ab_3}$ and $\mathtt{ab_1} \vee \mathtt{ab_2}$, the pair of arguments $\Delta_1 = \{\neg\mathtt{ab_1}\}$ and $\Delta_2 = \{\neg\mathtt{ab_2}\}$

constitute a stable cover. Since such a cover supports $\mathtt{ab_3}$, $\mathtt{ab_3}$ is causally entailed.

5.7 Architecture

The proof-theory above permits us to compute the consequences of a causal theory by considering only the fragment of the theory that is relevant to the query. For example, if the query is whether p is entailed, we will try to build stable arguments or covers that support p; if we succeed, we will answer yes, if we fail, we will answer no. Building stable arguments and covers, however, is far from trivial. Part of the complexity stems from having to test whether an argument Δ is protected from a conflicting argument Δ'. This involves finding a subset Δ'' of Δ' which is *not* in conflict with Δ and which together with Δ explains the complement of each of the assumptions in $\Delta' - \Delta''$. In addition, an argument Δ may be protected from two conflicting arguments Δ_1 and Δ_2 and still *not* be protected from their union $\Delta_1 + \Delta_2$.[18]

In order to make causal theories a practical language for representing and reasoning with defaults, we will thus have to find reasonable restrictions on the types of *theories* that we are going to consider and the types of *inferences* that we expect to uncover. In this section we will focus on such restrictions and the *procedures* that exploit them.[19]

The Language. The types of theories we will consider will be called *simple causal theories,* or SCT's for short, and will be comprised of two types of statements: *causal rules*

$$A_1 \wedge \cdots \wedge A_n \wedge \neg B_1 \wedge \cdots \wedge \neg B_m \Rightarrow CC$$

and *constraints*

$$A_1 \wedge \cdots \wedge A_n \Rightarrow \textbf{false}$$

where A_i's, B_i's and C are all atoms, n and m are greater than or equal to zero, and free variables are assumed to be universally quantified (**false** is an special atom which is false in every model).

[18] For example, in the theory $T = \{\neg\mathtt{s} \wedge \neg\mathtt{a} \Rightarrow C\mathtt{b}\ ,\ \neg\mathtt{s} \wedge \neg\mathtt{b} \Rightarrow C\mathtt{c}\ ,\ \neg\mathtt{s} \wedge \neg\mathtt{c} \Rightarrow C\mathtt{a}\}$, where $\mathtt{a}$, $\mathtt{b}$, $\mathtt{c}$, and $\mathtt{s}$ are all abnormalities, the argument $\Delta = \{\neg\mathtt{s}\}$ is protected from every minimal conflicting argument but it is not protected from their union $\Delta' = \{\neg\mathtt{a}, \neg\mathtt{b}, \neg\mathtt{c}\}$.

[19] The discussion below is sketchy at times. For more details see [Gef91] and the forthcoming paper [Gef92]

We will also assume that the predicates which appear negated in the body of some rule do not appear unnegated in the body of the same or another rule or in the body of a constraint. Since negated literals will act as 'normality' assumptions, this means that 'abnormality' predicates will appear either negated in the body of the rules, or unnegated in their head; which is normally the case. We will refer to theories complying with this restriction as *open* theories.

Semantics. SCT's are causal theories so the same semantics applies. As suggested above, all positive ground literals will be treated as 'abnormalities' (i.e., all predicates will be minimized), or what amounts to the same, all negative literals will be regarded as assumptions. This convention may seem strange in principle (e.g., why would a literal like $\neg$`loaded` be assumed to be true?). It does no harm, though, given the restrictions above plus the fact that we will only be interested in atoms p which are *explained.* Only 'true' assumptions, i.e., negative literals which appear in the body of some rule, will provide the grounds for accepting a conclusion.[20]

The convention of regarding all ground atoms as abnormalities will permit us to simplify the semantics of simple causal theories, replacing SCT's by *logic programs*,[21] and arbitrary classes of models by *Herbrand* models.[22] Indeed, for a simple causal theory T with rules

$$A_1 \wedge \cdots \wedge A_n \wedge \neg B_1 \wedge \cdots \wedge \neg B_m \Rightarrow CC$$

and constraints

$$A_1 \wedge \cdots \wedge A_n \Rightarrow \mathbf{false}$$

we will define the logic program $P[T]$ as the collection of rules

$$C \leftarrow A_1, \ldots, A_n, \neg B_1, \ldots, \neg B_m$$

and constraints

$$\leftarrow A_1, \ldots, A_n$$

[20]Other negative literals would have to be rewritten as atoms, e.g., $\neg$`pacifist`(x) would be rewritten as `non_pacifist`(x), and the latter would be declared incompatible with `pacifist`(x).

[21]We will consider the relation between causal theories and logic programs in more detail in Section 6.1. For an introduction to logic programming see [Llo84].

[22]A Herbrand interpretation over a language $\mathcal{L}$ is an interpretation whose domain is the ground terms in $\mathcal{L}$, and where each function and constant symbol is assigned to itself. A Herbrand model is a Herbrand interpretation which satisfies the formulas in the theory. A Herbrand model can and is usually represented by the ground atoms that it makes true.

Then, if $\mathcal{C}_M$ refers to the class of models of T with gap M,[23] we obtain the following result:

Proposition 5.1 $\mathcal{C}_M$ is a minimal class of the theory T if and only if M is a minimal Herbrand model of the logic program $P[T]$.

Let us also define the program P_Δ, where Δ is a set of negative literals, as the program that results from collecting all the rule instances of P whose negative literals are among those of Δ (i.e., P_Δ stands for the rules in P 'enabled' by Δ), and let P^+_Δ be the *positive* program that results from P_Δ by discarding all negative literals.[24] Let us also say that given a program P, an atom p is *supported* by Δ if p is a logical consequence of the positive program P^+_Δ; and that p is *supported by P in a model M* if there is a collection Δ of assumptions true in M that supports p. Then the second result that we need to relate simple causal theories to logic programs is the following:

Proposition 5.2 A ground atom p is *explained* in the minimal class $\mathcal{C}_M$ of T if and only if p is supported by $P[T]$ in the minimal model M.

Propositions 5.1 and 5.2 permit us to replace the (minimal) classes $\mathcal{C}_M$ of models of the theory T by the (minimal) Herbrand models M of the program $P[T]$, and to test whether an atom p is explained in $\mathcal{C}_M$ by testing whether p is supported by $P[T]$ in M. Hence, if the program $P[T]$ is interpreted in a suitable way, the conclusions sanctioned by the theory T and the program $P[T]$ would be the same and we would be able to replace the theory T itself by the program $P[T]$. The interpretation for logic programs that we need is similar to the interpretation of causal theories (Section 5.3).

Definition 5.9 (Semantics of Logic Programs) 1) A Herbrand model M of a program P is *at least as preferred as* a Herbrand model M', if every atom p in $M - M'$ is supported by P in M. 2) A collection $\mathcal{B}$ of Herbrand models of P is a *basis* for P if no minimal Herbrand model M *outside* $\mathcal{B}$ is at least as preferred as a model M' *inside* $\mathcal{B}$, and for every

[23] That is, $\mathcal{C}_M = \{M' \mid M' \models T \text{ and } A[M'] \subseteq M\}$, where $A[M']$ stands for the set of abnormalities sanctioned by M'. Since we are assuming all ground atoms are abnormalities, $A[M']$ is simply the collection of all the ground atoms true in M'.

[24] This transformation is similar to the one used by Gelfond and Lifschitz [GL88] for defining the stable model semantics of logic programs. Note that the constraints in P play no role in the transformation.

M *outside* $\mathcal{B}$ there is a model M' *inside* $\mathcal{B}$ which is at least as preferred as M'. 3) A program P *entails* an atom p if p *holds* in every model of a basis $\mathcal{B}$ of P; P *supports* an atom p if p is *supported* by P in every model of a basis $\mathcal{B}$ of P.

This semantics coincides with the standard semantics for logic programs when the set of constraints is empty and the program is stratified. Later on we will discuss this relationship in more detail (cf. Section 6.1). For the time being our interest will be in the relation between the program $P[T]$ and the causal theory T. The correspondence between the former and the latter can now be expressed as follows:

Theorem 5.3 The theory T causally entails an atom p iff the program $P[T]$ entails p. T causally entails $\mathrm{C}p$ iff the program $P[T]$ supports p.

Obviously, the same correspondences hold for the proof-theoretic notions:

Proposition 5.3 1) A set of assumptions Δ is consistent with T iff Δ is consistent with $P[T]$. 2) Δ is an argument for an atom p in T iff Δ is an argument for p in $P[T]$. 3) Δ *explains* an atom p in T iff Δ *supports* p in $P[T]$.

From now on we will take advantage of these correspondences and consider the programs $P[T]$ instead of the simple causal theories T. The results above show that no information will be lost in the translation.

Procedures. So far we have focused on the restrictions on the causal theories that we are going to consider, and the simplified semantics and proof-theory that result. We will now turn to the development of procedures that exploit these restrictions. The procedures will be *sound* but *incomplete*. This is because computing all the conclusions entailed by a causal theory (even a *simple* causal theory) is too expensive. The procedures thus aim to strike a 'reasonable' balance between computational and completeness concerns. Roughly, we want to identify a class of simple patterns of inference which can be computed efficiently, and ignore for the time being the patterns that are more complex (e.g., reasoning by cases).

As with conditional entailment (cf. Section 4.8), our focus will be on the propositions that are supported by stable arguments. From Theorem 5.2 we know that the only propositions that are entailed but are *not* supported by stable arguments are those which are supported by *disjunctive* collection of arguments or covers. However, even computing stable arguments remains too expensive: checking whether an argument Δ is protected from a conflicting argument Δ' involves finding a subset Δ'' which is both consistent with Δ and which together with Δ explains the negation of each assumption in Δ' but not in Δ''. There may be too many subsets of Δ' to test and each test is potentially expensive.

Thus, instead of focusing on the propositions supported by arbitrary *stable* arguments, we will focus on the propositions supported by a subclass of stable arguments which we call *linear*. *Linear arguments* are stable arguments whose assumptions can be ordered as a list $\{\alpha_1, \ldots, \alpha_n\}$ such that each prefix $\{\alpha_1, \ldots, \alpha_i\}$, $i = 1, \ldots, n$ is stable as well:

Definition 5.10 A *list of assumptions* $\Delta = \{\alpha_1, \ldots, \alpha_n\}$ is *linearly stable* if each prefix $\Delta_i = \{\alpha_1, \ldots, \alpha_i\}$ $i = 1, \ldots, n$ is stable. An argument is *linearly stable* or linear, for short, if it can be written as a list of assumptions which is linearly stable.

In other words, a linear argument can be constructed by adding assumptions, one at a time, to an argument which is either empty or stable. For example, the argument $\Delta = \{\neg \texttt{cp}_1(\texttt{0}), \neg \texttt{pv}_1(\texttt{1})\}$ in the Yale Shooting Problem (Example 5.8, page 114) is linear, since it is stable and either prefix $\{\neg \texttt{cp}_1(\texttt{0})\}$ and $\{\neg \texttt{pv}_1(\texttt{1})\}$ is stable as well.

Most stable arguments can be proven one assumption at a time, and thus, are linear. Non-linear stable arguments, on the other hand, require one assumption for proving a second assumption, and the second assumption for proving the first. Not surprisingly, linear stable arguments are easier to compute than non-linear ones.[25]

For computing linear arguments, the order in which the assumptions are proven matters. We will thus assume that we are given an argument and the way the assumptions in the argument are ordered. The procedures thus accept a *list of assumptions* and test whether the list

[25] An example of a non-linear argument can be obtained from a variation of the Yale Shooting Problem involving a duel between two people A and B. Both A and B are alive at time $t = 0$, and if they reach time $t = 1$ alive they will shoot at each other. Moreover, if either one is shot, he dies an instant later. Given this information, both A and B should reach time $t = 1$ alive, shoot each other, and die at time $t = 2$. Indeed, each of the arguments $\Delta_1 = \{\neg \texttt{ab}(\texttt{a}, \texttt{0})\}$, $\Delta_2 = \{\neg \texttt{ab}(\texttt{b}, \texttt{0})\}$ and $\Delta_3 = \Delta_1 + \Delta_2$, where $\neg \texttt{ab}(\texttt{i}, \texttt{j})$ means "i remained alive from $t = j$ to $t = j+1$", is linear. Yet, if both A and B are *confirmed* to be dead at time $t = 2$, Δ_1 and Δ_2 would no longer be stable, while Δ_3 would remain stable but no longer *linear*.

is linearly stable or not. Later on we will discuss how these procedures can be used for testing whether a proposition is supported by a linear stable *argument*, which is our main goal.[26]

The methods below for testing whether a list is linearly stable are variations of Definition 5.10. We will write $\Delta \succeq \Delta'$ to express that the argument Δ is *protected* from a conflicting argument Δ', and $\Delta \succ \Delta'$ to express that Δ is protected from Δ' but Δ' is not protected from Δ. An argument Δ is thus stable if for every conflicting argument Δ' the relation $\Delta \succ \Delta'$ holds. Similarly, the stability of a *list of assumptions* can be expressed as follows:

Lemma 5.2 A list of assumptions $\Delta = \{\neg\beta_1, \ldots, \neg\beta_n\}$ is linearly stable iff for every argument Δ' in conflict with $\Delta_i = \{\neg\beta_1, \ldots, \neg\beta_i\}$, $i = 1, \ldots, n$, $\Delta_i \succ \Delta'$ holds.

Furthermore, if we say that an argument Δ *implies* an atom β when β is a logical consequence of Δ given $P[T]$, regardless of whether β is supported or not, the above condition can be recast as follows:

Lemma 5.3 A list of assumptions $\Delta_n = \{\neg\beta_1, \neg\beta_2, \ldots, \neg\beta_n\}$ is linearly stable iff for every argument Δ' and $i = 1, \ldots, n$

[A.1] if Δ' supports β_i, then $\Delta_{i-1}, \Delta' \vdash$ **false** , and
[A.2] if Δ implies β_i, then $\Delta_i \succeq \Delta'$

This method for testing linear stability has the advantage of being incremental, although still relies on expensive computations: checking the consistency of $\Delta_{i-1} + \Delta'$ and whether Δ_i is protected from Δ'. The next step is to eliminate both tests.

For that purpose, let us denote the collection of rules in a program P by the symbol R, and let N stand for the collection of constraints. Let us also say that a collection of assumptions Δ is *self-defeating* when Δ supports the complement β of some assumption $\neg\beta$ in Δ, and that Δ is contradicted by a constraint, or *contradicted,* for short, when Δ supports each of the atoms A_i in a ground instance $\leftarrow A_1, A_2, \ldots, A_n$ of

[26]Since the assumptions in an argument can be arranged in various ways, testing whether an *argument* is linearly stable is different from testing whether a *list of assumptions* is linearly stable. In the theory $T = \{\neg \mathsf{a} \Rightarrow \mathsf{Cb}\ ,\ \neg \mathsf{b} \Rightarrow \mathsf{Cc}\}$, for example, the list $\Delta_1 = \{\neg\mathsf{a}, \neg\mathsf{c}\}$ is linearly stable, but the list $\Delta_2 = \{\neg\mathsf{c}, \neg\mathsf{a}\}$, which contains the same assumptions, is not. This is because to prove $\neg\mathsf{c}$ we need to prove the assumption $\neg\mathsf{a}$ first. Indeed, $\{\neg\mathsf{a}\}$ is stable, but $\{\neg\mathsf{c}\}$ is not, because it is not protected from $\Delta' = \{\neg\mathsf{b}\}$.

a constraint in N. Let us also say that a set of assumptions is *admissible* when it is neither self-defeating nor contradicted.

Provided with certain assumptions on the program which we will spell out in detail below, the conditions [A.1] and [A.2] in Lemma 5.3 can be replaced by the following simpler conditions:

Theorem 5.4 (Π_1) A list of assumptions $\Delta_n = \{\neg\beta_1, \neg\beta_2, \ldots, \neg\beta_n\}$ is linearly stable iff for every *admissible* Δ' and $i = 1, \ldots, n$:

[B.1] if Δ' supports β_i, then $\Delta' + \Delta_{i-1}$ is self-defeating, and
[B.2] if $\Delta' + \{\neg\beta_i\}$ is contradicted, then $\Delta' + \Delta_i$ is self-defeating

The new method for testing the stability of a list, which we call Π_1, is a generalization of the 'negation as failure' rule used in logic programs. If $N = \emptyset$, for example, Π_1 sanctions every assumption that is sanctioned by the well-founded semantics (see Section 6.1 and [Gef91]).[27]

The procedure Π_1 is also closely related to the procedures used in argument systems in which competing arguments of different strengths are allowed to rebut and defeat each other [Pol87, SL90]. In Π_1, an argument Δ' can rebut an argument $\Delta = \{\neg\beta_1, \ldots, \neg\beta_n\}$ in two ways: Δ' may rebut Δ by supporting β_i for some $1 \leq i \leq n$, or by making $\Delta' + \Delta$ contradicted. Rebuttals of the first type are defeated when $\Delta' + \Delta_{i-1}$ is self-defeating, and rebuttals of the second type are defeated when $\Delta' + \Delta_i$ is self-defeating. Only minimal rebuttals Δ' need to be considered.

This dialectical view of Π_1 provides the right intuition for *building* the lists of assumptions that support the propositions of interest. For example, in order to prove an atom p, we will have to find a list of assumptions Δ that supports p. If no Δ' rebuts Δ, we are done; otherwise, we will have to find a defeater Δ'' of Δ' and repeat the same process with the new list $\Delta'' + \Delta$ and so on.

Note that all the tests involved in Π_1 are simple; they only require checking whether certain atoms p are consequences of a positive logic program P^+_Δ for suitable chosen p's and Δ's. This operation, as is well known, is linear in the size of P, if P is propositional [DG84]. Likewise, we no longer need to test explicitly whether Δ_i is protected from Δ', and the condition that Δ' be an argument (i.e., consistent) has been replaced

[27] For the well-founded semantics, see [VRS88].

by the *equivalent* condition that Δ' be *admissible* (i.e., not self-defeating and not contradicted).

For Theorem 5.4 to hold, however, the program P must comply with a condition that we call *complete stability.* A program P is completely stable when the collection of rules P_Δ enabled by any set of assumptions Δ possesses a stable model.[28] [29] The key feature of completely stable programs is that any self-defeating set of assumptions Δ always contains a non-self-defeating subset Δ' that supports the complement of each of the assumptions in $\Delta - \Delta'$. Note that the complete stability of a program depends on rules in the program but does *not* depend on the constraints. Stratified programs are completely stable. More general conditions for complete stability will be given later on.

Example 5.9 As an illustration of the procedure Π_1, let us consider again the 'battery problem' discussed in Example 5.7 (page 113), now encoded as a program $P[T]$:

```
starts ← turn_key , ¬ab1
no_starts ← turn_key , battery_dead , ¬ab2
ab1 ← turn_key , battery_dead , ¬ab2
battery_dead ← lights_were_on , ¬ab3
lights_were_on ←
turn_key ←
← starts , no_starts
```

In order to prove `no_starts`, we find that the only (minimal) argument that supports `no_starts` is $\Delta = \{\neg \mathtt{ab}_2, \neg \mathtt{ab}_3\}$. Thus, we can prove `no_starts` by showing that the *list* $\Delta_2 = \{\neg \mathtt{ab}_2, \neg \mathtt{ab}_3\}$ is linearly stable. We prove first the sublist $\Delta_1 = \{\neg \mathtt{ab}_2\}$. Since there are no supports for $\mathtt{ab}_2$, we need to consider the (minimal) arguments Δ' such that $\Delta' + \{\neg \mathtt{ab}_2\}$ is contradicted. The only such argument is $\Delta' = \{\neg \mathtt{ab}_1, \neg \mathtt{ab}_3\}$ which together with $\neg \mathtt{ab}_2$ supports both `starts` and `no_starts`. $\Delta' +$

[28]Recall that P_Δ is given by the ground rules of P whose negative literals all belong to Δ.

[29]If a program P is completely stable, then P must have a stable model, but not vice versa. For example, the program $P = \{\mathtt{a} \leftarrow \neg \mathtt{b}\ ,\ \mathtt{b} \leftarrow \neg \mathtt{a}\ ,\ \mathtt{p} \leftarrow \neg \mathtt{a}\ ,\ \mathtt{p} \leftarrow \neg \mathtt{p}\}$ from [VRS88] has a stable model but it is not completely stable, because P_Δ, for $\Delta = \{\neg \mathtt{p}, \neg \mathtt{b}\}$, does not have a stable model.

Δ_1, however, is self-defeating as $\Delta' + \Delta_1$ supports the atom $\mathtt{ab_1}$ whose negation belongs to Δ'. Therefore, from Theorem 5.4, we can conclude that the list Δ_1 is stable. By similar considerations, it is possible to show that the assumption $\neg\mathtt{ab_3}$ can be appended to the list Δ_1, and thus, that the argument Δ is stable as well. Consequently, due to the two way correspondence between the causal theory T and the program $P[T]$, the propositions supported by Δ, e.g., `no_starts` and `battery_dead`, are causally entailed by T.

Reasoning Forward vs. Reasoning Backward

The conditions [B.1] and [B.2] in Π_1 capture two different forms of reasoning. When we test for arguments Δ' that support β_i, we are reasoning *forward,* as we are rebutting the assumption $\neg\beta_i$ by reasoning along the direction of the rules. When we test whether $\Delta' + \{\neg\beta_i\}$ is contradicted, we are reasoning *backward,* as we are rebutting $\neg\beta_i$ by *reductio ad absurdum,* implicitly relying on the *contraposition* of the rules. In the first case, we obtain *direct* arguments and information flows only along the direction of the rules; in the second case, we obtain *indirect* arguments, and information flows both forward, along the direction of the rules, and backward, from the constraints.

Most procedures used in rule-based systems and logic programming only reason forward because they do not accommodate explicit negative information (constraints). Yet, some architectures, like inheritance networks, handle a limited form of negative information (conflicting links) and still are able to reason forward only. Since reasoning forward is more efficient than reasoning both backward and forward, it would be interesting to see whether there are conditions under which Π_1 can be reduced to a forward reasoning procedure. Since as we said earlier condition [B.1] captures forward reasoning while condition [B.2] backward reasoning, the conditions should be such that [B.2] does not have to be tested. For that, if a set of assumptions Δ is contradicted, then Δ must *automatically* be self-defeating. When such a condition holds, information will flow forward only, and when a contradiction is met the information would not 'bounce' but would be 'absorbed'.

When will a set of assumptions which is contradicted be self-defeating? If one could identify a class of programs $P[T]$ in which this holds, Π_1 could be simplified by removing the condition [B.2] without affecting the inferences that are captured. Without loss of generality we will consider programs which are *ground*, i.e., in which expressions with variables have been replaced by the collection of all their ground instances (we will still use variables as abbreviations though). It is well known that for the purpose of answering existential queries both programs are equivalent [CL73].

We will also assume that $P[T]$ encodes the *closure* of the causal theory T (Sections 5.4 and 5.5). This assumption is crucial because it guarantees that if $p_i \leftarrow A_i$, $i = 1, \ldots, n$ is a collection of rules in head-to-head conflict, then the sets of assumptions Δ which support those rules will be self-defeating (because $P[T]$ must then include a rule $q_j \leftarrow A_1, \ldots, A_n$ for some negative literal $\neg q_j$ in A_j, $1 \leq j \leq n$).[30] [31]

Since all rules in $P[T] = R[T] + N[T]$ stand for causal rules in the theory $T = \langle K, E \rangle$, a collection of rules $p_i \leftarrow A_i$, $i = 1, \ldots, n$ in $P[T]$ will be in head-to-head conflict only when $\leftarrow p_1, \ldots, p_n$ is a constraint in $N[T]$. The opposite, however, is not necessarily true; for the above rules to be in head-to-head conflict the corresponding constraint in T, $p_1 \wedge \cdots \wedge p_n \Rightarrow$ **false**, must belong to the background K. Yet, this can be guaranteed if we assume that *there are no constraints in* E, or what amounts to the same, that there are not negative observations. We will say in this case that no constraints in $P[T]$ are *evidential.*

With these assumptions showing that every set Δ which is contradicted is self-defeating is straightforward. Indeed, if Δ is contradicted, there must be some constraint $\leftarrow p_1, \ldots, p_n$ in $N[T]$ such that Δ supports each p_i, $i = 1, \ldots, n$. For that to be the case, however, there must be rules $p_i \leftarrow A_i$ in $P[T]$ supported by Δ. But such rules must be in head-to-head conflict, and therefore, from the remarks above, Δ must be self-defeating. The simplified method for computing linear stable arguments can then be described as follows:

Theorem 5.5 (Π_1^-) If the program $P[T]$ encodes the *closure* of a simple causal theory $T = \langle K, E \rangle$ and no constraints in $P[T]$ are *evidential,* then $\Delta_n = \{\neg\beta_1, \ldots, \neg\beta_n\}$ will be linearly stable iff for any Δ' which supports β_i, $1 \leq i \leq n$, $\Delta' + \Delta_{i-1}$ is self-defeating.

[30] A set of assumptions Δ supports a rule $\gamma \leftarrow \alpha_1, \ldots, \alpha_n, \neg\beta_1, \ldots, \neg\beta_m$, when Δ supports each positive literal α_i and includes each negative literal $\neg\beta_i$.

[31] We are assuming that one of the rules $p_i \leftarrow A_i$ is 'defeasible'; i.e. A_i contains a negative literal $\neg\beta_j$.

The new method captures a significant aspect of causal inference; namely, that reasoning can be proceed forward, along the direction of the rules, as long as no prediction is refuted by an *observation* (see the discussion on page 109).

To illustrate the simplified procedure Π_1^-, let us look again at the battery problem. The formulation in Example 5.9 (page 125) required us to check twice that the set $\Delta = \{\neg ab_1, \neg ab_2, \neg ab_3\}$ which supports both starts and no_starts is self-defeating; one for proving $\neg ab_2$, and the other for proving $\neg ab_3$. Both tests can now be eliminated because the program complies with the restrictions in Theorem 5.5. We can now prove both $\neg ab_2$ and $\neg ab_3$ because neither ab_2 or ab_3 are supported.

The same procedure applied to the YSP would give us the expected result in the same fashion. Likewise, if we are also given that the person was found not to be dead after the shooting (i.e., $\leftarrow$ dead(2)), the conditions in Theorem 5.5 would not be satisfied, and condition [B.2] in Π_1 would have to be tested. Yet even in those cases we can limit the constraints that need to be tested to those which originate in E (i.e., $\leftarrow$ dead(2)).[32]

Computing Bottom-up

A further simplification of the procedure Π_1 will take us closer to the type of algorithms used in inheritance hierarchies and argument systems (e.g., [HTT87, Nut88b, GV89]). Many of those algorithms can be captured by the scheme:

$$\text{If } \mid\!\sim p,\ p \rightarrow q, \text{ and all arguments for } {\sim}q \text{ are } \textbf{defeated,} \text{ then } \mid\!\sim q$$

where '$\mid\!\sim p$' means that p is derivable, and arguments are 'defeated' when they are in conflict with 'better' arguments. Those schemes can be implemented efficiently by iterative, bottom-up procedures, in which each rule is triggered when its antecedents have been derived and all conflicting arguments have been defeated.

[32] We should point out that asserting alive(2) $\leftarrow$ instead of $\leftarrow$ dead(2) would yield a different result. For while the second expression corresponds to the the plain formula $\neg$dead(2), the first expression corresponds to the causal rule **true** $\Rightarrow$ Calive(2). The encoding of the fact alive(2), however, is wrong. To fix it, it is necessary to extend the language of simple causal theories so that causal rules can be distinguished from *positive facts* (as things are now, every expression is either a constraint or a causal rule). Then, since rules in $P[T]$ which correspond to positive facts would no longer participate in head-to-head conflicts, Theorem 5.5 would need to be qualified requiring that no positive fact occurs in a constraint in $N[T]$ either. See [Gef92] for details.

We will now show that under the conditions in Theorem 5.5, the procedure Π_1 can be implemented in a similar fashion. The advantages of this additional simplification of the procedure Π_1, which we call Π_2, are several. First of all, *there will be no need to establish an order on the assumptions a priori:* there will be no *lists* of assumptions to prove. Second, and equally important, *the program $P[T]$ will no longer have to represent the closure of the theory T explicitly;* the new procedure Π_2 will interpret $P[T]$ as if the rules corresponding to the closure of T were already present.

For the sake of simplicity, we will assume that all rules are defeasible (strict rules can be given priority over non-strict rules) and that constraints contain exactly two atoms. If p is one such atom then we will use the notation $\sim p$ to refer to the other atom. We also need to assume that if a literal $\neg\beta_i$ occurs in the body of some rule, then no rule has β_i as its head (i.e., explicit 'cancellation' axioms are not allowed), and if $\neg\beta_i$ occurs in the body of two or more rules, then the bodies of all such rules, although not their heads, have to be identical (again, neither restriction is significant).

Furthermore, for a program P that represents a causal theory T, we will refer by the *closure of* P to the program that represents the closure of T. With these conventions the procedure Π_1 can be simplified as follows:[33]

Theorem 5.6 (Π_2) An atom q is supported by a linear stable argument in the *closure* of a program P, if $\mid\!\approx_P q$ is derivable from the following rules:

1. If $p \leftarrow \in P$, then $\mid\!\approx_P p$
2. If $p \leftarrow A \in P$, $\mid\!\approx_P p_i$ for each atom p_i in A, and every support Δ' for $\sim p$ is *defeated,* then $\mid\!\approx_P p$

where an argument Δ' is *defeated* either when Δ' supports q and $\sim q$ is derivable, or when the only rules $\sim p \leftarrow A'$ supported by Δ' have lower priority than the rule $p \leftarrow A$ being rebutted (we are assuming that each rule r_i contains a single assumption $\neg\beta_i$, and that the priority of r_i is

[33] The simplified procedure Π_2 is sound but not complete; namely, there may be linear arguments which are not uncovered by Π_2. However, such cases seem to be rare. The precise conditions under which Π_2 is sound *and* complete are still to be worked out.

the priority of $\neg\beta_i$).[34]

For example, the program that corresponds to the causal theory of Example 5.9 is given by the expressions:

r_1 : starts $\leftarrow$ turn_key , $\neg$ab$_1$

r_2 : no_starts $\leftarrow$ turn_key , battery_dead , $\neg$ab$_2$

r_3 : battery_dead $\leftarrow$ lights_were_on , $\neg$ab$_3$

r_4 : lights_were_on $\leftarrow$

r_5 : turn_key $\leftarrow$

$\leftarrow$ starts , no_starts

The cancellation axioms in the closure of the theory no longer have to be made explicit. For this program, the first iteration of Π_2 yields both lights_were_on and turn_key, the second one yields battery_dead (due the absence of atoms $\sim$battery_dead in the program), and the third one yields no_starts (because r_1 has lower priority than r_2).

Complete Stability

A critical assumption we have made throughout this section is that the program $P[T]$ must be completely stable.[35] By this we meant that, for *any* set of assumptions Δ, the rule instances of P with assumptions among those of Δ must have a stable model. As we said before, stratified programs P are completely stable because every subset of P is also stratified and thus accepts a stable model. Yet, the class of stratified programs is too narrow for our purposes. For instance, the program that results from the closure of the so-called Nixon diamond:

pacifist $\leftarrow$ quaker , $\neg$ab$_1$

non_pacifist $\leftarrow$ republican , $\neg$ab$_2$

ab$_2$ $\leftarrow$ quaker , $\neg$ab$_1$

ab$_1$ $\leftarrow$ republican , $\neg$ab$_2$

[34] A rule $\sim p \leftarrow \alpha_1, \ldots, \alpha_n, \neg\beta_1, \ldots, \neg\beta_m$ is supported by Δ' when Δ' supports each positive literal α_i and includes each negative literal $\neg\beta_i$.

[35] More precisely, the assumption is that the program which encodes the *closure* of T must be completely stable. This assumption is required even for the procedure Π_2 in which the closure is not made explicit.

is not stratified because of the negative cycle $\mathtt{ab_1} \not\rightarrow \mathtt{ab_2} \not\rightarrow \mathtt{ab_1}$ in the dependency graph.[36] Indeed, whenever a pair of default rules are in head-to-head conflict and neither rule has priority over the other, the 'closed' program that results will never be stratified. Still such programs are often completely stable.

In the rest of this section we will sketch a class of completely stable programs which includes all *open* stratified programs as well as many non-stratified ones (recall that a program is *open* when the predicates that appear *negated* in the body of a rule do not appear appear *un-negated* in the body of the same or another rule, or in the body of a constraint). We will deal with programs with no constraints, as constraints play no role in the definition of complete stability. Likewise, for the sake of simplicity, we will assume that the programs are ground. In particular, all references to stratification below can be replaced by *local* stratification.[37]

First, given a program P, we will partition the rules into *cliques*, where a clique is a maximal collection of rules $r_i : p_i \leftarrow A_i$, $i = 1, \ldots, n$ such that each p_i occurs negated in the body of each rule r_j, for $j \neq i$, and all the sets $A_i + \{\neg p_i\}$, $i = 1, \ldots, n$ contain the same literals. Then, from this partition (which is not necessarily unique), we define the *disjunctive* program P_D where each clique $p_i \leftarrow A_i$, $i = 1, \ldots, n$ in P is replaced by the single disjunctive rule $p_1 \vee \cdots \vee p_n \leftarrow A$, where $A = A_i - \{\neg p_1, \ldots, \neg p_{i-1}, \neg p_{i+1}, \ldots, \neg p_n\}$.

For example, for the Nixon diamond above, the program P_D is given by the rules:

$$\mathtt{pacifist} \leftarrow \mathtt{quaker}, \neg \mathtt{ab_1}$$

$$\mathtt{non\_pacifist} \leftarrow \mathtt{republican}, \neg \mathtt{ab_2}$$

$$\mathtt{ab_1} \vee \mathtt{ab_2} \leftarrow \mathtt{quaker}, \mathtt{republican}$$

We will show next that P will be completely stable when the disjunctive program P_D is *stratified*. Since the standard definition of strat-

[36] The dependency graph of a program is the graph the results from connecting every predicate in the body of a rule to the predicate that appears in the head of the rule. Moreover, the link is negative if the first predicate occurs negated, and, positive, otherwise. A program is stratified when it its dependency graph does not contain cycles with negative links [ABW87]. We will say more about stratified programs in Section 6.1.

[37] The definition of local stratification is the same as for stratified programs, except that the links in the dependency graph are not among *predicates* but among ground *atoms* [Prz87].

ification only applies to non-disjunctive programs (see [ABW87]), we will first have to extend the definition of stratification to *disjunctive* programs.[38]

Let P_D be a disjunctive program given by the rules $D_i \leftarrow A_i$, $i = 1, \ldots, n$, where a head $D_i = p_1 \vee \cdots \vee p_n$ is *disjunctive* when $n > 1$. Let then group all the heads in P_D into classes, such that two heads D_i and D_j will belong to the same class when they have one or more atoms in common. Furthermore, for each class C_j which contains a disjunctive head let us introduce a new atom ξ_j, and let P_D^* be the non-disjunctive program that results from P_D by replacing each disjunctive head D_i in C_j as well as each atom p_j in D_i by the new atom ξ_j.
For example, for the disjunctive program P_D, P_D^* is given as follows:

$\texttt{pacifist} \leftarrow \texttt{quaker}, \neg\xi_1$

$\texttt{non\_pacifist} \leftarrow \texttt{republican}, \neg\xi_1$

$\xi_1 \leftarrow \texttt{quaker}, \texttt{republican}$

We will say that the disjunctive program P_D is *stratified* when the *non-disjunctive* program P_D^* is stratified.

Definition 5.11 A disjunctive program P_D is *stratified* when the non-disjunctive program P_D^* is stratified.

Then, if the original program P does not contain *self-defeating rules*, i.e., rules of the form $p \leftarrow \neg p, A$ and the disjunctive program P_D obtained from P is stratified, P will be completely stable.

Theorem 5.7 An open program P is *completely stable* if P does not contain self-defeating rules and the disjunctive program P_D obtained from P is *stratified.*

This result permits us to assert that the 'Nixon' program P is completely stable even though P is not stratified. This is because, P does not contain self-defeating rules and P_D^* is stratified. If P were extended with the rule:

$\texttt{republican} \leftarrow \texttt{pacifist}$

[38]The definition below aims to encompass only the type of disjunctive programs P_D that can be derived when P is open. In such programs, the predicates which occur *unnegated* in the body of a rule cannot appear in a disjunctive head $p_1 \vee \cdots \vee p_n$, $n > 1$, nor in a negative literal (i.e., disjunctions only involve 'abnormalities').

though, the program P^*_D would no longer be stratified, because of the negative cycle $\xi_1 \not\rightarrow$ `pacifist` $\rightarrow$ `republican` $\rightarrow \xi_1$ in the resulting dependency graph. More generally, it is not difficult to show that for programs P which represent acyclic inheritance networks, P^*_D would be stratified and thus P would be completely stable.[39]

5.8 Related Work

The causal theories presented here are an elaboration of ideas originally presented in [Gef89] where we also discussed the notions of classes, coherence and explanations. The introduction of a *causal operator* has produced a simplified formulation with added expressive power, which can be given a proof-theory and can be computed by a 'negation-as-failure' type of procedure. The adoption of the causal operator has been influenced by Pearl's proposal for distinguishing causal and evidential defaults [Pea88a], and the similarity between the ideas in [Gef89] and autoepistemic logic.[40]

Pearl's proposal is based on the observation that certain acceptable defaults, when chained, lead to unacceptable conclusions. He gives the example of two defaults 'if it rains, the grass is wet' and 'if the grass is wet, the sprinkler was on' which, although acceptable by separate, lead to the counterintuitive conclusion that 'if it rains, the sprinkler was on.' He argues that this problem is the result of using an *explanation giving* default (`rain` $\rightarrow$ `grass_wet`) to trigger an *explanation seeking* default (`grass_wet` $\rightarrow$ `sprinkler_on`). Pearl then proposes a system that has three main features: first, every default rule is labeled as either *causal* (e.g., `rain` $\rightarrow_{\mathrm{C}}$ `grass_wet`), or *evidential* (e.g. `grass_wet` $\rightarrow_{\mathrm{E}}$ `sprinkler_on`); second, the status of propositions p established on *causal* grounds, Cp, is distinguished from the status of propositions established on *evidential* grounds, Ep; and third, a calculus for reasoning with causal and evidential rules is introduced which purposely prevents deriving q from $p \rightarrow_{\mathrm{E}} q$ and Cp.

Though different in details and goals, the reading of the operator 'C'

[39] An example of a program P which is not completely stable even though P^*_D is stratified is the program $P = \{\mathtt{b} \leftarrow \neg\mathtt{a}, \neg\mathtt{b}\,;\ \mathtt{a} \leftarrow \neg\mathtt{b}, \neg\mathtt{a}\}$ which contains two self-defeating rules.

[40] I want to thank Michael Gelfond, Halina Przymusinska, and Kurt Konolige, for this observation.

in causal theories follows Pearl's intuitions. Pearl's focus, however, is on *evidential* reasoning, i.e., which *hypotheses* to adopt, while ours is on *default* reasoning, i.e., which *assumptions* to adopt. The difference is that hypotheses are adopted to explain observations (and thus the less the better), while assumptions are adopted in the absence of conflicting evidence (and thus the more the better). In fact, the problems discussed by Pearl can be avoided by capturing evidential reasoning in an *abductive* setting rather than in a *default reasoning* setting (e.g., [Poo87]; see also Section 6.4).

Causal theories are also closely related to Moore's [Moo85b] autoepistemic theories. For example, the autoepistemic encoding $L[P]$ [Gel87]

$$\alpha_1 \wedge \ldots \wedge \alpha_n \wedge \neg \mathrm{L}\beta_1 \wedge \ldots \wedge \neg \mathrm{L}\beta_m \Rightarrow \gamma$$

of a program P with rules:

$$\gamma \leftarrow \alpha_1, \ldots, \alpha_n, \neg\beta_1, \ldots, \neg\beta_m$$

turns out to be the reverse of the causal encoding $C_1[P]$:

$$\mathrm{C}\alpha_1 \wedge \ldots \wedge \mathrm{C}\alpha_n \wedge \neg\beta_1 \wedge \ldots \wedge \neg\beta_m \Rightarrow \mathrm{C}\gamma$$

That is, in the autoepistemic encoding $L[P]$ every *negated* atom is preceded by the *autoepistemic* operator 'L', while in the causal encoding $C_1[P]$ every *non-negated* atom is preceded by the *causal* operator 'C'. Moreover, both encodings sanction the same plain literals when P is stratified (Section 6.1). This suggests that the autoepistemic operator L can be understood as an *evidential* operator, with $\mathrm{L}\alpha$ meaning "there is evidence for α." More precisely, instead of using the *causal* operator C under the conventions that

$\neg\alpha$ is an assumption

$\mathrm{C}\alpha \Rightarrow \alpha$ must hold for every (plain) sentence α, and

α is *explained* in a class when $\mathrm{C}\alpha$ holds

we could have used an *evidential* operator E under the conventions that

$\neg\mathrm{E}\alpha$ is an assumption

$\alpha \Rightarrow \mathrm{E}\alpha$ must hold for every (plain) sentence α, and

$\mathrm{E}\alpha$ is *explained* in a class when α holds.

The *evidential* encoding of a logic program would then be identical to the *autoepistemic* encoding except for the presence of E's instead of L's. Moreover, both encodings would sanction an equivalent semantics for stratified programs. For non-stratified programs, however, as for most default theories, the duality between causal and autoepistemic disappears. First, default theories may lack stable models;[41] and second, the prefix ¬L, unlike any causal prefix, "generates" the assumptions that are needed.

The fact that the operator 'C' induces a preference on assumptions raises the question of whether the semantics of causal theories can be understood in terms of prioritized circumscription [McC86]. The answer is a qualified no: there are causal theories for which no priority order on the assumptions will yield the same behavior. The causal theory

$$\neg \mathsf{a} \wedge \neg \mathsf{b} \Rightarrow \mathsf{Cc} \wedge \mathsf{Cd} \qquad \neg \mathsf{c} \wedge \neg \mathsf{d} \Rightarrow \mathsf{Ca} \wedge \mathsf{Cb}$$

for abnormalities a, b, c, and d, is one such example. Still, the semantics of such theories could in principle be captured by defining priorities over more complex formulas (e.g., *conjunctions* of assumptions).

Also related to theories treated in this chapter are Shoham's causal theories [Sho88]. Shoham's causal theories are epistemic theories designed for efficient reasoning about change. They are interpreted by a preference criterion which rewards models in which "as little as possible is known for as long as possible." Although there is no direct correspondence between our causal theories and Shoham's, his idea of chronological minimization can be understood in terms of the ideas of explanation and coherence. If we recall that we regard an abnormality α as explained in a class $\mathcal{C}$ when $\mathcal{C}$ validates a set of assumption Δ which supports the truth of $C\alpha$, chronological minimization presumes α explained by Δ instead, when Δ logically entails α without involving assumptions about times past α. A consequence of this definition is that conclusions can be computed by reasoning forward in time even when some of the predictions are refuted by observations. It is well known, however, that this is not always correct; for example, if p is a fluent which was true at $t = 1$ and false at $t = 3$, there is no reason for assuming that p was clipped in the first interval as opposed to the second. Yet, that is what chronological minimization is bound to produce.

[41] But see the extensions proposed in [Mor89] and [GP89].

As discussed in Section 5.8, the architecture of causal theories is closely related to logic programs with negation as failure (e.g., [VRS88]), and argument systems [Pol88b, Lou87a]. Likewise, when priorities are allowed and the conditions in Theorem 5.6 hold, the resulting semantics and procedures are similar to those in Laenens' and Vermeir's ordered logic [LV90].

The notions of conditionals, causes, and explanations have also been of central importance in philosophy [Pit88, Gar88]. For the most part, however, philosophers have been concerned with making the meaning of such notions precise, while we have been concerned with exploiting the basic intuitions for designing better knowledge representation languages and semantics. Both goals, however, are highly interrelated, and a closer interaction between them is to be expected.

6 Applications

An adequate framework for representing and reasoning with defaults must provide three features: an expressive language that enables knowledge to be encoded in a natural way, an intuitive semantics that captures what the user has in mind, and a practical architecture that processes the knowledge in an efficient and correct manner. In this chapter we will illustrate how causal theories fare with regard to these issues by considering three standard classes of default theories: logic programs with negation as failure, inheritance hierarchies, and theories for reasoning about change. We will show how these theories can be expressed as causal theories, study the resulting behavior, and discuss how the procedures used in each of these domains compares with those developed for causal theories (Section 5.7).

In the final section we will focus on *abductive* reasoning. Abductive reasoning is a non-monotonic form of inference whose aim is to restore the coherence to a set of beliefs by seeking explanations for observed anomalies. Abductive inferences account for how a physician makes sense of the symptoms of a patient; how a technician makes sense of the measurements of a faulty circuit, and how people find motivations in the actions of other people. We will build a framework for abductive reasoning that exploits the distinction between true and explained propositions in causal theories, and then compare the resulting account with other proposals in the literature.

6.1 Logic Programming

Logic programs are collections of rules of the form $A \leftarrow L_1, L_2, \ldots, L_n$, where A is an atom, called the head of the rule, and each L_i, $i = 1, \ldots, n$, $n \geq 0$, is a literal in the rule's body (see [Llo84]). When all the literals are positive, the programs are said to be *positive* and their semantics can be understood in terms of the classical theories that they represent (the symbol '$\leftarrow$' stands for material implication, empty bodies stand for the atom **true**, and variables are assumed to be universally quantified). When some of the literals L_i are negative though, things are not so simple and the declarative reading of logic programs is often dropped. *General logic programs,* as programs with negative literals are called, are normally understood in procedural terms, with the proviso that negative literals $\neg A_i$ are assumed to be derivable when every derivation for A_i

fails. This interpretation of negation has been found highly useful in programming languages such as Planner [Hew72] and Prolog [Rou75], and is known as *negation as failure.* Negation as failure is different from classical negation and, in particular, behaves *non-monotonically:* a literal $\neg A$ may be derivable from a program P and yet *not* be derivable from a program P' that *extends* P (e.g., q follows from the program $\{q \leftarrow \neg p\}$ but not from the program $\{q \leftarrow \neg p\,;\, p \leftarrow\}$).

While the straightforward declarative reading of logic programs does not legitimize the behavior of negation as failure, more adequate accounts have been developed. One of these proposals, due to Clark [Cla78] is based on a small but significant modification of the semantics of *positive* programs. The key idea is to assume that the rules $A \leftarrow L_1, \ldots, L_n$ for an atom A provide not only the *sufficient* conditions for A to hold, but also the *necessary* conditions. Thus, for example, the semantics of a program P comprised of the rules $p \leftarrow \neg q$ and $q \leftarrow r$ is identified with the semantics of the *completion* of P, given by the sentences $p \Leftrightarrow \neg q$ and $q \Leftrightarrow r$ and $r \Leftrightarrow$ **false**. As a result, the truth of p and the falsehood of q and r are sanctioned, in agreement with negation as failure.

Clark's completion approach provides a good logical description of the negation as failure rule in interpreters such as Prolog. However, *describing* how a rule behaves is different than *prescribing* how it *should* behave. In this regard, Clark's account is not completely satisfactory. For example, a rule like $p \leftarrow p$ which should be harmless from a logical point of view, makes a difference between the programs $P = \{q \leftarrow \neg p\}$ and $P' = \{q \leftarrow \neg p, p \leftarrow p\}$. In the first program, the derivation of p fails and thus $\neg p$ and q follow; in the second program, the derivation of p 'loops' and thus neither $\neg p$ nor q follow.

In recent years different semantics of general logic programs have been developed which overcome the problems in Clark's approach and which show interesting connections to the non-monotonic formalisms developed in AI [She87, PP89]. Below we will explore this relationship further and show, in particular, that general logic programs can be regarded as a special class of causal theories. This will shed some light on the implementation of causal theories as well as on the semantics and procedures of a larger class of logic programs in which both rules and constraints (i.e., rules with no heads) are allowed.

Logic Programs and Causal Theories

In Section 5.7 we considered a mapping of simple causal theories T into logic programs and showed that the mapping preserved the 'meaning' of T. In this section, we will be interested in the inverse mapping: given a general logic program P we will define a causal theory $C[P]$ which captures the 'meaning' of P. As before, we will assume that all atoms in $C[P]$ are 'abnormalities' (i.e., all predicates are minimized), so that the gap $A[M]$ of an interpretation M will be simply the collection of all ground atoms that M makes true. Similarly, we will write $\mathcal{C}_M$ to refer to the class of models M' whose gaps $A[M']$ are contained in M (i.e., the models M' in $\mathcal{C}_M$ sanction 'abnormalities' from M only). The first mapping we will consider, $C_1[\cdot]$, translates each rule

$$\gamma \leftarrow \alpha_1, \ldots, \alpha_n, \neg\beta_1, \ldots, \neg\beta_m$$

in a program P, where $n \geq 0$ and $m \geq 0$, and α's, β's and γ are atoms, into a *causal* rule of the form

$$\mathrm{C}\alpha_1 \wedge \ldots \wedge \mathrm{C}\alpha_n \wedge \neg\beta_1 \wedge \ldots \wedge \neg\beta_m \Rightarrow \mathrm{C}\gamma$$

For example, if P is given by the rules:

$$\mathsf{c} \leftarrow \mathsf{a}, \neg\mathsf{b}$$

$$\mathsf{d} \leftarrow \neg\mathsf{c}$$

$$\mathsf{a} \leftarrow$$

$C_1[P]$ will be given by the causal rules:

$$\mathrm{C}\mathsf{a} \wedge \neg\mathsf{b} \Rightarrow \mathrm{C}\mathsf{c}$$

$$\neg\mathsf{c} \Rightarrow \mathrm{C}\mathsf{d}$$

$$\mathbf{true} \Rightarrow \mathrm{C}\mathsf{a}$$

The program P has two minimal Herbrand models: $M_1 = \{\mathsf{a}, \mathsf{c}\}$ and $M_2 = \{\mathsf{a}, \mathsf{b}, \mathsf{d}\}$, while the causal theory $C_1[P]$ has two minimal *classes* of models, $\mathcal{C}_{M_1}$ and $\mathcal{C}_{M_2}$. Moreover, M_1 is preferred to M_2, according to the perfect model semantics [Prz87], and similarly, $\mathcal{C}_{M_1}$ is preferred to $\mathcal{C}_{M_2}$, according to the semantics of causal theories (Section 5.3). Hence, P sanctions the atoms a and c, while $C_1[P]$ sanctions the atoms a and c, as well as the causal formulas $\mathrm{C}\mathsf{a}$ and $\mathrm{C}\mathsf{c}$. Therefore, if causal formulas are discarded, the same conclusions are sanctioned by both P and $C_1[P]$.

This correspondence between a program P and the causal theory $C_1[P]$ extends in fact to any program P which is *stratified.*[1]

Theorem 6.1 If P is stratified, then M is the canonical Herbrand model of P if and only if $\mathcal{C}_M$ is the single preferred class of $C_1[P]$.

As mentioned above, this implies that the *non-causal literals* sanctioned by M and $\mathcal{C}_M$ are the same. Also, if we say that a class of models $\mathcal{C}_M$ is *perfectly coherent* when every atom in M is explained, then the perfectly coherent classes $\mathcal{C}_M$ of $C_1[P]$ correspond exactly to the *stable models* M of P [GL88], even for programs P which are *not* stratified:

Theorem 6.2 M is a *stable* model of an arbitrary program P if and only if $\mathcal{C}_M$ is a perfectly coherent class of the causal theory $C_1[P]$.

In spite of this correspondence the semantics of causal theories $C_1[P]$ and the stable semantics of logic programs P diverge outside the family of non-stratified programs. First, P may lack stable stable models. For example, the program $\mathtt{p} \leftarrow \neg\mathtt{p}$ does not have stable models but the causal theory $\neg\mathtt{p} \Rightarrow \mathtt{Cp}$ has a single preferred class $\mathcal{C}_p$ where p is true but unexplained. Second, $C_1[P]$ may have several preferred classes even when P has a single stable model. For example, the program $P = \{\mathtt{a} \leftarrow \neg\mathtt{b}\,,\, \mathtt{b} \leftarrow \neg\mathtt{a}\,,\, \mathtt{p} \leftarrow \neg\mathtt{b}\,,\, \mathtt{p} \leftarrow \neg\mathtt{p}\}$ [VRS88] has a single stable model $M = \{\mathtt{a}, \mathtt{p}\}$, while $C_1[P]$ has two preferred classes $\mathcal{C}_M$ and $\mathcal{C}_{M'}$, with $M' = \{\mathtt{b}, \mathtt{p}\}$.

In all these examples, in spite of the differences with stable models, the semantics of a program P defined by the gaps M of the preferred classes $\mathcal{C}_M$ of $C_1[P]$ is appealing and well-justified. The problem of defining the semantics of P in this manner, however, is that the gaps M of the preferred classes of $C_1[P]$ are not always models of P. For example, for $P = \{\mathtt{p} \leftarrow \neg\mathtt{p}, \mathtt{q} \leftarrow \mathtt{p}\}$, the resulting causal theory is $C_1[P] = \{\neg\mathtt{p} \Rightarrow \mathtt{Cp}\,,\, \mathtt{Cp} \Rightarrow \mathtt{Cq}\}$, whose single preferred class $\mathcal{C}_M$ has a gap $M = \{\mathtt{p}\}$ which is not a model of P.

[1] Stratified programs are programs in which the use of negation adheres to certain constraints. Roughly, a program is stratified when the rules can be partitioned in layers $L_0, \ldots, L_n$ such that the rules in which a predicate p occurs in the head appear before or in the same layer as the rules in which p occurs unnegated in the body, and before the rules in which p occurs *negated* in the body [ABW87]. The semantics of stratified programs is well-agreed upon, and is defined by a single minimal Herbrand model which corresponds to either the *canonical, perfect, stable,* or *felicitous* model of the program (see [ABW87], [Prz87],[GL88], and [Fin89]).

A simple way for handling this problem is by extending the causal theories $C_1[P]$ with the logical encoding of the program P itself. In the resulting theories, $C_2[P]=C_1[P]+P$, the rules in P (which do not involve the operator C) act as constraints, while the rules in $C_1[P]$ establish the preferences on models. Since the gaps M of the minimal classes $\mathcal{C}_M$ of $C_2[P]$ are always models of P, the semantics defined by the preferred gaps of $C_2[P]$ will always be consistent with P. For example, for the program $P = \{\mathtt{p} \leftarrow \neg\mathtt{p}\,,\, \mathtt{q} \leftarrow \mathtt{p}\,,\, \mathtt{r} \leftarrow\}$, the preferred class of $C_2[P]$ is $\mathcal{C}_M$, with $M = \{\mathtt{p}, \mathtt{q}, \mathtt{r}\}$. Furthermore, in $\mathcal{C}_M$, the atom r is explained but the atoms p and q are true but unexplained. The result is thus similar to the three-valued semantics of logic programs where r is true, and p and q are unknown.

Logic Programs and Causal Networks

We considered above the semantics of causal theories that result from mapping the rules

$$\gamma \leftarrow \alpha_1, \ldots, \alpha_n, \neg\beta_1, \ldots, \neg\beta_m$$

in a program P into causal rules of the form

$$\mathrm{C}\alpha_1 \wedge \ldots \wedge \mathrm{C}\alpha_n \wedge \neg\beta_1 \wedge \ldots \wedge \neg\beta_m \Rightarrow \mathrm{C}\gamma$$

In the remainder of this section we will investigate the semantics associated with a different mapping $C_3[\cdot]$ which maps each rule

$$\gamma \leftarrow \alpha_1, \ldots, \alpha_n, \neg\beta_1, \ldots, \neg\beta_m$$

into a causal rule of the form:

$$\alpha_1 \wedge \ldots \wedge \alpha_n \wedge \neg\beta_1 \wedge \ldots \wedge \neg\beta_m \Rightarrow \mathrm{C}\gamma$$

The difference between the theories $C_3[P]$ and $C_1[P]$ is that positive antecedents no longer need to be 'explained' (i.e., $\mathrm{C}\alpha$'s are replaced by α's). This makes the models $C_3[P]$ models of $C_1[P]$ but not vice versa. As a result, the behavior of both theories may differ even when P is stratified (e.g., for $P = \{\mathtt{q} \leftarrow \neg\mathtt{p}\,,\, \mathtt{p} \leftarrow \mathtt{r}\,,\, \mathtt{r} \leftarrow \mathtt{p}\}$, $C_1[P]$ sanctions q but $C_3[P]$ doesn't). However, if P is not only stratified but also *acyclic,* i.e., P's dependency graph does not contain either negative or positive cycles, then $C_1[P]$ and $C_3[P]$ will be equivalent:

Theorem 6.3 For an acyclic program P, M is the canonical model of P iff $\mathcal{C}_M$ is the single preferred class of $C_1[P]$, $C_2[P]$, and $C_3[P]$.

In other words, once recursion is disallowed the three causal mappings behave identically, and are equivalent to the accepted semantics of logic programs. While the requirement of acyclicity is unacceptably strong in the domain of programming, it is common among network representational languages, such as inheritance hierarchies [Tou86] and causal networks [Pea88b].

For the theories $C_1[P]$, $C_2[P]$ and $C_3[P]$ to be equivalent, however, it is not necessary for the program P to be acyclic, but it is sufficient that P be *open:*

Theorem 6.4 The causal theories $C_1[P]$, $C_2[P]$, and $C_3[P]$ are equivalent for any program P which is *open.*

Remember that P is open when no predicate appears *negated* in the body of some rule and *unnegated* in the body of the same or another rule in P. The *simple causal theories* studied in Section 5.7 are open causal theories of the form $C_3[P]$ augmented by constraints (i.e., formulas which do not involve the operator C). In those theories, the negated predicates act as 'abnormality' predicates and the 'openness' restriction amounts to ruling out derivations based on *positive* abnormalities.

Provided that negative literals which are not assumptions are rewritten as *positive* literals (e.g., $\texttt{non\_pacifist}(x)$), most 'abnormality' default theories are open in this sense. More generally, non-open programs can be 'opened' by introducing auxiliary predicates ξ and rewriting rules $\gamma \leftarrow \alpha_1, \ldots, \alpha_n, \neg\beta_1, \ldots, \neg\beta_m$ as $\gamma \leftarrow \alpha_1, \ldots, \alpha_n, \neg\xi$ together with $\xi \leftarrow \beta_i$, for $i = 1, \ldots, m$. The open and the un-opened version of a program will often have a different semantics, although it is possible that programmers really mean the 'opened' versions of the programs they write. Few logic programmers would be surprised by the conclusion $\neg\texttt{c}$ from the program $P = \{\texttt{c} \leftarrow \texttt{a}\,, \texttt{b} \leftarrow \neg\texttt{a}\,, \leftarrow \texttt{b}\}$ where $\leftarrow \texttt{b}$ means it is not the case that $\texttt{b}$ (cf. Section 5.7). Indeed, while $\neg\texttt{c}$ is inconsistent with P, it is a legitimate conclusion of the 'opened' version P' of P: $P' = \{\texttt{c} \leftarrow \texttt{a}\,, \texttt{b} \leftarrow \neg\xi\,, \xi \leftarrow \texttt{a}\,, \leftarrow \texttt{b}\}$.

Procedures

So far we have focused on the semantics of logic programs that result from various translations of logic programs into causal theories. We will now add a few remarks about the relation between the *procedures* used in logic programs and those developed for causal theories (Section 5.7; see also [Gef91]).

The procedure Π_1 described in Section 5.7 (page 124) operates on programs P comprised of a collection R of rules and a collection N of constraints. Constraints are represented as positive rules $\leftarrow p_1, \ldots, p_n$ with no head, and express that some atom in the body has to be false. The procedure Π_1 tests whether a list $\Delta = \{\neg\beta_1, \ldots, \neg\beta_n\}$ of assumptions (i.e., negative ground literals) is linearly stable, and thus whether atoms supported by Δ can be accepted.[2]

Procedure Π_1

$\Delta_n = \{\neg\beta_1, \neg\beta_2, \ldots, \neg\beta_n\}$ is derivable if for $\forall$ *admissible* Δ' and i

[1] if Δ' supports β_i, then $\Delta' + \Delta_{i-1}$ is self-defeating, and
[2] if $\Delta' + \{\neg\beta_i\}$ is contradicted, then $\Delta' + \Delta_i$ is self-defeating

Recall that Δ *supports* an atom p in a program $P = R + N$ if p is a logical consequence of the positive program P^+_Δ obtained from the rules of P, by dropping first all rule instances with assumptions not in Δ, and then all assumptions from the remaining instances. Likewise, Δ is *self-defeating* if it supports an atom β_i whose complement belongs to Δ; Δ is *contradicted* if it supports each of the atoms p_i in a ground instance $\leftarrow p_1, \ldots, p_n$ of a constraint in N; and Δ is *admissible* when it is neither self-defeating nor contradicted.

There are two main differences between Π_1 and Prolog's negation as failure rule (NAF) or SLDNF [Llo84]. The first is that Π_1, unlike NAF or SLDNF, can handle negative information; namely, we can assert that an atom is false or that several atoms are incompatible, and have this information be taken into account. On the other hand, unlike Prolog's NAF and SLDNF, Π_1 is not a full-fledged procedure; all details about control e.g., how to build the list Δ_n, which rebuttal Δ' to try first, etc. are left unspecified. However, as suggested in page 124 a layer of control can be added to Π_1. For example, to prove an atom p, we could look for sets Δ of assumptions which support p and accept p if no rebuttal Δ' for Δ is found. Otherwise we will have to find a defeater Δ'' of Δ' and repeat the process for the set $\Delta'' + \Delta$, and so on.

[2] Δ_i stands for the list $\{\neg\beta_1, \ldots, \neg\beta_i\}$, when $i > 0$, and for the empty list otherwise.

Yet, even if these two differences are bridged, i.e., constraints in N are removed and a layer of control is added to Π_1, the results will not be the same. In fact, the well-founded semantics [VRS88] which captures every conclusion sanctioned by SLDNF [Prz89] can be shown to be 'sound' but not 'complete' with respect to Π_1.

Theorem 6.5 If an atom p is true in the well-founded model of P, then p is supported by a list of assumptions Δ derivable from P by Π_1.

For example, in the program P:

$$\mathsf{f} \leftarrow \neg\mathsf{c}$$

$$\mathsf{c} \leftarrow \neg\mathsf{a}, \neg\mathsf{b}$$

$$\mathsf{b} \leftarrow \neg\mathsf{d}, \neg\mathsf{a}$$

$$\mathsf{a} \leftarrow \neg\mathsf{d}, \neg\mathsf{b}$$

Π_1 sanctions the list $\{\neg\mathsf{c}\}$ which supports the atom `f`, yet `f` is not derivable by SLDNF nor it is true in the well-founded model of P.

A simple restriction on Π_1, however, yields a procedure which is equivalent to the well-founded semantics. The new procedure, which we call Π_0, is obtained from Π_1 by eliminating the second condition (it is assumed that $N = \emptyset$), and by replacing the condition "$\Delta' + \Delta_{i-1}$ is self-defeating" by the stronger condition "Δ_{i-1} supports β', for some $\neg\beta'$ in Δ'." For Π_0, the following result can be shown:

Theorem 6.6 An atom p is true in the well-founded model of P if and only if p is supported by a list of assumptions Δ derivable from P by Π_0.

Under the conditions spelled out in Section 5.7, namely that P is open and completely stable, both Π_1 and Π_0 are *sound* with respect to the semantics of the causal theories $C_i[P]$, for $i = 1, 2, 3$, but neither one is complete. Π_1, in particular, computes all and only linear stable arguments ignoring non-linear stable arguments and covers (see Section 5.6). For example, in the program:[3]

$\mathsf{a} \leftarrow \neg\mathsf{c}$	$\mathsf{d} \leftarrow \neg\mathsf{a}$
$\mathsf{b} \leftarrow \neg\mathsf{d}$	$\mathsf{d} \leftarrow \neg\mathsf{c}$
$\mathsf{c} \leftarrow \neg\mathsf{b}$	$\mathsf{c} \leftarrow \neg\mathsf{d}$

[3]This program is due to Alberto Torres.

the argument $\Delta = \{\neg\mathtt{a}, \neg\mathtt{b}\}$ is stable but not linear, so it cannot be computed by either Π_1 or Π_0. In light of the equivalence above, Δ cannot be captured either by the well-founded semantics.

Truth-Maintenance Systems

Truth maintenance systems (TMSs) keep track of dependencies among propositions and often perform additional forms of non-monotonic inference (e.g., [Doy79, dK86]). Recently it has been shown that Doyle's TMSs are equivalent to propositional logic programs, where rules replace justifications, constraints replace nogoods, and negative literals replace OUT-justifiers (see [Elk88, RDB89, GM90]).[4] In spite of this result, however, the *procedures* used in non-monotonic TMSs (e.g., [Dre88, Jun89]), remain quite different from those used in logic programs. In particular, TMS procedures are "credulous" (they compute 'preferred' models), while NAF procedures are "skeptical" (they compute what's is true in *all* preferred models).

Since computing one model is easier than computing all models, it may appear that TMSs should be more efficient than logic programs. This is not true, however, and can be explained in terms of the proof-theory developed in Section 5.6: TMSs compute the atoms supported by arguments Δ which are *protected* from every conflicting arguments Δ';[5] logic programs, on the other hand, compute the atoms supported by *linear stable arguments.* Although linear stable arguments $\Delta_n = \{\neg\beta_1, \ldots, \neg\beta_n\}$ must be protected from every conflicting argument Δ', by virtue of being *linear*, they are also *decomposable.* Thus we can prove Δ_n by proving each assumption $\neg\beta_i$ in sequence. The same decomposition is not achievable in TMSs, and thus, although TMSs compute atoms supported by *non-linear* stable arguments as well, they are overall less efficient. A proposal for less powerful, although more efficient TMSs, has been recently advanced in [Wit91].

[4] The equivalence between Doyle's TMSs and logic programs holds when the meaning of the program is given by its stable or 'generalized' stable models (see [KM90, GM90]).

[5] If M is an stable model, the collection of assumptions sanctioned by M is protected from every conflicting argument Δ'.

6.2 Reasoning about Change

We will now focus on the application of causal theories for representing and reasoning about change. Theories for reasoning about change must contain rules representing the effect of actions, the conditions which can prevent actions from achieving their normal effects, and the tendency of certain aspects of the world (fluents) to remain stable (see [McD82]). We will call the first type of rules *change* rules, the second type *cancellation* rules, and the third type *persistence* rules.

Change, cancellation, and persistence rules can interact in various ways. The Yale shooting scenario illustrates a problem that results from spurious interactions between change and persistence rules. We showed, however, that this problem could be avoided by expressing the Yale shooting problem as a causal theory. We will now present general guidelines for locally mapping any basic theory for reasoning about change into a causal theory. The guidelines do not depend on the temporal notation used. For the sake of simplicity, we will use a simple reified temporal language, although other notations could be used as well (see the discussion in [Sho88]). The notation $p(x)_t$ will be used as an abbreviation for the sentence $Holds(p(x), t)$, to read "fluent $p(x)$ holds at time t." We will assume a discrete time where t precedes $t+1$ and so on.

First we specify the encoding of rules about change. A rule describing the effect $e(x)$ of an action $a(x)$ under the condition $p(x)$ will be encoded as the formula:

$$p(x)_t \wedge a(x)_t \wedge \neg \texttt{pv}_i(x) \Rightarrow \mathrm{C}e(x)_{t+1}$$

if the rule is defeasible, and as the formula:

$$p(x)_t \wedge a(x)_t \Rightarrow \mathrm{C}e(x)_{t+1}$$

if the rule is strict. The predicates $\texttt{pv}_i$'s, read "the effect of the action is prevented," are abnormality predicates used for distinguishing rules about change from other defeasible rules. The expression $\mathrm{C}e(x)_t$ can be understood as stating that $e(x)$ has been *caused to hold* at time t, or that $e(x)$ has been 'initiated' at time t, as in Kowalski and Sergot's event calculus [KS86].

The persistence of a fluent $f(x)$ (e.g., $\texttt{on(a,b)}$) will be similarly expressed by rules of the form:

$$f(x)_t \wedge \neg \texttt{cp}_i(x)_t \Rightarrow \mathrm{C}f(x)_{t+1}$$

where $\mathtt{cp}_i$ is another type of abnormality predicate, read "the fluent is clipped." The effect of backward persistence, e.g., concluding $f(x)_t$ from $f(x)_{t+1}$, would be achieved by contraposing the persistence axiom corresponding to the complement $\overline{f(x)}$ of $f(x)$.

The reason for appealing to two different types of abnormality predicates, $\mathtt{pv}_i$ and $\mathtt{cp}_i$, is for giving the defaults about change priority over the defaults about persistence (see Example 5.8, page 114). Indeed, by assuming that the literals $\neg\mathtt{pv}_i(x)$ have priority over the literals $\neg\mathtt{cp}_j(x)$, the closure of any theory about change will contain cancellation axioms of the form (see page 112):

$$p(x)_t \wedge a(x)_t \wedge f(x)_t \wedge \neg\mathtt{pv}_i(x)_t \Rightarrow \mathrm{C}\mathtt{cp}_j(x)_t$$

for any pair of rules

$$p(x)_t \wedge a(x)_t \wedge \neg\mathtt{pv}_i(x)_t \Rightarrow \mathrm{C}e(x)_{t+1}$$
$$f(x)_t \wedge \neg\mathtt{cp}_j(x)_t \Rightarrow \mathrm{C}f(x)_{t+1}$$

which are in head-to-head to conflict in the theory.[6]

Provided with conditions such as that the antecedent of each rule is a conjunction of literals, observations are atoms and so on, the resulting theories are what we called simple causal theories in Section 5.7. As we showed, simple causal theories can be expressed as logic programs augmented by negative constraints, and procedures like Π_1 can be used for computing with them. A property highlighted by these procedures (e.g., Π_1^- in page 127) is that as long as no set of assumptions is refuted by an *observation*, reasoning can proceed forward, along the direction of the rules, ignoring conflicts that take place in the future (e.g., in the YSP, we can get $\mathtt{loaded(2)}$ from $\mathtt{loaded(1)}$, ignoring that $\mathtt{loaded(2)}$ triggers a default $\mathtt{shoot(2)} \wedge \mathtt{loaded(2)} \rightarrow \mathtt{dead(2)}$ which is in conflict with $\mathtt{alive(1)} \rightarrow \mathtt{alive(2)}$). Under those conditions temporal default reasoning is similar to *simulation.*

The causal encoding of the YSP was illustrated in Example 5.8 above.

[6] The notion of head-to-head conflicts defined in Section 5.4 only deals with rules $p_i(x) \wedge \alpha_i(x) \Rightarrow \mathrm{C}q_i(x)$ in which $p_i(x)$ and $q_i(x)$ have at most a single free variable (see page 106). Below we will need a more general definition in which $x = \{x_1, \ldots, x_m\}$ may be a *tuple* of variables. More precisely, we will assume that a collection of temporal rules $p_i(x)_t \wedge \alpha_i(x)_t \Rightarrow \mathrm{C}q_i(x)_t$, $i = 1, \ldots, n$, are in head-to-head conflict when 1) the arity of each term $q_i(x) = q_i(x_1, \ldots, x_m)$ is the same, 2) every free variable x_j in the antecedent expression $p_i(x)$ also appears in the term $q_i(x)$, and 3) the constraints in K logically entail the formula $\forall x, t. \neg(q_1(x)_t \wedge \cdots q_n(x)_t)$.

Below we will consider a slightly richer example due to Ginsberg and Smith [GS88].

Example 6.1 Let us assume that there is a room with some ducts for ventilation. If the ducts become blocked, the room becomes stuffy. Objects can be moved and if an object sits on a duct, the duct gets blocked. This information can be encoded in a background K with rules:[7]

$$\mathtt{duct}(x) \wedge \exists y.\, \mathtt{on}(y,x)_t \Rightarrow C\mathtt{blocked}(x)_t$$
$$\mathtt{move\_to}(x,y)_t \wedge \neg \mathtt{pv_1}(x,y)_t \Rightarrow C\mathtt{on}(x,y)_{t+1}$$
$$[\forall x. \mathtt{duct}(x) \Rightarrow \mathtt{blocked}(x)_t] \Rightarrow C\mathtt{stuffy}_{t+1}$$

The persistence of the fluents $\mathtt{blocked}(x)$, $\mathtt{on}(x,y)$, and $\mathtt{stuffy}$ can be expressed as stipulated above by means of axioms of the form:

$$\mathtt{blocked}(x)_t \wedge \neg \mathtt{cp_1}(x)_t \Rightarrow C\mathtt{blocked}(x)_{t+1}$$
$$\mathtt{on}(x,y)_t \wedge \neg \mathtt{cp_2}(x,y)_t \Rightarrow C\mathtt{on}(x,y)_{t+1}$$
$$\mathtt{stuffy_t} \wedge \neg \mathtt{cp_3}()_t \Rightarrow C\mathtt{stuffy}_{t+1}$$

If we use the notation $\overline{f(x)}$ to express the 'complement' of a fluent $f(x)$, the persistences associated with the 'negated' fluents can be expressed as:[8]

$$\overline{\mathtt{blocked}(x)}_t \wedge \neg \mathtt{cp_4}(x)_t \Rightarrow C\overline{\mathtt{blocked}(x)}_{t+1}$$
$$\overline{\mathtt{on}(x,y)}_t \wedge \neg \mathtt{cp_5}(x,y)_t \Rightarrow C\overline{\mathtt{on}(x,y)}_{t+1}$$
$$\overline{\mathtt{stuffy}}_t \wedge \neg \mathtt{cp_6}()_t \Rightarrow C\overline{\mathtt{stuffy}}_{t+1}$$

The incompatibility of a fluent $f(x)$ and its complement $\overline{f(x)}$, in turn, can be captured by a schematic constraint

$$f(x)_t \Rightarrow \neg \overline{f(x)}_t$$

All rules above determine also three cancellation axioms

$$\mathtt{duct}(x) \wedge \exists y.\, \mathtt{on}(y,x)_t \wedge \overline{\mathtt{blocked}(x)}_t \Rightarrow C\mathtt{cp_4}(x)_t$$
$$\mathtt{move\_to}(x,y)_t \wedge \neg \mathtt{pv_1}(x,y)_t \wedge \overline{\mathtt{on}(x,y)}_{t+1} \Rightarrow C\mathtt{cp_5}(x,y)_t$$
$$[\forall x. \mathtt{duct}(x) \Rightarrow \mathtt{blocked}(x)_t] \wedge \overline{\mathtt{stuffy}}_{t+1} \Rightarrow C\mathtt{cp_6}()_t$$

[7] For simplicity, we treat some of the rules as strict. No significant change would arise, however, from treating them as defaults.

[8] Recall that fluents are terms; e.g., $\mathtt{blocked}(x)_t$ is an abbreviation of the *atom* $Holds(\mathtt{blocked}(x), t)$.

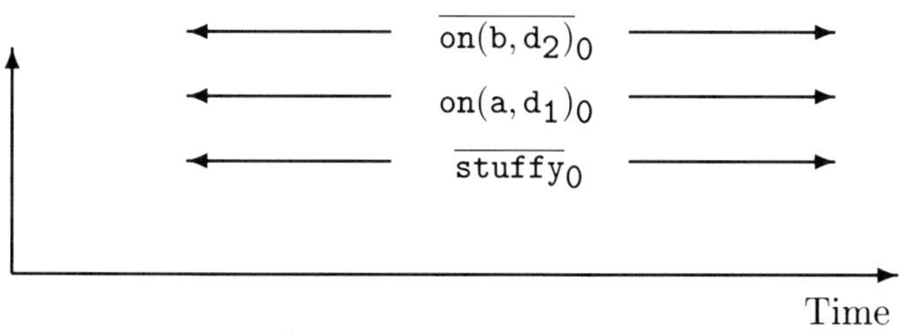

Figure 6.1
Initial scenario: Forward and backward persistences

which are automatically included in the closure of the theory due to the head-to-head conflicts between the rules about change and the rules about persistence (see Sections 5.4 and 5.5).[9]

Given this background, let us consider a scenario $T = \langle K, E \rangle$ describing a room with two ducts $\texttt{d}_1$ and $\texttt{d}_2$. At time $t = \texttt{0}$ the room is not stuffy, a block $\texttt{a}$ is sitting on top of duct $\texttt{d}_1$, and a block $\texttt{b}$ is sitting on a place different than $\texttt{d}_2$:

$$E = \{\texttt{duct}(x) \Rightarrow x = \texttt{d}_1 \vee x = \texttt{d}_2, \overline{\texttt{stuffy}_0}, \texttt{on}(\texttt{a}, \texttt{d}_1)_0, \overline{\texttt{on}(\texttt{b}, \texttt{d}_2)_0}\}$$

Figure 6.1 depicts this situation and the backward and forward projections that are legitimized. Let us now assume that at time $t = \texttt{0}$ the block $\texttt{b}$ is moved to duct $\texttt{d}_2$. The new context is $T' = \langle K, E' \rangle$, with $E' = E + \{\texttt{move\_to}(\texttt{b}, \texttt{d}_2)_0\}$. The conflicts in this context are depicted in Fig. 6.2. These conflicts produce three minimal classes of models: the intended class $\mathcal{C}_1$ where the action is successful and, as a result, the two ducts get blocked and the room becomes stuffy; the class $\mathcal{C}_2$, where the action is successful but somehow the block $\texttt{a}$ has been removed from duct $\texttt{d}_1$; and the class, $\mathcal{C}_3$, where the action is unsuccessful and the block $\texttt{b}$ remains in a place other than $\texttt{d}_2$. The result is that $\mathcal{C}_1$ is the only class that explains the abnormalities it introduces, and thus, it is preferred over $\mathcal{C}_2$ and $\mathcal{C}_3$. Therefore, T' predicts that block $\texttt{a}$ stays in place and that the room becomes stuffy. The formulation thus captures the intended behavior without relying on explicit cancellation axioms.

[9]For an implementation point of view, these axioms do not necessarily have to be added to the theory, see page 129.

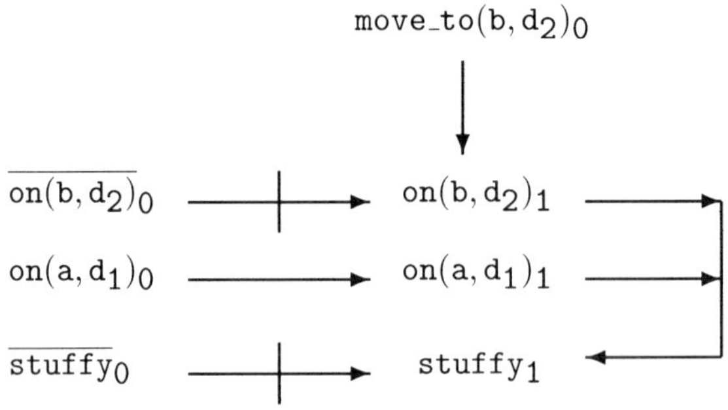

Figure 6.2
Final scenario: Conflicts among defaults

6.3 Inheritance Hierarchies

Inheritance hierarchies are devices for organizing knowledge about prototypical classes of individuals [Tou86]. They are represented as directed graphs, where links connecting a node a to a node b indicate that a is a member of b — if a is an individual — and that members of a are normally members of b — if a stands for a class. For *negated* links, the same relation is understood in terms of a and the *complement* of b. In an inheritance hierarchy Γ, the task of an inheritance algorithm is to determine the properties of a given individual p, a task which amounts to finding the classes which have p as member. The difficulty in this task is that the links stand for default relations, so there may be paths suggesting that p is a member of a class b and paths suggesting exactly the opposite. Thus, an inheritance algorithm must decide which paths to 'believe', or, as it is more often said, which paths are *supported.* The main criterion for chosing paths is *specificity:* more specific paths are 'preferred' over less specific ones (see [Tou86], [HTT87] and [GV89], among others).

Causal theories with priorities provide a suitable architecture for reasoning with inheritance hierarchies and similar types of structures. A link $a \rightarrow b$ can be expressed as a rule $a \wedge \neg \mathtt{ab}_i \Rightarrow Cb$, while a negated link $a \not\rightarrow d$ can be expressed as a rule $a \wedge \neg \mathtt{ab}_j \Rightarrow Cd'$ along with a

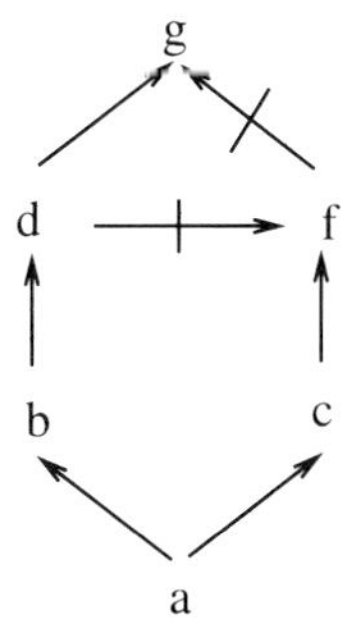

Figure 6.3
Inheritance hierarchies as simple causal theories

constraint $d \wedge d' \Rightarrow$ **false**. The priorities among rules can be obtained from conditional considerations as in Section 4.3.

The resulting theories will belong to the class of simple causal theories considered in Section 5.7 which can be expressed and processed as logic programs with negative constraints. For example, the program that corresponds to the network depicted in Figure 6.3 will look as follows:

$\mathtt{b} \leftarrow \mathtt{a}, \neg \mathtt{ab}_1$	$\mathtt{g} \leftarrow \mathtt{d}, \neg \mathtt{ab}_5$
$\mathtt{c} \leftarrow \mathtt{a}, \neg \mathtt{ab}_2$	$\mathtt{g}' \leftarrow \mathtt{f}, \neg \mathtt{ab}_6$
$\mathtt{d} \leftarrow \mathtt{b}, \neg \mathtt{ab}_3$	$\mathtt{f} \leftarrow \mathtt{d}, \neg \mathtt{ab}_7$
$\mathtt{f} \leftarrow \mathtt{c}, \neg \mathtt{ab}_4$	$\leftarrow \mathtt{g}, \mathtt{g}'$

Furthermore, since the default $\mathtt{d} \rightarrow \mathtt{g}$ is in conflict with the set of defaults $\{\mathtt{d} \rightarrow \mathtt{f}, \mathtt{f} \rightarrow \mathtt{g}'\}$, and similarly, the default $\mathtt{d} \rightarrow \mathtt{f}$ is in conflict with the set $\{\mathtt{d} \rightarrow \mathtt{g}, \mathtt{f} \rightarrow \mathtt{g}'\}$, it follows then that both $\mathtt{d} \rightarrow \mathtt{g}$ and $\mathtt{d} \rightarrow \mathtt{f}$ must have higher priority than $\mathtt{f} \rightarrow \mathtt{g}'$ (cf. Section 4.3).

As long the networks are *acyclic*, the conditions in Theorem 5.6 hold, and the supported inheritance paths can be computed by means of the procedure Π_2 (cf. page 129):

Procedure Π_2

1. If $p \leftarrow \; \in P$, then $\mid\!\sim_P p$
2. If $p \leftarrow A \in P$, $\mid\!\sim_P p_i$ for each atom p_i in A, and every support Δ' for $\sim\!p$ is *defeated*, then $\mid\!\sim_P p$

Recall that $\mid\!\sim_P p$ means that the atom p is derivable from the program P; $\sim\!p$ refers to any atom p' incompatible with p (i.e., an atom p' such that

$\leftarrow p, p' \in P$), and Δ' is *defeated* either when it supports the complement $\sim q$ of an atom q derivable from P, or when it only supports rules $\sim p \leftarrow A'$ that have lower priority than $p \leftarrow A$.[10]

In the program above, if we are given $\mathtt{a} \leftarrow$ (e.g., some individual belongs to class a), Π_2 produces a in the first iteration (by application of the first rule); b, c, d, and f in the second and third iterations (because the complements of these atoms do not occur anywhere in the theory), and g in the fourth iteration (because the only support Δ' for $\sim$g involves the rule $\mathtt{g}' \leftarrow \mathtt{f}, \neg\mathtt{ab}_6$ which has lower priority than $\mathtt{g} \leftarrow \mathtt{d}, \neg\mathtt{ab}_5$).

Besides providing an architecture for inheritance hierarchies, the procedure Π_2 also provides valuable insights regarding the scope and limitations of other inheritance schemes. This is because we can assess the soundness and completeness properties of Π_2 relative to the more general framework of causal theories. We will illustrate the advantages of this in a pair of examples.

Example 6.2 (Cycles and Strict Links) Let us consider first the cyclic network depicted in Figure 6.4, where the link $\mathtt{c} \not\rightarrow \mathtt{b}$ is the only 'strict' link (for the sake of simplicity, strict links are encoded as defeasible links with priority higher than any true defeasible link). The program P encoding the network has the following rules:

$$r_1 : \mathtt{b} \leftarrow \mathtt{a}, \neg\mathtt{ab}_1$$
$$r_2 : \mathtt{c} \leftarrow \mathtt{b}, \neg\mathtt{ab}_2$$
$$r_3 : \mathtt{b}' \leftarrow \mathtt{c}, \neg\mathtt{ab}_3$$
$$\leftarrow \mathtt{b}, \mathtt{b}'$$

with rule r_3 having higher priority than rule r_1. Given $\mathtt{a} \leftarrow$, Π_2 produces a, b, c and b′. In other words, both b and b′ are derived even though they are jointly inconsistent. It is simple to show though that the causal theory that corresponds to the program does not authorize these conclusions; indeed, b is entailed but b′ is not. This means that the behavior of Π_2 is not sound, and thus, that P does not satisfy the conditions of Theorem 5.6 (P also violates the condition of Theorem 5.4 regarding the soundness of Π_1, see page 125). The condition violated by P is the one that requires that the *closure of P be completely stable.*

[10] Remember that a rule $\sim p \leftarrow \alpha_1, \ldots, \alpha_n, \neg\beta_1, \ldots, \neg\beta_m$ is supported by Δ' when Δ' supports each positive literal α_i and includes each negative literal $\neg\beta_i$.

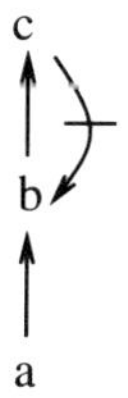

Figure 6.4
Inconsistent cyclic network

Indeed, since the rules r_1 and r_3 are in head-to-head conflict and r_3 has higher priority than r_1, the closure of P contains the rule

$$r_4 : \mathtt{ab_1} \leftarrow \mathtt{c}, \mathtt{a}, \neg \mathtt{ab_3}$$

which together with the rules r_1, r_2, r_3 and $\leftarrow$ a does not have a stable model.[11]

Since most inheritance schemes behave like Π_2, our example shows that *cyclic* inheritance networks with *strict* links would need special care. In any case, the mapping of inheritance networks into causal theories provides possible soundness and completeness criteria to meet.

Example 6.3 (Non-Linear Arguments) The previous example illustrates a case in which Π_2 fails to be sound. We will now show a case in which Π_2 fails to be complete. Recall that Π_2 aims to compute the atoms supported by *linear stable arguments* even though atoms supported by non-linear stable arguments and stable covers are entailed as well (Section 5.6). The theory for the network depicted in Fig. 6.5 contains in fact an atom which is entailed but which is not supported by a linear stable argument.

We will assume that the rule corresponding to the more 'specific' link B $\not\rightarrow$ G has priority over the rule for the less 'specific' link D $\rightarrow$ G, and similarly, that the rule corresponding to the link C $\not\rightarrow$ G has priority over the rule for the link F $\rightarrow$ G. Given A, Π_2 will derive B, C, D, and F, but neither G nor its complement G$'$. This is because the link F $\rightarrow$ G rebuts the link B $\not\rightarrow$ G but is not defeated; and similarly, the link D $\rightarrow$ G rebuts the link C $\not\rightarrow$ G but is not defeated either.

Intuitively, G$'$ should be derivable because for each path from A to G there is another path from A to G$'$ which is more 'specific'. Indeed, the

[11]Note also that the closure of P does not comply with the conditions for complete stability established by Theorem 5.7, page 132).

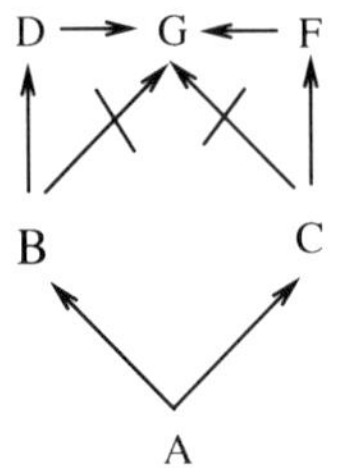

Figure 6.5
Non-linear stable arguments

causal theory for the network entails $\mathtt{G}'$, and $\mathtt{G}'$ is furthermore supported by the *stable argument* which corresponds to the *union* of the paths $\mathtt{A} \to \mathtt{B} \not\to \mathtt{G}$ and $\mathtt{A} \to \mathtt{C} \not\to \mathtt{G}$. However, this argument is not *linearly* stable: the first path is needed for defeating the rebuttals of the second path, and the second path is needed for defeating the rebuttals of the first path; thus both 'paths' have to be established jointly, not in sequence. As a result, since Π_2 only computes atoms supported by linear stable argument, $\mathtt{G}'$ is not sanctioned by Π_2. The same limitation applies to other procedures which prove arguments incrementally, one default at a time (e.g., [Nut88b]). Procedures such as those in [HTT87] and [GV89] can handle these networks because they implicitly embed assumptions about the restricted language of inheritance hierarchies (e.g., that each atom p participates in a single binary constraint $\leftarrow p, p'$). Yet, if some of these restrictions are raised, these procedures would be subject to the same limitation.

6.4 Abductive Reasoning

Work in non-monotonic reasoning has been motivated by the goal of providing a formal account of some of the pervasive patterns of common-sense inference. Our focus so far has been on the patterns of *default* inference, namely, on patterns of *deductive* inference that rely on *assumptions* which may be proven wrong. Yet, there are other common forms of inference which are also non-monotonic but which do not rely on defaults. Some of these inferences are called *abductive* [Pei55, CM85, Har86] and their purpose is to restore the coherence of a set of beliefs by seeking explanations for observed anomalies. Abductive inferences account for how a physician makes sense of the symptoms of a patient; how a technician makes sense of the measurements of a faulty circuit, and how people find motivations in the actions of other people. In this section we will take a closer look at this type of inferences and develop a framework for abductive reasoning which exploits the distinction between true and explained propositions in causal theories. We will also discuss a number of issues in abductive reasoning and compare the resulting account with other proposals in the literature.

For simplicity, we will deal with causal theories that comply with two conditions: first, all atoms are 'abnormalities' (i.e., all predicates are minimized), and second, the only formulas that involve C's are causal rules of the form:

$$\alpha_1 \wedge \cdots \wedge \alpha_n \wedge \neg\beta_1 \wedge \cdots \neg\beta_m \Rightarrow C\gamma$$

where α's, β's, and γ are atoms, $n \geq 0$ and $m \geq 0$, and variables are assumed to be universally quantified.[12] We will call the resulting theories *normal causal theories,* as most default theories of interest can be expressed in this form. Normal causal theories are thus a generalization of the class of simple causal theories studied in Section 5.7, where constraints (i.e., non-causal formulas) were required to be negative clauses, and causal rules were required to be 'open'. The penalty that we will pay for this generalization is that computing with normal causal theories will be harder than computing with simple causal theories. The additional expressive power is especially needed in abductive reasoning.

The semantics of *normal* causal theories can be simplified by replacing *classes* of models by *Herbrand models*. Indeed, if T is a normal causal theory, $\mathcal{C}_M$ will be a minimal class of T iff M is a minimal Herbrand model of the theory T' that results from T by stripping off all C's.[13] Also, an atom p will hold in $\mathcal{C}_M$ iff p holds in M, while p will be *explained* in $\mathcal{C}_M$ iff there is a rule instance

$$\alpha_1 \wedge \cdots \wedge \alpha_n \wedge \neg\beta_1 \wedge \cdots \neg\beta_m \Rightarrow Cp$$

in T whose body is satisfied in M.

[12] Considering a predicate p as 'abnormal' (i.e., minimizing p) has no effect on other predicates when p only occurs positively in the theory (i.e., as positive antecedent or head). Otherwise, the literals $\neg p(x)$ can be prevented from acting as default assumptions by introducing a new atom $q(x)$ incompatible with $p(x)$.

[13] Recall that $\mathcal{C}_M$ stands for the non-empty collection of models M' that sanction abnormalities from the set M only.

We will take advantage of these correspondences and talk about the preferred (Herbrand) *models* of a normal causal theory rather than about the preferred *classes* of models. We will also find useful to use C-rules of the form:

$$\gamma \leftarrow_c \alpha_1, \ldots, \alpha_n, \neg\beta_1, \ldots, \neg\beta_m$$

to express causal formulas:

$$\alpha_1 \wedge \cdots \wedge \alpha_n \wedge \neg\beta_1 \wedge \cdots \wedge \neg\beta_m \Rightarrow \mathrm{C}\gamma$$

and E-rules of the form:

$$\beta_1 \vee \cdots \vee \beta_m \leftarrow_e \alpha_1, \ldots, \alpha_n$$

to express non-causal formulas

$$\alpha_1 \wedge \cdots \wedge \alpha_n \Rightarrow \beta_1 \vee \cdots \vee \beta_m$$

in the *evidence set* (i.e., evidential statements).[14] When the same non-causal formulas occur in the *background context,* we will express them by means of K-rules:[15]

$$\beta_1 \vee \cdots \vee \beta_m \leftarrow_k \alpha_1, \ldots, \alpha_n$$

Since any classical formula can be expressed as a collection of clauses, any normal causal theory T with background K and evidence set E can be expressed as a collection of C, E, and K-rules. Examples of rules expressed in this form are:

$$\texttt{wet\_lawn}(t{+}1) \leftarrow_c \texttt{rain}(t), \texttt{uncovered}(t)$$
$$\texttt{covered}(t{+}1) \leftarrow_c \texttt{covered}(t), \neg\texttt{ab}_1(t)$$
$$\texttt{covered}(t) \vee \texttt{uncovered}(t) \leftarrow_k$$
$$\leftarrow_k \texttt{covered}(t), \texttt{uncovered}(t)$$
$$\texttt{rain}(1) \leftarrow_e$$
$$\texttt{covered}(0) \leftarrow_e$$

The first pair of rules encode explanations, the second pair encode background constraints, and the third pair encode observations.

[14]The C-rule and E-rule notation is from [Pea88a] (see Section 5.8).

[15]The distinction between E-rules and K-rules is needed for determining the closure of T (Sections 5.4 and 5.5). Likewise, K-rules like $p \leftarrow_k q$, unlike similar E-rules, make p explained when q is explained (this is not captured by our account; see footnote in page 99).

In addition to an underlying causal theory, an abductive theory involves *hypotheses* and *observations.* Roughly, the observations are the propositions that call for explanation, while the hypotheses are the propositions that we are willing to adopt for providing those explanations. The explanations, in turn, permit us to classify situations for the purpose of taking appropriate actions. In medical diagnosis, for example, *diseases* explain abnormal *symptoms* and permit a physician to select the right *therapy.*

We will denote the set of all possible hypotheses by $\mathcal{H}$, and the set of all possible observations by $\mathcal{O}$.[16] For the rules above, for example, we may select $\mathcal{H}$ to be given by the atoms rain(t) and covered(0), uncovered(0), and $\mathcal{O}$, by all other atoms. There is no need though for the sets $\mathcal{H}$ and $\mathcal{O}$ to be orthogonal or complementary, or for the hypotheses to be mutually exclusive or exhaustive.

When the the sets $\mathcal{H}$ and $\mathcal{O}$ of hypotheses and observations are not given, we will make the assumption that both are equal to the set of all ground atoms. This assumption will cause no harm because hypotheses and observations will be *ranked* and, *by default,* the ranks will be such that hypotheses in $\mathcal{H}$ will (almost) never be worth adopting, and observations in $\mathcal{O}$ will never be worth explaining.

Abductive reasoning consists in the adoption of *hypotheses* much like default reasoning consists in the adoption of *assumptions.* The *grounds* on which hypotheses are adopted, however, will be different from the grounds on which assumptions are adopted. Assumptions do not need justification; they are adopted as long no evidence suggests otherwise. Hypotheses, on the other hand, are adopted only for increasing the coherence of a set of beliefs by providing explanations for observed anomalies.

The criteria for selecting hypotheses will be made precise by means of the notion of *belief states.* A *belief state* $\mathcal{S} = \langle T, H \rangle$ will refer to the *hypothetical* context that results from adopting a consistent set of hypotheses H in a context $T = \langle K, E \rangle$. This hypothetical context, which we also denote as $T + H$, has the same background as T, and an evidence set E' given by the firm evidence E together with the *causal* formulas CH_i for the hypotheses H_i in H. The hypotheses are preceded with the operator C to indicate that by adopting an hypothesis H_i, H_i requires

[16] The observation vocabulary is from the abductive framework in [Kon90].

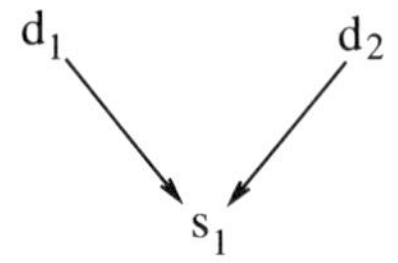

Figure 6.6
Simple causal network

no further explanation.

For example, the causal theory depicted in Figure 6.6, where $\mathcal{H}$ contains the 'diseases' d_i's, $\mathcal{O}$ contains the 'symptoms' s_i's, and each link $d_i \rightarrow s_j$ denotes the causal rule $s_j \leftarrow_c d_i$, the observation $s_1 \leftarrow_e$, gives rise to four belief states $\mathcal{S}_i = \langle T, H_i \rangle$, $i = 1, \ldots, n$, where $H_1 = \{d_1\}$, $H_2 = \{d_2\}$, $H_3 = \{d_1, d_2\}$, and $H_4 = \emptyset$. The first two states explain s_1, and the other two states leave s_1 unexplained.

Belief states $\mathcal{S}$ will be ranked by a scalar measure $Bel(\mathcal{S})$ which aims to reflect how *unlikely* the state $\mathcal{S}$ is; namely, the lower $Bel(\mathcal{S})$, the more likely the state $\mathcal{S}$, and the higher $Bel(\mathcal{S})$, the less likely the state $\mathcal{S}$. A belief state $\mathcal{S}$ is *preferred* to a belief state $\mathcal{S}'$ when $Bel(\mathcal{S}) < Bel(\mathcal{S}')$. $\mathcal{S}$ will be an *optimal* belief state when no state is preferred to $\mathcal{S}$. Multiple optimal belief states will be common because the ranks $Bel(\mathcal{S})$ will not be known with precision.

The rank $Bel(\mathcal{S})$ of a belief state $\mathcal{S} = \langle T, H \rangle$ will depend on two factors: how likely the hypotheses set H is, and how well H accounts for the observations. We will call the first factor the *prior ranking* of H and denote it by $\pi(H)$, and call the second one the *coherence* of $\mathcal{S}$, and denote it by $\lambda(\mathcal{S})$.[17] Our approach thus mimics probabilistic approaches, where the probability $P_K(E\&H)$ of $E + H$ is given the prior $P_K(H)$ of H and the likelihood ratio $P_K(E \mid H)/P(E)$. The reason we will not rely explicitly on probabilities is because the precision required does not appear to justify the effort of providing and computing with all the relevant numbers. Probabilistic languages like Bayesian Networks [Pea88b] have ameliorated this problem, but except for well-structured domains are not yet an alternative to logic-based languages.[18]

[17]The π and λ notation is borrowed from [Pea88b], where a similar notation is used for expressing prior and evidential support in Bayesian Networks.

[18]This does not mean that probability theory is not a good tool for *analysis* or good source of intuitions, but rather that it is not always a good *representation language*. A good representation language should embed the assumptions people find natural; yet, languages based on probabilities usually accommodate few of those assumptions

The parameters $\pi(H)$ and $\lambda(\mathcal{S})$ will be computed from the ranks $\pi(\mathrm{H}_i)$ corresponding to the *individual* hypotheses H_i in $\mathcal{H}$, and the ranks $\lambda(\mathrm{O}_i)$ corresponding to the *individual* observations O_i in $\mathcal{O}$ respectively.[19] The values of $\pi(\mathrm{H}_i)$ and $\lambda(\mathrm{O}_i)$ are either supplied by the user or are assumed by default. They intend to reflect the 'cost' of adopting the hypothesis H_i and the 'cost' of leaving the observation O_i unexplained, respectively. We will say more about the meaning and use of these parameters later on.

For the sake of convenience we will assume that the prior ranks $\pi(\mathrm{H}_i)$ corresponding to the individual hypotheses H_i in $\mathcal{H}$ all take values within the interval $I_1 = [1, 10] + \{\infty\}$. Moreover, we will assume that those ranks are equal to *infinity* unless otherwise specified (i.e., by default, the 'cost' of adopting an hypothesis will be very high). The ranking of *sets* of hypotheses set H will then be computed from the weighted sum:

$$\pi(H) = \sum_{j \in I_1} k_j * n_j(H)$$

where k_j's are multiplying weights, and $n_j(H)$ is the number of individual hypotheses H_i in H with a ranking $\pi(\mathrm{H}_i) = j$. We do *not* adopt the more standard aggregation rule:

$$\pi(H) = \sum_{\mathrm{H}_i \in H} \pi(\mathrm{H}_i)$$

or variations of it, because those rules are *too committed:* any two sets of hypotheses will either be equally ranked or one will be preferred to the other. In our formulation, the resulting ranking will only be *partially* specified. This will be accomplished by providing only *partial constraints* on the values of the weights k_j's:

[K.1] $k_j > 0$

[K.2] $k_{j-1} < k_j$

[K.3] $k_\infty > 1000 * k_j$, for $j \neq \infty$

Since we will seek to minimize $\pi(H)$, the first constraint says that, other things being equal, the fewer the hypotheses, the better. The second one says that lower ranked hypotheses are preferred to higher ranked

(e.g., Bayesian Networks), when they accommodate any assumption at all.

[19] This presumes hypotheses to be independent. Later on we will show how correlation effects can be accommodated.

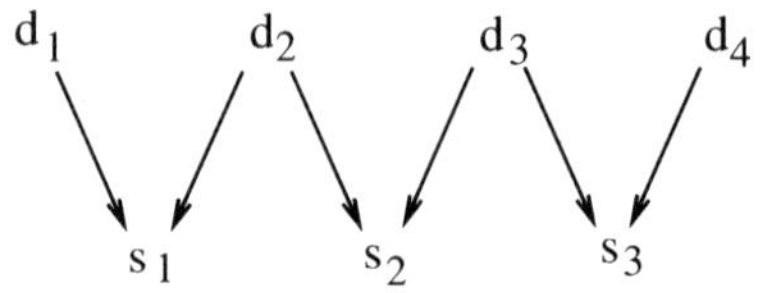

Figure 6.7
Computing prior support

hypotheses (it does *not* say though that *several* hypotheses of lower rank are preferred to a *single* hypotheses of higher rank, nor vice versa). Finally, the last constraint says that any combination of finitely ranked hypotheses will be preferred to any hypothesis with infinite rank (the number 1000 is arbitrary, any other very large number will do).[20]

For example, if the ranks of the 'diseases' $\mathtt{d}_i$ in Figure 6.7 are such that $\pi(\mathtt{d}_i) = i$, then the prior ranks corresponding to the (minimal) sets of hypotheses that explain *all* the 'symptoms' $\mathtt{s}_i$, $i = 1, 2, 3$ will be:

$$\pi(\{\mathtt{d}_1, \mathtt{d}_3\}) = k_1 + k_3 \;,\; \pi(\{\mathtt{d}_2, \mathtt{d}_3\}) = k_2 + k_3 \;,\; \pi(\{\mathtt{d}_2, \mathtt{d}_4\}) = k_2 + k_4$$

Since the constraint [K.2] tells us that $k_1 < k_2 < k_3 < k_4$, the hypotheses set $H_{1,3} = \{\mathtt{d}_1, \mathtt{d}_3\}$ has the minimal ranking and is thus preferred to both $H_{2,3}$ and $H_{2,4}$.

The second factor in determining the rank $Bel(\mathcal{S})$ of a belief state $\mathcal{S} = \langle T, H \rangle$ is the parameter $\lambda(S)$ which measures the *(in)coherence* of $\mathcal{S}$; i.e., how well the *observations* in the context $T + H$ are accounted for. For example, other things being equal, a state that explains why a patient has **high_temperature** will be more coherent than a state in which **high_temperature** is true but unexplained.

The parameter $\lambda(\mathcal{S})$ will be computed from the ranks $\lambda(\mathrm{O}_i)$ of the *unexplained* observations O_i in the state $\mathcal{S}$. These ranks intend to reflect how important it is to explain O_i when it is observed, or alternatively, how much evidential support accrues from explaining O_i in those situations. For example, in a medical application, explaining high-temperature is important but explaining why the temperature is exactly one hundred and four degrees is not. This will be captured by setting $\lambda(\mathtt{high\_temperature})$ high and $\lambda(\mathtt{temp} = 104^{\circ})$ low. The ranks $\lambda(\mathrm{O}_i)$ will be assumed to take values within the interval $I_0 = [0, 10] + \{\infty\}$

[20] Yet $k_\infty = \infty$ would not be good, because it would make several hypotheses with infinite ranks to be as preferred as a single hypothesis with the same rank.

and their default value will be *zero* (i.e., by default we don't care about explaining observations).

The coherence $\lambda(\mathcal{S})$ of a state $\mathcal{S} = \langle T, H\rangle$ will be given by the least coherent models in the set $\mathcal{M}$ of *preferred* models of $T + H$:[21]

$$\lambda(\mathcal{S}) = \max_{M \in \mathcal{M}} \lambda(M)$$

where the coherence of a model M is given by the weighted sum

$$\lambda(M) = \sum_{j \in I_0} k'_j * n'_j(M)$$

In analogy to prior rankings, k'_j's are multiplying weights and $n_j(H)$ is the number of observations O_i with rank $\lambda(\mathrm{O}_i) = j$ which are *unexplained* in M (recall that O_i is unexplained in a minimal model M if O_i is true in M but there is no instance $\mathrm{O}_i \leftarrow_c A$ of a C-rule in $T + H$ whose body A holds in M).[22]

The constraints on the evidential weights k'_j will be similar to those on the prior weights k_j:

$[\mathrm{K}'_1]$ $k'_j > 0$, if $j > 0$

$[\mathrm{K}'_2]$ $k'_{j-1} < k_j$

$[\mathrm{K}'_3]$ $k'_\infty = \infty$

$[\mathrm{K}'_4]$ $k'_0 = 0$

The first constraint says that it pays to explain observations which have ranks greater than zero. The second one says that, other things being equal, it is preferable to explain an observation with rank j than an observation with rank $j-1$. The third constraint says that observations with infinite ranks *must* be explained.[23] The last constraint makes observations with zero rank 'don't care's: they will never trigger an hypothesis.

[21] Both $\lambda(\mathcal{S})$ and $\lambda(M)$ are actually measures of *in*coherence; i.e., the smaller the value of $\lambda(\mathcal{S})$ and $\lambda(M)$, the more coherent the state $\mathcal{S}$ and the model M, respectively.

[22] The choice of the *least* coherent models in $\mathcal{M}$ as opposed to the *most* coherent ones (or some other combination) gives the resulting account a conservative bias. For example, given a disjunction $\mathrm{O}_1 \vee \mathrm{O}_2$, where O_1 is an observation that we care to explain (i.e., $\lambda(\mathrm{O}_1)$ is high), and O_2 is an observation that we don't care to explain (i.e., $\lambda(\mathrm{O}_2)$ is low), we will assume the 'worst' scenario and thus look for an explanation for either O_1 or O_2. On the other hand, if we had chosen the most coherent models in the definition of $\lambda(\mathcal{S})$, the disjunction $\mathrm{O}_1 \vee \mathrm{O}_2$ would be treated as the low ranked observation O_2, and thus, no explanations will be sought.

[23] We assume that $k'_\infty * n$ is equal to infinity if $n \neq 0$, and zero otherwise.

For example, in the theory above (Fig. 6.7), if each of the observations $\mathtt{s}_i$, $i = 1, \ldots, 3$, has a rank $\lambda(\mathtt{s}_i) = \infty$, the (in)coherence of a state will be zero, if all observations are explained, and infinite otherwise. Thus, the hypotheses will have to be sought among those which explain all the observations. On the other hand, if $\lambda(\mathtt{s3}) = 0$, explaining $\mathtt{s3}$ will make no difference, and thus, the hypothesis $\mathtt{d2}$ which explains both $\mathtt{s1}$ and $\mathtt{s2}$ will be preferred. In general, when the value of the evidential ranks $\lambda(\mathrm{O}_j)$ is neither zero or infinity, the hypotheses sets H that are 'optimal' will result from a trade-off between the prior ranks of H and the coherence of the state that results from adopting H.

Formally, the rank $Bel(\mathcal{S})$ of a belief state $\mathcal{S} = \langle T, H\rangle$ is defined as:

$$Bel(\mathcal{S}) \stackrel{\text{def}}{=} \lambda(\mathcal{S}) + \pi(H)$$

where $\pi(H)$ stands for prior ranking of H and $\lambda(\mathcal{S})$ stands for the coherence of $\mathcal{S}$. Small ranks indicate more likely states. Like in probabilities, the measure $Bel(\mathcal{S})$ is given by two terms: $\lambda(\mathcal{S})$, which captures *evidential support,* and $\pi(H)$, which captures *prior support.* Unlike probabilities, however, these terms are determined by fewer parameters and more assumptions.[24]

To accommodate tradeoffs between the prior and evidential sources of support we will assume that the prior and evidential weights k_i and k'_j are related by the inequality:

$$n * k_i < k'_i, \text{ for all } i \in I_1 = [1, 10] + \{\infty\}$$

where n is some large number. Thus, while we will be able to explain a high ranked (i.e., important) observations in terms of either low or high ranked hypotheses, we will only be able to explain low ranked observations in terms of low ranked hypotheses. For example, if T is given by a single causal rule $\mathrm{O} \leftarrow_c \mathrm{H}_1, \mathrm{H}_2$, and O is observed, the belief state $\mathcal{S}_H = \langle T, \{\mathrm{H}_1, \mathrm{H}_2\}\rangle$ that results from adopting the hypotheses H_1 and H_2 will be preferred to the belief state $\mathcal{S}_0 = \langle T, \emptyset\rangle$ that results from adopting no hypothesis (i.e., $Bel(\mathcal{S}_H) < Bel(\mathcal{S}_0)$), if the rank $\lambda(\mathrm{O})$ is higher than both $\pi(\mathrm{H}_1)$ and $\pi(\mathrm{H}_2)$. Otherwise, the state with lower rank will be undetermined and both states would be equally preferred (a state $\mathcal{S}$ is preferred to a state $\mathcal{S}'$ only if its rank is lower).

[24]It may be right to say that the proposed framework does not aim to provide a language for modeling uncertainty in the world, but a representation language for modeling uncertainty in the 'user's head'.

The *optimal belief states* in an abductive theory $A = \langle T, \mathcal{H}, \mathcal{O}\rangle$, where T is a causal theory, $\mathcal{H}$ is a ranked set of hypotheses, and $\mathcal{O}$ is a ranked set of observations, will then be simply the states $\mathcal{S}$ with minimal ranks $Bel(\mathcal{S})$. We will refer to the optimal belief states $\mathcal{S} = \langle T, H\rangle$ as *admissible states,* and to the hypotheses sets H as *admissible hypotheses sets.* The optimal belief states aim to reflect the plausible scenarios that a rational agent with the information in T may consider.[25] We will also say that p is an *abductive* conclusion in the abductive theory A if p holds in all optimal belief states, and that p is *evidentially supported* if p holds in some optimal state. We assume that p does not hold in T, though.

We will illustrate these definitions with the scenario depicted in Figure 6.6. The scenario involves two diseases $\mathtt{d_1}$ and $\mathtt{d_2}$ and a symptom $\mathtt{s_1}$:

$$\mathtt{s_1} \leftarrow_c \mathtt{d_1}$$
$$\mathtt{s_1} \leftarrow_c \mathtt{d_2}$$
$$\mathtt{s_1} \leftarrow_e$$

That is to say, $\mathtt{s_1}$ has been observed and $\mathtt{d_1}$ and $\mathtt{d_2}$ are two possible causes of it. Since symptoms usually call for explanation we will choose a high value for $\lambda(\mathtt{s_1}) = \lambda_1$, and similarly, since we are willing to hypothesize diseases in order to explain symptoms, we will choose a low value for $\pi(\mathtt{d_1}) = \pi_1$ and $\pi(\mathtt{d_2}) = \pi_2$. There are three belief states $\mathcal{S}_i = \langle T, H_i\rangle$ to consider, where $H_1 = \{\mathtt{d_1}\}$, $H_2 = \{\mathtt{d_2}\}$ and $H_3 = \emptyset$, whose ranks are:

$$Bel(\mathcal{S}_1) = k_{\pi_1} \ , \ Bel(\mathcal{S}_2) = k_{\pi_2} \ , \ Bel(\mathcal{S}_3) = k'_{\lambda_1}$$

From the assumptions about the values π_1, π_2 and λ_1, i.e., $\pi_1 < \lambda_1$ and $\pi_2 < \lambda_1$, and from the relation between the prior and evidential weights k_j's and k'_j's, it follows that $\mathcal{S}_1$ and $\mathcal{S}_2$ are preferred to $\mathcal{S}_3$, and thus that H_1 and H_2 are the only admissible hypotheses sets. If, in addition, π_1 is smaller than π_2, only H_1 would be admissible, because $Bel(\mathcal{S}_1)$ would be smaller than $Bel(\mathcal{S}_2)$.

We will consider now variations of this example that illustrate how this framework accommodates some of the features characteristic of proba-

[25] Obviously, if there are *utilities* involved, less plausible belief states may have to be considered as well (as in the example in [LS89], where the decision is whether to drop Tweety off a cliff). (see Section 7.3)

bilistic approaches (e.g., strength of the evidence, different priors, correlations, explaining away, etc.).

The meaning of λ. The parameters $\lambda(O_i)$ are a measure of how important it is to explain the evidence O_i once it is observed: if $\lambda(O_i)$ is low, only likely hypotheses will be triggered; if $\lambda(O_i)$ is high, any hypothesis which can explain O_i will be triggered. In the example above, we assumed λ_1 high and π_1 and π_2 low, so once s_1 is observed, one of the hypotheses d_1 or d_2 is adopted.

If we had chosen $\lambda_1 < \pi_1$ and $\lambda_1 < \pi_2$ instead, the state in which s_1 is left without explanation would no longer be less preferred than the states in which s_1 is explained by either d_1 or d_2 (because neither k_{π_1} or k_{π_2} would be smaller than k'_{λ_1}). Intuitively, this should happen when the causal model is known to be *incomplete,* either because s_1 often arises with no apparent reason, or because there are explanations for s_1 which are as good as or better than d_1 and d_2 but which have not been made explicit in the theory. This suggests that the value $\lambda(O)$ for an observation O is in relation to the probabilistic ratio $P(O)/P(H^*)$, where $P(O)$ is the prior of O, and $P(H^*)$ is the probability of the best explanation for O *which is not in the model.* In other words, the less surprising the observation or the more incomplete the model, the smaller $\lambda(O)$, and therefore, the smaller the evidential support that will result from explaining O.[26]

π's and λ's. The behavior above can also be captured by regarding s_1 as an *hypothesis* with a rank comparable to the ranks of d_1 and d_2. Indeed, most abductive frameworks do not rank observations but only hypotheses (e.g., [Gel89b]). This approach may work in many cases but it obscures the meaning of the parameters $\pi(H)$. Indeed, since the prior probability of s_1 has to be greater than the prior probabilities of d_1 and d_2 (because both d_1 and d_2 imply s_1), we could either no longer associate the rank $\pi(H)$ with the prior of H, or we could never hypothesize d_1 or d_2 to explain s_1 (because $\pi(s_1)$ would be smaller than both $\pi(d_1)$ and $\pi(d_2)$).

Uncertain relations. If the relations between the diseases d_1 and d_2

---

[26]Charniak and Shimony [CS90] draw a similar interpretation of the parameters used in the abductive scheme of Hobbs *et al.* [HSME88].

and the symptom s_1 is expressed by means of *defaults* rules:

$$s_1 \leftarrow_c d_1, \neg ab_1$$
$$s_2 \leftarrow_c d_2, \neg ab_2$$

the same results would follow. The only difference would be that each of the states $\mathcal{S}_i$ would give rise to more *minimal* models. However, the *preferred* models and, therefore, the coherence and rank of each state $\mathcal{S}_i$ would remain the same.

More interesting are relations that are neither strict nor defeasible but simply *uncertain,* like 'smoke causes cancer'. Although we do not want to predict 'cancer' given 'smoke', we still want the latter to be evidence for the former. As it has been suggested in various places (e.g., [LL89]), these uncertain relations can be represented by means of auxiliary hypotheses. 'Smoke causes cancer', for example, can be represented by the rule

$$\texttt{cancer} \leftarrow_c \texttt{smoke}, h_1$$

where h_1 is an auxiliary hypothesis. Then the observation $\texttt{cancer} \leftarrow_e$ would provide evidential support for `smoke` and h_1, because the hypothesis set $H = \{\texttt{smoke}, h_1\}$ would be admissible.

Since uncertain relations are common, we will find it useful to abbreviate them as in

$$\texttt{cancer} \leftarrow_c \texttt{smoke} \ [\texttt{j}]$$

where `j` is the rank of the auxiliary hypothesis h_1, which can now be omitted.

Correlations. The problem with encoding uncertain relations by means of auxiliary hypotheses is that these hypotheses are not necessarily independent (e.g., see [Pea89b]). We therefore need a means for expressing correlations. Recall first that two hypotheses H_1 and H_2 are said to be positively (resp. negatively) correlated when their joint probability $P(H_1, H_2)$ is larger (resp. smaller) than the product of their marginal probabilities $P(H_1)$ and $P(H_2)$. Obvious cases of correlations arise when one hypothesis or its negation is a deductive or defeasible consequence of the other hypothesis. These correlations can be represented in our framework in an straightforward way (e.g., as $H_2 \leftarrow_c H_1$). We will examine the more interesting cases where the correlations are not so clear cut.

First, let us consider the case of two hypotheses H_1 and H_2 which are *positively* correlated and for which $\pi(\mathrm{H}_1) \leq \pi(\mathrm{H}_2)$. The correlation between H_1 and H_2 can then be represented by means of an auxiliary hypothesis H'_2 whose rank $\pi(\mathrm{H}'_2)$ is smaller than $\pi(\mathrm{H}_2)$ and which together with H_1 explains H_2:

$$\mathrm{H}_2 \leftarrow_c \mathrm{H}_1, \mathrm{H}'_2$$

Since the states that result from adopting H_1 and H'_2 are identical to the states that result from adopting H_1 and H_2 (except for H'_2) but have smaller rank, the net effect of this rule is to decrease the joint rank of $\mathrm{H}_1 + \mathrm{H}_2$, correctly reflecting the positive correlation between H_1 and H_2.

The case of negative correlations can be handled in an analogous way. When H_1 and H_2 are *negatively* correlated, we want the states that result from adopting H_1 and H_2 to have a higher rank than when H_1 and H_2 are independent. This can be captured by means of an auxiliary *observation* O' which is *evidentially* introduced when both H_1 and H_2 hold:

$$\mathrm{O}' \leftarrow_e \mathrm{H}_1, \mathrm{H}_2$$

Then if $\lambda(\mathrm{O}') = \lambda\ (\neq 0)$, the states in which *both* H_1 and H_2 hold will have their rank increased by the positive amount k'_λ (because the observation O' is true but is not explained). Notice that the ability to express this type of information is made possible by the distinction between causal and evidential rules. We will illustrate later on other cases in which such a distinction is crucial.

Explaining Away. Let us consider the following causal model T describing some diseases $\mathtt{d}_i$ and some symptoms $\mathtt{s}_j$:

$$r_1 : \mathtt{s}_1 \leftarrow_c \mathtt{d}_1 \ [4]$$
$$r_2 : \mathtt{s}_1 \leftarrow_c \mathtt{d}_2 \ [5]$$
$$r_3 : \mathtt{s}_2 \leftarrow_c \mathtt{d}_2 \ [6]$$

The numbers in square brackets are the ranks of the auxiliary hypotheses that have been omitted (see above). Let us also assume that the ranks for the symptoms and diseases are as follows:

$$\pi(\mathtt{d}_1) = 3 \ , \ \pi(\mathtt{d}_2) = 2 \ , \ \lambda(\mathtt{s}_1) = 7 \ , \ \lambda(\mathtt{s}_2) = 8$$

Then if we observe $\mathtt{s}_1$ (i.e., $\mathtt{s}_1 \leftarrow_c$), two hypotheses sets would be admissible: $H_1 = \{\mathtt{d}_1, h_1\}$ and $H_2 = \{\mathtt{d}_2, h_2\}$, where h_1 and h_2 are the auxiliary hypotheses in rules r_1 and r_2 respectively. Indeed, the ranks of the belief states are:

$$Bel(\langle T, H_1\rangle) = k_3 + k_4\ ,\ Bel(\langle T, H_2\rangle) = k_2 + k_5\ ,\ Bel(\langle T, \emptyset\rangle) = k'_7$$

and since $k_{i-1} < k_i$ and $n * k_i < k'_i$, $Bel(\langle T, H_1\rangle) < Bel(\langle T, \emptyset\rangle)$ and $Bel(\langle T, H_2\rangle) < Bel(\langle T, \emptyset\rangle)$. The result is that the observation $\mathtt{s}_1$ provides evidential support for both $\mathtt{d}_1$ and $\mathtt{d}_2$.

If $\mathtt{s}_2$ is also observed, the evidential support shifts from $\mathtt{d}_1$ to $\mathtt{d}_2$. This is because $\mathtt{d}_2$ can explain $\mathtt{s}_2$ while $\mathtt{d}_1$ cannot ($H'_2 = \{\mathtt{d}_2, h_2, h_3\}$ becomes the single admissible hypotheses set). The effect of $\mathtt{s}_2$ is thus to increase the support for $\mathtt{d}_2$ who now *explains away* the symptom $\mathtt{s}_1$ and hence removes the support for the other possible cause of $\mathtt{s}_1$, $\mathtt{d}_1$ [Pea88b].

Wellman and Henrion [WH91] noted recently that this pattern of interaction among different causes of a single observation is not universal. There are conditions in which an increase in support for one of the possible causes of an observation does not translate into a decrease in support for the other possible causes. For example, if $\mathtt{d}_1$ and $\mathtt{d}_2$ *together* provide a better explanation for $\mathtt{s}_1$ than each one alone, e.g.,

$$r_4 : \mathtt{s}_1 \leftarrow \mathtt{d}_1, \mathtt{d}_2\ [3]$$

the observation of $\mathtt{s}_2$ would still increase the support for $\mathtt{d}_2$ (which would hold in all admissible belief states), but this increase in support would no longer translate into a decrease of support for the 'competing' cause of $\mathtt{s}_1$, $\mathtt{d}_1$ (which would still hold in one admissible belief state with hypotheses $\mathtt{d}_1$, $\mathtt{d}_2$, h_3, and h_4). This apparent violation of the 'explain away' principle can itself be explained if we assume that the causes for $\mathtt{s}_1$ are not two but *three;* i.e., $\mathtt{d}_1$, $\mathtt{d}_2$ *and* $\mathtt{d}_1 \wedge \mathtt{d}_2$. From such a perspective, it is clear that an increase in support for the last cause cannot translate into a decrease of support for any of the other two 'competing' causes.

Special Cases. Abduction is sometimes construed as the search for hypotheses that explain a given observation O (e.g., [Poo87]). In our terms this corresponds to the special case in which O is the single observation that we care to explain, and can be captured by means of a single evidential parameter $\lambda(\mathrm{O})$ whose value is set to infinity. More generally, in an abductive theory whose only evidential ranks $\lambda(O_i)$ are infinite, the resulting belief states will be either *completely coherent,* if they explain all observations, and *completely incoherent* otherwise. The result is that abduction in those theories reduces to finding hypotheses that explain the observations. Moreover, if all the hypotheses have the same prior rank, the resulting account is similar to *minimal cardinality abduction* (i.e., hypotheses sets with minimum cardinality are preferred), while if the prior ranks are not known, the result is similar to *minimal set abduction* (i.e., hypotheses sets which are minimal are preferred) (see [PR90] for a discussion of these and other forms of abduction). Furthermore, if the only non-causal rules in the underlying theory are of the form $O_i \leftarrow_e$, for observations O_i, $i = 1, \ldots, n$, an hypotheses set H would provide a minimal explanation for the observations iff $H + \cup_{i=1,n} O_i$ is a minimal model of the *completed* theory.[27]

On the other hand, when there are *no causal rules,* the result turns out to be similar to what is usually called *consistency-based diagnosis.* In fact, when there are *no causal rules,* the only way for explaining an 'observation' O is by adopting the 'hypothesis' O. So, if T represents a circuit, and the 'abnormality' atoms $\mathtt{ab}_i(a)$ used for representing the 'normal' behavior of components (see [Rei87b]) are chosen as both 'observations' (with infinite λ's) and hypotheses,[28] the sets H of 'abnormalities' that render the theory consistent with all other normality assumptions $\neg\mathtt{ab}_i(a)$ for $\mathtt{ab}_i(a) \notin H$ would correspond exactly to the hypotheses sets H that make the state $\langle T, H\rangle$ completely coherent. The different variations discussed above can be accommodated by suitable selection of the prior ranks (e.g., if all prior ranks are equal, then the result is minimal cardinality consistency-based diagnosis, and so on).

Abduction and Priorities. In causal theories in which the sets $\mathcal{H}$ and $\mathcal{O}$ of hypotheses and observations are identified with the set of abnormalities $\mathtt{ab}_i(a)$, prior ranks $\pi(\mathrm{H})$ on hypotheses play a role similar to *priorities* among assumptions. For example, in the theory T

$$\mathtt{invited}(x) \leftarrow_c \mathtt{friend}(x), \neg\mathtt{ab}_1(x)$$

[27]If the causal rules are either propositional or do not contain function symbols, the 'completed' theory is the theory that results from extending each causal rule $q \leftarrow_c p_1, \ldots, p_n$ with its 'inverse' $p_1 \vee \cdots \vee p_n \leftarrow_e q$. See [Kau87] and [CDT89] for more details on this approach.

[28]Observations here mean the formulas in the set $\mathcal{O}$; the observations in diagnostic applications normally refer to measurements.

$$\texttt{attend}(x) \leftarrow_c \texttt{invited(x)}, \neg\texttt{ab}_2(x)$$

$$\texttt{friend(tom)} \leftarrow_e$$

$$\leftarrow_e \texttt{attend(tom)}$$

with $\pi(\texttt{ab}_2(x)) > \pi(\texttt{ab}_1(x))$, the hypothesis $\texttt{ab}_2\texttt{(tom)}$ would be preferred to $\texttt{ab}_1\texttt{(tom)}$, and thus both the assumption $\neg\texttt{ab}_1\texttt{(tom)}$ and the proposition invited(tom) will hold in the single optimal state. The result is similar to the one obtained from assuming the priority of the default $\texttt{friend}(x) \rightarrow \texttt{invited}(x)$ to be higher than the priority of the default $\texttt{invited}(x) \rightarrow \texttt{attend}(x)$.

Proving vs. Explaining. Our final example is from [Kon90] (see also [Pea88a]). The background is given by the causal rules:

$$\texttt{wet\_lawn}(t+1) \leftarrow_c \texttt{rain}(t), \texttt{uncovered}(t)$$

$$\texttt{wet\_lawn}(t+1) \leftarrow_c \texttt{wet\_lawn}(t), \neg\texttt{ab}_1(t)$$

$$\texttt{dry\_lawn}(t+1) \leftarrow_c \texttt{dry\_lawn}(t), \neg\texttt{ab}_2(t)$$

$$\texttt{covered}(t+1) \leftarrow_c \texttt{covered}(t), \neg\texttt{ab}_3(t)$$

$$\texttt{uncovered}(t+1) \leftarrow_c \texttt{uncoveredt}, \neg\texttt{ab}_4(t)$$

and the constraints $\texttt{uncovered}(t) \equiv \neg\texttt{covered}(t)$ and $\texttt{wet\_lawn}(t) \equiv \neg\texttt{dry\_lawn}(t)$ expressed as the following K-rules:

$$\texttt{covered}(t) \vee \texttt{uncovered}(t) \leftarrow_k$$

$$\texttt{dry\_lawn}(t) \vee \texttt{wet\_lawn}(t) \leftarrow_k$$

$$\leftarrow_k \texttt{covered}(t), \texttt{uncovered}(t)$$

$$\leftarrow_k \texttt{dry\_lawn}(t), \texttt{uncovered}(t)$$

We will assume that the set of possible hypotheses $\mathcal{H}$ is given by the atom $\texttt{rain}(t)$, for any t, and the fluents $\texttt{wet\_lawn}(t)$, $\texttt{dry\_lawn}(t)$, $\texttt{covered}(t)$, and $\texttt{uncovered}(t)$ for $t = 0$. For $t \neq 0$, the same fluents and all the abnormalities comprise the set $\mathcal{O}$ of possible observations. To simplify matters, we will also assume that all evidential ranks $\lambda(\mathrm{O})$, for $\mathrm{O} \in \mathcal{O}$, are infinite (i.e., all observations *must* be explained).
In this context, the evidence

$$\texttt{rain(1)} \leftarrow_e \ , \ \texttt{dry\_lawn(0)} \leftarrow_e \ , \ \texttt{wet\_lawn(2)} \leftarrow_e$$

yields a single admissible state with hypotheses $H = \{\texttt{uncovered(0)}\}$. If the evidence is:

$$\texttt{rain(1)} \leftarrow_e \quad , \quad \texttt{covered(1)} \leftarrow_e$$

the single admissible hypotheses set becomes $H = \{\texttt{covered(0)}\}$. As Konolige notes, if explanations for a proposition p are construed as arguments for p (rather than as arguments for Cp, as in causal theories), the hypotheses set $H' = \{\texttt{dry\_lawn(0)}\}$ would also be admissible in this last scenario. Indeed, from dry_lawn(0) and the persistence assumptions $\neg\texttt{ab}_2\texttt{(0)}$ and $\neg\texttt{ab}_2\texttt{(1)}$, we can derive the atom dry_lawn(2), and using the constraints and the contrapositive of the 'rain' rule, we can also derive covered(1). This explanation, however, is not causal. Konolige proposes to prune those explanations by disallowing the contraposition of causal rules. Within the framework of causal theories the approach is different: causal rules are not weaker than non-causal rules but stronger; their antecedents allow us both to establish their consequents and to explain them. And since the contraposition of a causal rule is *not* a causal rule, the hypotheses set H' makes covered(1) true, but does not explain it; so H' is not admissible.

7 Conclusion

7.1 Summary

We have addressed the linguistic, semantic, and computational issues involved in representing and reasoning with defaults. The result is an architecture in which defeasible knowledge can be encoded in a natural way, and which does well in capturing the intuitions of the user, both in terms of *what* conclusions are sanctioned and *how* they are obtained.

For *representing* defaults we have found two distinctions essential. The distinction between *background* and *evidence* was used to derive q from $p \rightarrow q$ when p represents all the *evidence*, and to explain the violation of defaults $p' \rightarrow q'$ whose consequents are incompatible with q *given the background constraints.* Similarly, the distinction between *causal* and *evidential* relations was used for determining which default violations are *explained* and thus, what the *intended* models of a set of defaults are.

For analyzing the *semantics* of defaults, we turned to both probabilities and models, and showed that the same inferences are sanctioned by interpreting a default $p \rightarrow q$ as stating that the *probability of q is high given p* or that *q is true in the preferred models of p.* The same inferences are also captured by the system of five rules of inference which we called the *core.*

The virtues and limitation of these *conditional* interpretations of defaults are orthogonal to those of the standard, *extensional* interpretations, in which defaults are prescriptions for extending one's set of beliefs. The former capture arguments of *specificity* (e.g., 'penguins don't fly in spite of being birds') and the latter, arguments of *irrelevance* (e.g., concluding '*red* birds fly' from 'birds fly'). The two interpretations were then combined, first, by extending the core with an *irrelevance rule* to derive assumptions of independence, and then, by restricting the orderings on models compatible with a set of defaults. We showed that the first approach was an approximation of the second approach, called *conditional entailment.* In conditional entailment the preferences on models are derived from *priorities* among the defaults which in turn are extracted from the information in the knowledge base. Conditional entailment can be characterized proof-theoretically in terms of interacting *arguments,* and we took advantage of this characterization for exploring an implementation of conditional entailment in terms of an assumption-based truth system.

Since conditional entailment provides a precise specification of the behavior that can be expected from defaults when only *minimality* and *conditionality* considerations are taken into account, examples which are not handled correctly by conditional entailment point to the necessity of taking other aspects of defaults into consideration rather than to tinker further with priorities or irrelevance rules.

That is what we did when we addressed the *causal* aspects of defaults by introducing *causal default theories* in which *explanatory* and *evidential* relations are distinguished. We developed a semantics for causal theories based on model-preference, a proof-theory based on arguments, and different architectures. We also discussed the application of causal theories to logic programs with negation as failure, inheritance hierarchies, theories for reasoning about change, and abductive reasoning.

The *architectures* for causal theories consist of restrictions on the formulas that can be expressed and the inferences that aim to be captured, and of procedures that exploit those restrictions. These procedures have many elements in common with the algorithms used in logic programs with negation as failure, truth-maintenance systems, argument systems, and inheritance hierarchies.

7.2 Loose Ends

There are some relevant problems which have not received a satisfactory treatment in this work. I will discuss these problems briefly.

Causal and Conditional Preferences. In Chapters 2, 3 and 4 we addressed the conditional aspects of defaults and accounted for them by means of a priority ordering on defaults. In Chapter 5 we discussed the causal aspects of defaults and accounted for them by means of causal default theories. The two accounts were combined by allowing priorities in causal theories. This solution is adequate for most practical purposes but it is *not* adequate from a formal point of view: the priorities in causal default theories are not interpreted in the same way as in regular default theories, and thus, causal entailment is not an extension of conditional entailment (Section 5.5). The question then is how *global* priorities among assumptions (as in conditional entailment and circumscription) can be accommodated in the framework of causal theories. This question needs to be addressed at three levels: the semantics of causal theories, the proof-theory, and the inference procedures.

Architectures. Procedures like Π_1 developed for causal theories remain too abstract and their optimal implementation is yet to be worked out. It would be desirable to explore the scope of procedures like Π_1^- and Π_2 which simplify Π_1 and can be implemented more easily. There are also variations of these procedures that seem worth exploring, such as a 'credulous' version of Π_1 aimed at computing propositions that hold in *one* preferred model as opposed to all of them (like TMSs), and versions able to accommodate disjunctive heads and disjunctive forms of reasoning (in accordance with the results in Section 5.7).

Abduction. There are a number of unanswered questions with regard to the abductive framework developed in Section 6.4. First of all, we only sketched the probabilistic interpretation of the π and λ parameters used, but we did not provide a detailed account. It would also be interesting to test the suitability of the framework vis-a-vis Bayesian and non-Bayesian approaches in commonsense domains like language comprehension [CG89, HSME88]. In particular, it would be useful to assess the merits and limitations of producing *likelihood judgements* in terms of the ranking on belief states (e.g., p is very likely if p holds in all preferred belief states; p is likely if it holds in some preferred belief state, and so on). For any of this, however, we need suitable *procedures.* Sound and complete procedures are bound to be very expensive and it seems worth exploring approximations as we did for causal theories.

7.3 Open Problems

Two related problems that I haven't addressed at all in this work are the *projection* problem in reasoning about change, and the *utility* problem in planning. Both problems have been addressed in the literature but the solutions that have been proposed so far are not entirely compelling.

The Projection Problem

Consider the following story in relation to the frame problem:[1]

> Eloise glances at her window and sees Abelard standing in the courtyard, wearing a hat, leaning against the chestnut tree and speaking to her father ... Soon one of her brothers enters and tells her that Abelard has departed. Now Eloise has to reasses her beliefs. Minimally, she must delete her belief that Abelard is in the courtyard. But what of his hat? ...

Intuitively, if Abelard left and he was wearing a hat, he must have left with his hat on, and therefore, it is natural to conclude that the hat is no longer in the courtyard. However, the hat *was* in the courtyard, and there is no explicit information in conflict with the assumption that it *remained* in the courtyard. Thus, if the location of the hat is regarded as a fluent (namely, a time or situation dependent property [MH69, McD82]), and the persistence of fluents is assumed by default, we would be led to the counterintuitive conclusion that the hat remained in the courtyard. On the other hand, if we do *not* regard the location of the hat as a persistent fluent, we wouldn't be able to predict the location of the hat if Abelard had dropped it in the courtyard.

The *projection problem* — to be distinguished from the more general problem of temporal projection or prediction (e.g., [HM87]) — is the problem of identifying the fluents which can be assumed to persist by default in a given context. In the scenario above, Abelard's location is a projectible fluent, but the location of the the hat is not. We will call the fluents which can be assumed to persist by default, the *projectible* fluents.

The proposals in the literature regarding the projection problem range from those which assume that the projectible fluents have been identified by the user (e.g., [McD82, KS86]), to those in which persistence defaults contain appropriate censors (e.g., [MS88b]). Some approaches determine the projectibility of a fluent by its (explicit) appearance in the context in question (e.g., [GS88]), while others assume all fluents to be equally projectible (e.g., [Win88]). None of these proposals, however, seems to address the projection problem in its full generality as *the problem of*

[1] The story is from [Mal88]. For the the frame problem see [MH69].

identifying the independent fluents in a given context. For instance, $\texttt{above}(\texttt{a},\texttt{b})$ is projectible in a context which does not contain other information, but is not projectible in a context in which both $\texttt{on}(\texttt{a},\texttt{c})$ and $\texttt{on}(\texttt{c},\texttt{b})$ hold. Similarly, $\neg\texttt{on}(\texttt{a},\texttt{table})$ is projectible if alone, but is not projectible when augmented with the fluent $\texttt{on}(\texttt{a},\texttt{c})$. In each case, we need to conjecture what *depends* on what and project only what we regard as *independent*. The projection problem is the problem of elucidating the nature and logic of these conjectures.

The Utility Problem

The framework developed in this book aims to provide an account of how people reason with defaults and how machines ought to do so. Yet, people do not only reason but they also *act*. Moreover, when we reason about which actions to perform we are not only influenced by what is *likely,* but also about what is *desirable* and/or *difficult.* For example, if the lights in the car don't light up, we would certainly try to turn the ignition key even though it is unlikely that the car will start. Although the chances are low, the payoff is high and the difficulty of trying it out is negligible.

The trade-offs between actions, chances and payoffs have been studied thoroughly in decision theory (e.g., [Jef83]) and the importance of dealing with these trade-offs in AI have been lately emphasized by a number of authors [HBH88, Doy90, Wel90, LS89, Kle89]. Insofar as these proposals rely on probabilities for modeling beliefs and utilities for modeling preferences, they are subject to the same criticism that motivated this work: probabilistic languages as well as utility functions do not embed the assumptions common in everyday discourse and thus do not provide a framework in which knowledge can be represented in a natural (i.e., modular, incremental, purpose-free) way.[2]

For example, consider the following scenarios (from [Wil83]):

1. John wanted to read the newspaper. Since it was raining, he took his raincoat and left.
2. John was in a hurry to get to Las Vegas but noticed that there were a lot of cops around, so he stuck to the speed limit.

[2]Some of these same points have been raised by Breese *et al.* [BGW91], who intend to develop better representation languages from which the relevant decision models could be derived.

3. John's wife called him and told him that they were all out of milk. He decided to pick up some on his way home from work.

All these scenarios are about trade-offs involving probabilities and preferences. However, the representation in terms of the standard decision-theoretic models is likely to look awkward. Let's take a look at the first example. First, we would have to provide utilities for the different states: e.g., being wet with a newspaper, being dry without the newspaper, being less wet with both the raincoat and the newspaper, and so on. Then we would have to provide the necessary probabilities: e.g., the prior chances of being dry, the chances that John will actually get the newspaper, and so on.

It seems that a better representation framework for this type of inferences could be obtained by modifying the architecture for abductive reasoning developed in Section 6.4. For example, variations of the classical planning paradigm, in which there are no preferences but just goals (i.e., states to be achieved), can be captured by mapping goals G_i into *evidential* rules of the form $G_i \leftarrow_e$, and actions A_j into *hypotheses.* If the result of the actions A_j are encoded by means of *causal* rules, the most *coherent* states will be the states in which the actions achieve the goals (i.e., where the 'hypotheses' explain all the 'observations'). Moreover, context-dependent goals could be accommodated by means by evidential rules $G_i \leftarrow_e B$, while trade-offs among goals could be represented by suitable parameters π and λ which would stand for the costs of actions and the preferences among goals.

A different use of the same architecture may permit the representation of *preferences* and not just *goals* (e.g., it is preferable to be dry than wet unless otherwise specified). For example, if $\mathtt{good_1}$, $\mathtt{good_2}$, ..., $\mathtt{good_n}$, and $\mathtt{bad_1}$, $\mathtt{bad_2}$, ..., $\mathtt{bad_n}$ are special 'observations' such that the 'penalties' for failing to explain them are $\lambda(\mathtt{good}_i) = -i$ and $\lambda(\mathtt{bad}_i) = i$, we could then express statements like 'I like to read the newspaper' and 'I do not like being wet' by writing rules like $\mathtt{good}_j \leftarrow_e \mathtt{paper}$ and $\mathtt{bad}_i \leftarrow_e \mathtt{wet}$.[3] Then, since none of these 'observations' would be explained, actions which lead to good's will be automatically rewarded (they have a negative penalty, and thus, a reward), and actions that lead to bad's will be automatically penalized. The trade-offs between

[3]In Section 6.7 we only dealt with *positive* λ's. However the extension to accommodate negative λ's is straightforward.

`good`'s, `bad`'s, and action costs will be handled by the aggregation functions used for computing the rank of belief states when the prior ranks $\pi(\mathrm{H_i})$ of the hypotheses in $\mathcal{H}$ and the evidential ranks $\lambda(\mathrm{O_i})$ of the observations $\mathcal{O}$ are given (cf. Section 6.4).

This only scratches the surface of how a logic-based architecture that accommodates both preferences and uncertainty may look like. More work needs to be done to understand the scope, the limitations and the assumptions embedded in this type of architecture, and for developing suitable algorithms.

Appendix: Proofs

Theorem 2.2 If $E \mathrel{|\!\!\thickapprox_K} p$ and $K \subseteq K'$ then $E \mathrel{|\!\!\thickapprox_{K'}} p$

Proof The theorem can be proven by induction on the minimal length n of the derivation of $E \mathrel{|\!\!\thickapprox_K} p$. If $n = 1$, it means that p was derived from $T = \langle K, E\rangle$ either by Rule 1 or Rule 2. In either case p can also be derived from $T' = \langle K', E\rangle$. Let us thus assume that p is derivable in n steps, with $n > 1$, and that the theorem holds for all proofs with length $m < n$. The last step in the derivation must then involve one of the Rules 3–5, and thus, the antecedents of such rule must be derivable in a number of steps smaller than n. Therefore, these antecedents will also be derivable in K', and using the same rule, p will be derivable from T'. ∎

Theorem 2.3 If $E \mathrel{|\!\!\thickapprox_K} p$ then p is ϵ-entailed by $T = \langle K, E\rangle$.

Proof We prove that each rule in the core is sound with respect to ϵ-entailment. That is, for a rule with conclusion $E \mathrel{|\!\!\thickapprox_K} p$, we prove that for any ϵ-admissible probability distribution P which complies with the premises of the rule, $P(p \mid E)$ must approach one, as ϵ approaches zero. The **defaults** rule is sound by definition: if $p \rightarrow q$ is a default in K, then the admissibility of P requires of $P(p \mid q)$ to approach one as ϵ approaches zero. For **deduction**, if $E \vdash_K p$, then clearly $P(p \mid E) = 1$. For proving the soundness of **augmentation** and **reduction**, we need to show that if $P(p \mid E)$ approaches one, $P(q \mid E, p)$ approaches one iff $P(q|E)$ does. This, in turn, is a consequence of the probabilistic equality:

$$P(q \mid E) \;=\; P(q \mid E,p)\; P(p \mid E) \;+\; P(q \mid E, \neg p)\; P(\neg p \mid E)$$

Indeed, if $P(q \mid E)$ and $P(p \mid E)$ approach one, so must $P(q \mid E,p)$, since $P(\neg p \mid E)$ approaches zero and $P(q \mid E, \neg p)$ is bounded by one. On the other hand, since the value of $P(q \mid E)$ is bound from below by the product of $P(q \mid E, p)$ and $P(p \mid E)$, the former term must approach one when the latter two terms do. Finally, the soundness of **disjunction** rule follows from the soundness of **weak reduction**. Weak reduction is a derived rule which permits us to infer $E \mathrel{|\!\!\thickapprox_K} \neg p \vee r$ from $E, p \mathrel{|\!\!\thickapprox_K} r$. The soundness of weak reduction is obvious when $E \vdash_K \neg p$ holds. Otherwise, by Bayes rule we have:

$$P(\neg r \wedge p \mid E) \;=\; P(\neg r \mid E, p)\; P(p \mid E)$$

Hence, if $P(r \mid E, p)$ approaches one, $P(\neg r \mid E, p)$ must approach zero, and so must $P(\neg r \wedge p \mid E)$. As a result $P(\neg(\neg r \wedge p) \mid E)$ must approach one, and so must $P(r \vee \neg p \mid E)$, due to the logical equivalence between $\neg(\neg r \wedge p)$ and $r \vee \neg p$. The disjunction rule can be derived from weak reduction, augmentation and deductive closure, all sound rules relative to ϵ-entailment (deductive closure is a consequence of deduction, augmentation and reduction). By augmentation we can derive $E, p, p \vee q \mid\!\approx_K r$ and $E, q, p \vee q \mid\!\approx_K r$, from $E, p \mid\!\approx_K r$ and $E, q \mid\!\approx_K r$. By weak reduction we can further get $E, p \vee q \mid\!\approx_K r \vee \neg p$ and $E, p \vee q \mid\!\approx_K r \vee \neg q$. Finally, $E, p \vee q \mid\!\approx_K r$ follows by deductive closure. ∎

Theorem 3.1 If p is is derivable from $T = \langle K, E \rangle$ by Rules 1–5, then p is preferentially entailed by T.

Proof We need to show that Rules 1–5 are sound relative to preferential entailment. The first rule is sound by the definition of preferential entailment. **Deduction** is sound because if p is true in all models of E, p will be true in all *preferred* models of E. The soundness of **augmentation** and **reduction** follows from the fact that in any well-founded structure $\langle \mathcal{I}, < \rangle$ where p is true in all the preferred models of E, the preferred models of E and $E \cup \{p\}$ coincide. Assume otherwise, that there is a well-founded p-structure in which M is a preferred model of E but not of $E' = E \cup \{p\}$. Then, since M must a be model of E' because p holds in all preferred models of E, there must be a preferred model of M' of E' such that $M' < M$ (because of well-foundness). This, however, contradicts the assumption that M is a preferred model of E since M' is also a model of E. A similar contradiction results if we assume that there is an interpretation N that is a preferred model of $E' = E \cup \{p\}$ but not of E. Finally, **disjunction** follows from the fact that in any p-structure, the preferred models of $\alpha \vee \beta$ are among the preferred models of α and the preferred models of β. Indeed, if M is a preferred model of $\alpha \vee \beta$, M must satisfy either α or β. If M satisfies α but M is not a preferred model of α, by the well-foundedness assumption, there must be a preferred model M' of α such that $M' < M$. However, since M' is also a model of $\alpha \vee \beta$, this contradicts the assumption that M is a preferred model of $\alpha \vee \beta$. A analogous contradiction results if M satisfies β instead of α. ∎

Lemma 3.1 K is p-consistent if and only if K is l-consistent.

Proof We show first that given an admissible l-structure $\lambda = \langle \mathcal{W}, \kappa \rangle$, it is possible to construct a p-structure $\pi = \langle \mathcal{I}, < \rangle$ that is also admissible. For that purpose, we define $\mathcal{I}$ to be any minimal set of interpretations whose associated set of worlds is $\mathcal{W}$, and define the order '$<$' over $\mathcal{I}$ in such a way that $M < M'$ holds iff $\kappa(w(M)) < \kappa(w(M'))$, where $w : \mathcal{I} \mapsto \mathcal{W}$ is a function that maps an interpretation M into its corresponding world W (i.e., M and W satisfy the same sentences). We need to show that the structure π is admissible with $K = \langle L, D \rangle$ when λ is. First note that the mapping from worlds to interpretations preserves satisfiability. Also, since worlds have only non-negative ranks, the induced preferential structure π must be well-founded. Thus, if q is false in some *preferred* model M of p in $\mathcal{I}$, it means that there is a world W in which both p and $\neg q$ hold, and no world W' where p and q hold such that $\kappa(W') < \kappa(W)$. This, however, contradicts the assumption that the l-structure $\lambda = \langle \mathcal{W}, \kappa \rangle$ is admissible, and therefore, if λ is admissible, so is π.

To show that given an admissible p-structure $\pi = \langle \mathcal{I}, < \rangle$ it is possible to build an admissible l-structure $\lambda = \langle \mathcal{W}, \kappa \rangle$, we use a construction suggested by Lehmann [Leh89]. First, we define $\mathcal{W}$ to be the set of worlds that correspond to the interpretations in $\mathcal{I}$, and then for every interpretation M in $\mathcal{I}$ we let $height(M)$ stand for the length of the longest ascending chain of interpretations $M_0 < M_1 < \cdots < M_n$ in $\mathcal{I}$ for which $M_n = M$. The rank of a world W in $\mathcal{W}$ is then defined as $\kappa(W) = \min_{M \in \mathcal{I}_W} height(M)$, where $\mathcal{I}_W$ stands for the set of interpretations M in $\mathcal{I}$ such that $w(M) = W$. Since, again, the mapping from worlds to interpretations preserves satisfiability, to show the admissibility of λ we need only to show that for every default $p \rightarrow q$ in K, q is true in all the preferred worlds of p in λ. Let us assume otherwise, that there is a world W in $\mathcal{W}$ that satisfies both p and $\neg q$, and no world W' in $\mathcal{W}$ that satisfies both p and q such that $\kappa(W') < \kappa(W)$. Furthermore, let M be an interpretation in $\mathcal{I}$ such that $W = w(M)$ and $\kappa(W) = height(M)$ (by the construction of λ, there must be one such interpretation). Then, from the admissibility of the preferential structure π, it must be the case that there is an interpretation M' that satisfies both p and q and for which $M' < M$. This, however, implies that $height(M') < height(M)$ and, therefore, that $\kappa(W') < \kappa(W)$ for $W' = w(M')$, in contradiction with the assumption that W is a preferred world of p in λ. ∎

Lemma 3.2 K is ϵ-consistent if and only if K is l-consistent.

Proof (if part) We show that given an admissible l-structure $\langle \mathcal{W}, \kappa \rangle$ it is possible to build an ϵ-admissible probability distribution for any positive ϵ. Given the assumption of a finite number of worlds, we can assume that $\mathcal{W}$ contains n worlds and that the ranking κ divides $\mathcal{W}$ into $m+1$ non-empty layers $\mathcal{W}_0, \mathcal{W}_1, \ldots, \mathcal{W}_m$ of increasing rank, each with a number n_i of worlds. Clearly, since L has to be logically consistent, there is a probability distribution which is ϵ-admissible for any ϵ greater than or equal to one. We show below, that it is possible to construct a probability distribution P over $\mathcal{W}$ which is ϵ-admissible for any positive real ϵ smaller than one.

The probability distribution P is defined to assign to each world W in the layer $\mathcal{W}_i$, $0 \leq i < m$, a probability

$$P(W) = \delta^i (1-\delta)/n_i$$

where $0 < \delta \leq \epsilon \cdot [1 + n(1-\epsilon)]^{-1} < 1$, and to each world W in the last layer $\mathcal{W}_m$, a probability

$$P(W) = \delta^{m+1}$$

Due to the equality

$$1 - \delta^{m+1} = (1 + \delta + \delta^2 + \delta^3 + \ldots + \delta^m) \cdot (1 - \delta)$$

it is easy to show that the sum of P over all the worlds in $\mathcal{W}$ is equal to 1. We need to show that the probability distribution P is ϵ-admissible. First, note that since the structure $\langle \mathcal{W}, \kappa \rangle$ is admissible, every world W in $\mathcal{W}$ satisfies L, and for every default $p \rightarrow q$ in D there is a world where p holds. Thus, we are guaranteed that the probability $P(s)$ of any sentence s in L is one, and that the probability $P(p)$, for any default $p \rightarrow q$ in D, is greater than zero. We are thus left to show that the probability $P(q \mid p)$ for any default $p \rightarrow q$ in D is greater than $1 - \epsilon$. We know, however, by the admissibility of the structure $\langle \mathcal{W}, \kappa \rangle$, that there is a world W that satisfies both p and q which is better than any other world in which p is satisfied and q is not. Thus, in particular, if W belongs to $\mathcal{W}_m$, $P(q \mid p)$ must be equal to 1. Otherwise, W must belong to some layer $\mathcal{W}_i$, $0 \leq i < m$, from which $P(q \mid p) \geq 1 - \epsilon$ is obtained as follows:

$$P(q \mid p) = \frac{P(p,q)}{P(p,q) + P(p,\neg q)}$$

$$\geq \frac{\delta^i (1-\delta)}{\delta^i (1-\delta) + n\,\delta^{i+1}}$$

$$\geq \frac{1-\delta}{1+n\,\delta}$$

$$\geq 1-\epsilon \text{ , since } 0 < \delta \leq \frac{\epsilon}{1+n\,(1-\epsilon)} < 1$$

Proof (only if part) After the following lemma.

Lemma 3.3 A default theory $T = \langle K, \{p\}\rangle$ ϵ-entails (resp. p-entails, l-entails) a proposition q, if and only if the background obtained by adding the default $p \rightarrow \neg q$ to K, is ϵ-inconsistent (resp. p-inconsistent, l-inconsistent).

Proof (only for ϵ-entailment) The only-if part of the theorem follows from the monotonicity of '$\mathrel{|\!\!\!\approx_K}$' with respect to K. The other half is trivial when K itself is ϵ-inconsistent, as T would ϵ-entail any sentence in the language. We will thus assume that K is ϵ-consistent and show that p ϵ-entails q in K when K' is ϵ-inconsistent. We will follow the proof in Adams [Ada75], and rely on Lemma 3.5 to be proven below independently. From the half of Lemma 3.2 established above, if K' is ϵ-inconsistent, then K' is l-inconsistent, and from Lemma 3.5 below, if K' is l-inconsistent then K' must contain a clash D'. Furthermore, since K *is* consistent, the default $p \rightarrow \neg q$ must be a member of D'.
Now, consider the expression

$$U_P(D') = \sum_{i=1}^{n} 1 - P(q_i|p_i)$$

where $p_i \rightarrow q_i$, $i = 1, \ldots, n$, are the defaults in D', and the expression $U_P(\{C(D')\})$, where $C(D')$ is the quasi-conjunction of D' (Section 3.6), namely the default

$$p_1 \vee p_2 \vee \cdots \vee p_n \rightarrow (p_1 \Rightarrow q_1) \wedge (p_2 \Rightarrow q_2) \wedge \cdots \wedge (p_n \Rightarrow q_n)$$

The value of $U_P(\{C(D')\})$ is given by the sum of the probabilities of the worlds that violate defaults from D', while the value of $U_P(D')$ is given by a sum that includes all such probabilities possibly repeated several times (e.g., when a world violates more than one default in D'). Therefore, $U_P(D')$ is greater than $U_P(\{C(D')\})$. Moreover, since D' is clash, there is no world that verifies $C(D')$ and satisfies the sentences in L in the background K. Thus, if P is a probability distribution ϵ-admissible with K, $U_P(\{C(D')\} = 1$, and thus, $U_P(D') \geq 1$. Furthermore, as ϵ approaches zero all terms in $U_P(D')$ which correspond to defaults in D vanish, and thus $U_P(D')$ approaches $U_P(\{p \rightarrow \neg q\})$. Since $U_P(D') \geq 1$ and $U_P(\{p \rightarrow \neg q\}) = P(q \,|\, p)$, for any ϵ-admissible probability distribution P, $P(q \,|\, p)$ must approach one as ϵ approaches zero, so q is ϵ-entailed by p in K. ∎

Lemma 3.2 K is ϵ-consistent if and only if K is l-consistent.

Proof (only if part) We can now construct an admissible layered-structure $\langle \mathcal{W}, \kappa \rangle$ given an ϵ-consistent background context K. For a world W_i, $i = 1, \ldots, n$, we will refer by s_i to the sentence formed by conjoining all the positive and negative ground literals true in W_i; namely, s_i is the 'world' sentence associated with W_i. The ranking κ on worlds W_i will then be determined by defining an order on the sentences s_i. First, we collect in a set S all the defaults of the form $s_i \vee s_j \rightarrow \neg s_i$ and $s_i \vee s_j \rightarrow \neg s_j$, for s_i and s_j with $i < j$. The number of defaults in S is thus $l = n\,(n-1)$. We then incrementally construct a new ϵ-consistent background context $K' = \langle L, D \cup S' \rangle$, $S' \subseteq S$, as follows. Initially, we set $S^0 = S$, $D^0 = \emptyset$ and $K^0 = K$. Then until S^i is empty, for each $i = 1, \ldots, l$, we remove a default $p_i \rightarrow q_i$ from S^i and test whether $\neg q_i$ is ϵ-entailed by p_i in the background $K^{i-1} = \langle L, D \cup D^{i-1} \rangle$. If so, we set D^i to D^{i-1}; otherwise, we set D^i to $D^{i-1} \cup \{p_i \rightarrow q_i\}$. The resulting background context $K' = K^l$ must be ϵ-consistent because $K^0 = K$ is ϵ-consistent by assumption and each iteration preserves the ϵ-consistency of K^i (Lemma 3.3). We show next (1) that K' yields a *total* order over the sentences s_i, $i = 1, \ldots, l$, and (2) that the ranking κ on $\mathcal{W}$ determined by this order yields an admissible layered structure.

We show first that one and only one of the defaults $s_i \vee s_j \rightarrow \neg s_i$ or $s_i \vee s_j \rightarrow \neg s_j$, for each $i < j$, belongs to K'. Assume that $s_i \vee s_j \rightarrow \neg s_i$ belongs to K'. Then the disjunction $s_i \vee s_j$ ϵ-entails the sentence s_j and, by consistency arguments, the default $s_i \vee s_j \rightarrow \neg s_j$ cannot belong to K'. Otherwise, if $s_i \vee s_j \rightarrow \neg s_i$ does not belong to K', it must be the case that it is not consistent with some K^i, $0 \leq i \leq l$, and therefore, not consistent with K'. This means that the disjunction $s_i \vee s_j$ ϵ-entails the sentence s_i in K' (Lemma 3.3), and therefore, that $s_i \vee s_j$ ϵ-entails the sentence $\neg s_j$ since s_i and s_j are logically inconsistent. Thus, the default $s_i \vee s_j \rightarrow \neg s_j$ is ϵ-consistent with K' and, therefore, it must belong to

K'. Furthermore, from the soundness of core and 'or-transitivity' (i.e., the rule derivable from the core which permits us to conclude $p \vee r \mathrel{\substack{\sim\\K}} r$, given $p \vee q \mathrel{\substack{\sim\\K}} q$ and $q \vee r \mathrel{\substack{\sim\\K}} r$), it must also be the case that if K' includes the defaults $s_i \vee s_j \rightarrow \neg s_j$ and $s_j \vee s_k \rightarrow \neg s_k$, then K' includes the default $s_i \vee s_k \rightarrow \neg s_k$. Thus, K' determines a total order '$<$' on the sentences s_i, where $s_i < s_j$ holds iff either $s_i \vee s_j \rightarrow \neg s_j$ or $s_j \vee s_i \rightarrow \neg s_j$ belong to K'. We can thus define the ranking κ of a world W_i as the length of the maximal ascending chain $s_{i_1} < s_{i_2} < \ldots < s_{i_n}$, where $s_{i_n} = s_n$. We show now that the resulting l-structure $\lambda = \langle \mathcal{W}, \kappa \rangle$ is admissible with K. Note that by definition, $\mathcal{W}$ stands for the set of worlds that satisfy L. Furthermore, since $K = \langle L, D \rangle$ is ϵ-consistent, $\mathcal{W}$ must include worlds satisfying p for every default $p \rightarrow q$ in D. We are thus left to show that for every such default, q is true in all the preferred worlds of p in the l-structure λ. Assume otherwise, that there is a world W_i in which p holds and q does not, and no world W_j with smaller rank than W_i where both p and q hold. Moreover, let us assume that W_i is the single minimal such world (remember that κ imposes a total order on $\mathcal{W}$). Then, if s_i is the sentence which corresponds to W_i, K' must include either $s_j \vee s_i \rightarrow \neg s_j$ or $s_i \vee s_j \rightarrow \neg s_j$, for each $j \neq i$. However, since the disjunction of all the s_j sentences is logically entailed by p, this would imply that s_i, and thus, $\neg q$, are ϵ-entailed by p in K',[4] in contradiction with the ϵ-consistency of K'. Thus, there is no such a world W_i and the l-structure λ is admissible. ∎

Theorem 3.2 T ϵ-entails p iff T p-entails p iff T l-entails p.

Proof Immediate from Lemmas 3.1, 3.2 and 3.3. ∎

Theorem 3.3 A background context K is consistent if and only if there is a default ranking admissible with K.

Proof We prove the 'only if' part first. Assume that K is l-consistent, and that $\lambda = \langle \mathcal{W}, \kappa \rangle$ is a layered world structure admissible with K. We show that the default ranking $\sigma(p \rightarrow q) = \min_{W \in \mathcal{W}_p} \kappa(W)$, where $\mathcal{W}_p$ stands for the non-empty set of worlds in $\mathcal{W}$ that satisfy p, is admissible. Assume that σ is not admissible; i.e., there is a default $p \rightarrow q$ in D in

[4]This can be shown by means of 'or-monotonicity'; the rule derivable from the core which permits us to conclude $p \vee q \vee r \mathrel{\substack{\sim\\K}} \neg q$, given $p \vee q \mathrel{\substack{\sim\\K}} \neg q$.

conflict with a subset D' of D, such that

$$(*) \qquad \sigma(p \rightarrow q) \leq \min_{d' \in D'} \sigma(d')$$

Let then W be minimal ranked world in $\mathcal{W}$ that verifies $p \rightarrow q$.[5] By the admissibility of λ, we know that there must be at least one such world W, and that W must satisfy the sentences in L. From the conflict between $p \rightarrow q$ and D' though, one default in D', say $p' \rightarrow q'$, must be falsified by W. Again, by the admissibility of λ, W must be preceded by a world W' in which the default $p' \rightarrow q'$ is verified. This, however, implies $\sigma(p' \rightarrow q') < \sigma(p \rightarrow q)$ in contradiction with the assumption (*) above.

We prove now the 'if' part. We show that given an admissible default ranking over $K = \langle L, D \rangle$ it is possible to construct a layered structure $\langle \mathcal{W}, \kappa \rangle$ which is admissible with K. For that purpose, we select $\mathcal{W}$ as the set of all worlds consistent with L, and κ as the ranking $\kappa(W) = \max_{d \in D_W} \sigma(d)$, where D_W stands for the set of defaults falsified in W. We need to show that for any world W in $\mathcal{W}$ that falsifies a default $p \rightarrow q$ in D, there is a world W', $\kappa(W') < \kappa(W)$, that verifies it. First, note that if W falsifies the default $p \rightarrow q$ then, by the definition of κ, $\kappa(W)$ must be equal or higher than $\sigma(p \rightarrow q)$. Moreover, since σ is an admissible default ranking, every subset D_i of D in conflict with $p \rightarrow q$ must contain a default $p_i \rightarrow q_i$ such that $\sigma(p_i \rightarrow q_i) < \sigma(p \rightarrow q)$. Let D' be the set of all such defaults. It follows then that there must be a world W' in $\mathcal{W}$ that satisfies L, verifies $p \rightarrow q$ and only falsifies defaults in D'. This implies that the ranking of W' is such that $\kappa(W') < \sigma(p \rightarrow q)$ and, therefore, that $\kappa(W') < \kappa(W)$. Thus, the layered world structure $\langle \mathcal{W}, \kappa \rangle$ is admissible with K, and K is l-consistent. ∎

Lemma 3.4 A background context is consistent if and only if it does not contain a clash.

Proof We prove the 'only if' part first. Let us assume that there is an admissible ranking σ over $K = \langle L, D \rangle$ and that D', $D' \subseteq D$, is a clash in K. Let also $p \rightarrow q$ be a default in D' with minimal rank. There must be one such default in D' due to the nature of default rankings.

[5]Remember that a world W verifies $p \rightarrow q$ when W satisfies p and q, and that W falsifies $p \rightarrow q$ when W satisfies p but doesn't satisfy q.

However, by the definition of *admissible* default ranking, since $p \rightarrow q$ is in conflict with D', D' must contain a default with a rank smaller than $\sigma(p \rightarrow q)$, contradicting the minimality of $p \rightarrow q$. Thus, a consistent K cannot contain a clash.

Now, let us assume that K does not contain a clash. We show that it is possible construct an admissible default ranking by decomposing D into layers $D_0, D_1, \ldots, D_i, \ldots$ and by setting $\sigma(p \rightarrow q) = i$ iff $p \rightarrow q \in D_i$. Let $D^0 = D$. Since, in particular, D is not a clash in itself, there is a set D_0 of defaults in D^0 which are not in conflict with D^0. For $i = 1, 2, \ldots$, let D^i be set to $D^{i-1} - D_{i-1}$. Since $D^i \subseteq D$, D^i cannot be a clash and, therefore, there must be a non-empty set D_i of defaults in D^i which are not in conflict with D^i. Following this procedure, we obtain a layering $D_0, D_1, \ldots$ of defaults, such that (1) $D = \cup_i D_i$, and (2) every default in D_i is not conflict with defaults in $D^i = D_i \cup D_{i+1} \cup \cdots \cup D_n$. Thus, since D contains a finite number of default schemas whose instances all belong to the same layer, the default ranking $\sigma(p \rightarrow q) = i$ iff $p \rightarrow q \in D_i$ assigns an admissible rank to every default in D. ∎

Lemma 3.5 p entails q in a background context $K = \langle L, D\rangle$ if and only if the background $K' = \langle L, D + \{p \rightarrow \neg q\}\rangle$ contains a clash.

Proof From Lemma 3.3, p entails q iff K' is inconsistent, and from Lemma 3.4, K' is inconsistent iff K' contains a clash. ∎

Theorem 3.4 For a background context $K = \langle L, D\rangle$ with n defaults, there is a $\mathcal{O}(C(n) \times n^2)$ procedure for testing whether a sentence q is entailed by a sentence p in K, where $C(n)$ is the complexity associated with testing the satisfiability of n sentences in the language that contains the sentences in L, the material counterparts of the defaults in D, and the sentence $p \Rightarrow \neg q$ (e.g., $C(n) = \mathcal{O}(n)$ for Horn clauses).

Proof In order to test whether q is entailed by p, it is sufficient to test the consistency of the background K' as in Lemma 3.5. We can test the consistency of K' by following the construction given in the second part of the proof of Lemma 3.4. That is, we start with $D^0 = D$ and for each D^i we identify a set D_i of defaults which are not in conflict with D^i, and set D^{i+1} to $D^i - D_i$. We stop this iteration when one of the sets D^i or D_i is empty. If D^i is empty at the end, it means that we have not found a clash in D, and therefore, that K' is consistent and that p

does not entail q in K. Otherwise, D^i *is* a clash, and therefore, K' is inconsistent and q is entailed by p. Furthermore, there are at most $n+1$ iterations, each involving at most $n+1$ satisfiability tests. ∎

Lemma 3.6 Let $p \rightarrow q$ be a default in D, let D' be a subset of D, and let $C(D')$ be the quasi-conjunction of D'. Then, $p \rightarrow q$ clashes with D' in a background context $K = \langle L, D\rangle$, if and only if $p \rightarrow q$ clashes with $C(D')$ in the background context $K' = \langle L, D''\rangle$ with $D'' = \{C(D'), p \rightarrow q\}$.

Proof Let $p_0 = p$, $q_0 = q$, and let $p_i \rightarrow q_i$, $i = 1, \ldots, n$, be the defaults in D'. If $D' + \{p_0 \rightarrow q_0\}$ is a clash in K, we must have

$$p_i \vdash_K \neg(p_0 \Rightarrow q_0) \vee \neg(p_1 \Rightarrow q_1) \vee \cdots \vee \neg(p_n \Rightarrow q_n)$$

for each $i = 0, 1, \cdots, n$. Therefore, from the logical equivalence between:

$$\neg(p_1 \Rightarrow q_1) \vee \cdots \vee \neg(p_n \Rightarrow q_n) \quad \text{and}$$
$$\neg(p_1 \vee p_2 \vee \cdots \vee p_n \Rightarrow (p_1 \Rightarrow q_1) \wedge (p_2 \Rightarrow q_2) \wedge \cdots \wedge (p_n \Rightarrow q_n))$$

we get

$$p_0 \vdash_K \neg(p_0 \Rightarrow q_0) \vee \neg(p_1 \vee p_2 \vee \cdots \vee p_n \Rightarrow (p_1 \Rightarrow q_1) \wedge \cdots \wedge (p_n \Rightarrow q_n))$$

and

$$p_{1,n} \vdash_K \neg(p_0 \Rightarrow q_0) \vee \neg(p_{1,n} \Rightarrow (p_1 \Rightarrow q_1) \wedge \cdots \wedge (p_n \Rightarrow q_n))$$

where $p_{1,n}$ stands for the disjunction $p_1 \vee \cdots \vee p_n$. The last expression shows a clash between $p_0 \rightarrow q_0$ and the quasi-conjunction $C(D')$. The proof for the 'if' part involves the reverse steps. ∎

Lemma 3.7 Let $K = \langle L, D\rangle$ be a background context, and let D' be a non-empty subset of D. Then, if $r \rightarrow s$ stands for the quasi-conjunction $C(D')$ of D', $r \succsim_K s$.

Proof Let D' be the collection of defaults $p_i \rightarrow q_i$, $i = 1, \ldots, n$. Then by Rule 1 we can obtain $p_i \succsim_K q_i$. So, if we let r stand for the disjunction $p_1 \vee \cdots \vee p_n$, we can get $p_i, r \succsim_K q_i$ by augmentation, and $r \succsim_K p_i \Rightarrow q_i$ by weak reduction. Finally, $r \succsim_K s$, with $s = (p_1 \Rightarrow q_1) \wedge \cdots \wedge (p_n \Rightarrow q_n)$, follows by deductive closure. ∎

Lemma 3.8 Let $K = \langle L, D\rangle$ and $K' = \langle L, D'\rangle$ be two background contexts with the same set L of sentences. If $p \rightarrow \neg q$ clashes with $r \rightarrow s$ in K' and $r \succsim_K s$, then $p \succsim_K q$.

Proof From the definition of default clashes, by **deduction** it follows that $r, s \mathrel{|\!\!\approx}_K p \wedge q$ and $p, \neg q \mathrel{|\!\!\approx}_K r \wedge \neg s$. Furthermore, from $r \mathrel{|\!\!\approx}_K s$ and the first expression, we can obtain $r \mathrel{|\!\!\approx}_K p$, $r, p \mathrel{|\!\!\approx}_K q$, and therefore, by **weak reduction**, $p \mathrel{|\!\!\approx}_K \neg r \vee q$. Likewise, from the second expression we can obtain $p, \neg q \mathrel{|\!\!\approx}_K r$, and then by **weak reduction**, $p \mathrel{|\!\!\approx}_K r \vee q$. Combining the two results by **deductive closure**, $p \mathrel{|\!\!\approx}_K q$ follows. ∎

Proposition 3.1 For every consistent background $K = \langle L, D \rangle$ there is unique *minimal* admissible default ranking σ^*, such that for any default $p \rightarrow q$ in D and any admissible default ranking σ, $\sigma^*(p \rightarrow q) \leq \sigma(p \rightarrow q)$.

Proof Immediate from the fact that if σ_1 and σ_2 are two admissible default rankings, $\sigma_3(x) = \min\{\sigma_1(x), \sigma_2(x)\}$ is an admissible default ranking as well. ∎

Lemma 4.1 If the quadruple $\langle \mathcal{I}_{\mathcal{L}}, <, \mathcal{D}, \prec \rangle$ is a prioritized structure, then the pair $\langle \mathcal{I}_{\mathcal{L}}, < \rangle$ is a preferential structure.

Proof From Definition 4.2, $M < M'$ holds iff $D[M] \neq D[M']$, and for every d in $D[M] - D[M']$ there exists a d' in $D[M'] - D[M]$, such that $d \prec d'$, where '$\prec$' is an irreflexive and transitive relation which does not contain infinite ascending chains. First, note that the relation '$<$' must also be irreflexive. We next show that '$<$' is also transitive. Let M_1, M_2, and M_3 be three interpretations such that $M_1 < M_2$ and $M_2 < M_3$, and let

$$D_1 = D[M_1] \ , \ D_2 = D[M_2] \ , \ D_3 = D[M_3]$$

We will use the notation $\overline{D_i}$ to denote the complement of a set D_i , i.e., $\overline{D_i} = \mathcal{D} - D_i$, and write $D_{i_1, i_2, \ldots, i_n}$ to denote the intersection of the sets $D_{i_1}, \ldots, D_{i_n}$. Furthermore, when one of the indices i is preceded by a minus sign, D_i is to be replaced by its complement $\overline{D_i}$. Thus, for example, $D_{1,-2,3}$ stands for the intersection of the sets D_1, D_3 and the complement $\overline{D_2}$ of D_2. Similarly, $D_{-1,2}$ stands for the intersection of $\overline{D_1}$ and D_2.

To prove transitivity we need to show that for every default d in $D_{1,-3}$, there is a default d' in $D_{-1,3}$ such that $d \prec d'$.[6] First note that since '$\prec$' does not contain infinite ascending chains, it is sufficient to prove this for every *maximal* element d in $D_{1,-3}$. Let then d_1 be an arbitrary maximal element in $D_{1,-3}$. We need to consider two cases:

[6] A similar proof can be found in [Prz87].

1. if d_1 belongs to $D_{1,-2,-3}$, then d_1 must also belong to $D_{1,-2}$. Thus, since $M_1 < M_2$, there must be a default d_2 in $D_{-1,2}$ such that $d_1 \prec d_2$. Furthermore, let d_2 be the maximal such element. If $d_2 \in D_{-1,2,3}$ we are done. Otherwise, $d_2 \in D_{-1,2,-3}$, and then since $M_2 < M_3$, there must be a default $d_3 \in D_{-2,3}$ such that $d_2 \prec d_3$. Now, if $d_3 \in D_{1,-2,3}$, then from $M_1 < M_2$, there must be a d'_2 in $D_{-1,2}$ such that $d_3 < d'_2$, and therefore, $d_2 \prec d'_2$, in contradiction with the maximality of d_2. Thus, $d_3 \in D_{-1,3}$, and $d_1 \prec d_3$, by the transitivity of '$\prec$'.
2. if d_1 belongs to $D_{1,2,-3}$, then, since $M_2 < M_3$, there must be a d_3 in $D_{-2,3}$ such that $d_1 \prec d_3$. Moreover, if $d_3 \in D_{-1,-2,3}$ we are done. Otherwise, $d_3 \in D_{1,-2,3}$, and therefore, as a result of $M_1 < M_2$, there must be a d_2 in $D_{-1,2}$ such that $d_3 \prec d_2$. Let d_2 be a maximal such element. Then if d_2 belongs to D_3 we are done. Otherwise, $d_2 \in D_{-1,2,-3}$, and therefore, there must be a d'_3 in $D_{-2,3}$ such that $d_2 \prec d'_3$. Furthermore, d'_3 cannot belong to D_1; otherwise, there should be another element d'_2 in $D_{-1,2}$, such that $d'_3 \prec d'_2$, contradicting the maximality of d_2. So, $d'_3 \in D_{-1,3}$ and $d_1 \prec d'_3$ by transitivity of '$\prec$.' ∎

Lemma 4.2 In any prioritized structure, if M is a preferred model of a theory T, then M is *minimal* in $D[M]$, i.e. there is no model M' of T such that $D[M'] \subset D[M]$.

Proof If $D[M'] \subset D[M]$, then $D[M'] - D[M] = \emptyset$, and $M' < M$ would trivially hold in every prioritized structure, preventing M from being preferred. ∎

Theorem 4.1 If T preferentially entails p, then T also conditionally entails p.

Proof If T is logically inconsistent, the result is trivial. So let us assume that T is logically consistent. We will show that if $\xi = \langle \mathcal{I}_{\mathcal{L}}, <, \mathcal{D}, \prec \rangle$ is a prioritized structure admissible with $K = \langle L, D \rangle$, then $\pi = \langle \mathcal{I}_L, < \rangle$ will be a preferential structure admissible with K ($\mathcal{I}_L \subset \mathcal{I}$ stands for the collection of models of L), so if T does not conditionally entail p, T will not preferentially entail p either. Note that since we are assuming $\mathcal{L}$ to be a finite propositional language, the preferential structure π must be well-founded. We need to show that for every default $p \rightarrow q$ in D, q holds in the preferred models of the theory $T' = \langle K, \{p\}\rangle$ in π. Again the result is trivial if T' is logically inconsistent, so we will assume otherwise. Let then M' be a model of T' in which q does not hold, and therefore, where the default $d : p \rightarrow q$ is violated, i.e., $d \in D[M']$. We will now construct a model M of T' preferred to M' in which the default d is satisfied. Since the preference order '$<$' is well-founded, this will be sufficient to prove that q holds in all preferred models of T'. Let C stand for the collection of all minimal sets of defaults in conflict in T',[7] and let C' stand for the sets of defaults D_i in C such that $D_i \cap D[M'] = \{d\}$. Since the priority ordering '$\prec$' is admissible, any such set D_i must contain a default d' such that $d' \prec d$. Let D' stand for the collection of all such defaults d', and let us select M as an interpretation with a gap $D[M] = D[M'] + D' - \{d\}$ that satisfies T'. There must be one such interpretation because $D[M]$ is a *hitting set* for C (i.e., $D[M]$ contains at least one member of every set in C; see [Rei87b] for the terminology). Indeed, any set in C not 'hit' by a default from $D[M'] - \{d\}$ will certainly be 'hit' by a default from D'. Furthermore, $M < M'$ must hold, as $D[M] - D[M'] = D'$, $D[M'] - D[M] = \{d\}$, and for every d' in D', $d' \prec d$ holds. ∎

Theorem 4.2 A background K is *preferentially consistent* only if it is *conditionally consistent.*

Proof If K is preferentially consistent, then by Theorem 3.3 there must be a default ranking σ admissible with K. Hence, the priority ordering $\prec_\sigma$ defined as $p' \rightarrow q' \prec_\sigma p \rightarrow q$ iff $\sigma(p' \rightarrow q') < \sigma(p \rightarrow q)$ will also be admissible with K, and thus, K will be conditionally consistent. ∎

Lemma 4.3 A proposition q is *conditionally entailed* by a default theory $T = \langle K, E\rangle$ iff q holds in all preferred models of T of every *minimal* prioritized structure admissible with K.

Proof It is sufficient to show that if $\prec'$ is an admissible priority ordering that properly contains all the tuples in a *minimal* admissible priority ordering '$\prec$', then the preferred models in the structure $\xi' = \langle \mathcal{I}_\mathcal{L}, <', \mathcal{D}, \prec'\rangle$ will be a subset of the preferred models of the structure $\xi = \langle \mathcal{I}_\mathcal{L}, <, \mathcal{D}, \prec\rangle$. Assume otherwise, that M is a preferred model in ξ'

[7] A collection $D_0 \subseteq K$ of defaults is in conflict in a context $T = \langle K, E\rangle$, if every model of T violates one of the defaults in D_0.

but not in ξ. Then there must be a model M' such that $M' < M$. This means that for every default d in $D[M'] - D[M]$ there must be a default d' in $D[M] - D[M']$ such that $d \prec d'$. However, since $d \prec d'$ implies $d \prec' d'$, then M' would be preferred to M in ξ' as well, in contradiction with the minimality M in ξ'. ∎

Lemmas 4.4 and **4.5** are special cases of **Lemma 4.6**, and the latter is a special case of the 'if part' of Theorem 4.3 (D' is a stable argument iff $C = \{D'\}$ is a stable cover). Recall that we are assuming that the theories T under consideration give rise to a finite number of minimal conflict sets (a conflict set is a collection of defaults logically inconsistent with T). These theories are *well-founded* in the following sense (see [Eth88]):

Lemma 4.7 If $T = \langle K, E \rangle$ gives rise to a finite number of minimal conflict sets, and $\xi = \langle \mathcal{I}_{\mathcal{L}}, <, \mathcal{D}, \prec \rangle$ is a prioritized structure, then for every non-preferred model M of T there is a preferred model M' of T such that $M' < M$.

Proof If T is logically inconsistent, the lemma follows trivially. So let us assume that T is logically consistent and let C stand for the collection of all minimal conflict sets that T gives rise to. It is easy to show that for every hitting set D_i for C (see above) there is a model M_i of T such that $D[M_i] = D_i$, and that if M_i is a model of T then $D[M_i]$ must include a hitting set D_i for C. Furthermore, if there are only a finite number of minimal conflict sets, there must be a finite number of minimal hitting sets D_i, $i = 1, \ldots, n$. Thus let M_i, $i = 1, \ldots, n$, stand for n models of T such that $D[M_i] = D_i$ and let $\mathcal{M}$ stand for the collection of all such models. Furthermore, let $\mathcal{M}_p$ denote the *minimal* collection of models in $\mathcal{M}$ such that if $M \in \mathcal{M} - \mathcal{M}_p$ then $\mathcal{M}_p$ contains a model M_i such that $M_i < M$. It is simple to show that such collection of models $\mathcal{M}_p$ is unique. We will show that they each model M_i in $\mathcal{M}_p$ is a preferred model of T, and that for every model M not in $\mathcal{M}_p$ there is a model M_i preferred to M. Assume otherwise that there is a model M of T preferred to some M_i in $\mathcal{M}_p$. This implies that the gap $D[M]$ of M contains some hitting set D_j, and thus, that if M is preferred to M_i, so will be M_j, in contradiction with the selection of M_i. We are thus left to show that for every non-preferred model M of T there is a model in $\mathcal{M}_p$ preferred to M. Two cases need to considered. If $D[M] = D_i$, $1 \leq i \leq n$, then a model will be preferred to M if and only if it is preferred to M_i above. Since M is not a preferred model of T, then M_i must belong to $\mathcal{M} - \mathcal{M}_p$, and thus, there must be a model M_j in $\mathcal{M}_p$ preferred to M_i, and therefore, to M. If for no i, $1 \leq i \leq n$, $D[M] = D_i$, then there must be one such i for which $D[M] \supset D_i$. In that case, $M_i < M$, and since $\mathcal{M}_p$ must contain a model M_j preferred to M_i, by transitivity, $M_j < M$. ∎

Theorem 4.3 A proposition p is conditionally entailed if and only if p is supported by a stable cover.

Proof (if part) Since we are assuming that the theory T under consideration gives rise to a finite number of minimal conflict sets, by Lemma 4.7 above, it is sufficient to show that for any model M that violates defaults from every set (argument) D_i, $i = 1, \ldots, n$ in the cover, and any structure $\langle \mathcal{I}_\mathcal{L}, <, \mathcal{D}, \prec \rangle$ admissible with K, there is model M' preferred to M such that one of the sets D_i is satisfied. Without loss of generality we can select M to be a minimal model, so that the set D' of defaults validated by M is maximal. If there is no such a minimal model M, we are done, because as stated in the Lemma 4.7, there would be a minimal model M' that satisfies some D_i, such that $D[M'] \subset D[M]$, and thus, $M' < M$. We assume thus that D' is maximal and in conflict with every set D_i in the cover. Since the cover is stable, it must then contain a set D_i strongly protected from D'. That is, for every subset D'_j of D' in conflict with D_i, there must be a subset D_i^j of D_i in conflict with D', such that $D'_j \prec D_i^j$. That means that every set D'_j in D' in conflict with D_i contains a default d'_j such that $d'_j \prec d_i^j$, for some default d_i^j in both D_i^j and $D[M]$. Then, it is possible to build a model M' of T that satisfies D_i by making every d_i^j true and every d'_j false. Thus for every default d'_j in $D[M'] - D[M]$ there is a default d_i^j in $D[M] - D[M']$ such that $d_j \prec d_i^j$, and therefore, $M' < M$.

Proof (only if part) If T gives rise to a finite number of minimal conflict sets, then T is well-founded and there are only a finite number of preferred classes. Let D_1, D_2, ..., D_n, be the *maximal* sets of defaults validated by the preferred classes of T. Since p is conditionally entailed this means that every such set supports p. We will show now that the collection C of sets $D_1, \ldots, D_n$ constitutes a stable cover, i.e., that for any definite conflicting argument D', C contains an argument

D_i strongly protected from D'. For that purpose, let M be a model of T satisfying D' and let M_i be a preferred model of T satisfying D_i, $1 \leq i \leq n$, such that $M_i < M$. From Lemma 4.7, we know that there must be one such model. We show now that D_i is strongly protected from D'. Assume otherwise, i.e. there is a subset D'_j of D' in conflict with D_i such that for every set $D_i^j \subseteq D_i$ in conflict with D', $D'_j \not\prec D_i^j$. This implies that the set D_A of defaults d in D_i such that $D'_j \prec d$ is consistent with D'. Furthermore, since D' is a *definite* conflicting argument this means that $D_A \subset D'$, and therefore, that for every default d' in $D[M] - D[M_i]$, $D'_j \not\prec d'$. However, this contradicts $M_i < M$. Indeed, since D'_j is inconsistent with D_i, one of the defaults d'_j in D'_j must belong to $D[M_i] - D[M]$, and for $M_i < M$ to be true, another default d_i, such that $d'_j \prec d_i$ must belong to $D[M] - D[M_i]$. ∎

Theorem 4.4 For two sets of defaults D and D', the relation $D' \prec D$ holds in every priority ordering '$\prec$' admissible with a *consistent background* $K = \langle L, D_K \rangle$ if and only if D is part of a set D'' that *dominates* D' in K.

Proof (if part) Recall that we use the notation $D' \prec D$ to state that for every default d in D there exists a default d' in D' such that $d' \prec d$. Moreover, the relation '$\prec$' among *sets* of defaults remains irreflexive and transitive, and therefore, asymmetric. That is, for every priority ordering $D \not\prec D$, and if $D_1 \prec D_2$ and $D_2 \prec D_3$ hold, so does $D_1 \prec D_3$.

Let D stand for a collection of defaults d_i, $i = 1, \ldots, n$. We will use the notation $D_{i,j}$, for $i \leq j$, to stand for the set $\{d_i, d_{i+1}, \ldots, d_j\}$. If $j > n$, the notation $D_{i,j}$ is to be understood as $D_{i,n}$, and as the empty set, if $i > n$. We show first that if D dominates a set D' then the relation $D' \prec D$ must hold for any priority ordering '$\prec$' admissible with K. We show this by induction; the base case $D_{i+1,n} + D' \prec D_{1,i}$, for $i = 1$, first. Clearly, if D dominates D', the default d_1 must dominate $D_{2,n} + D'$, and thus, $D_{2,n} + D' \prec \{d_1\}$ must hold. Thus, if $n = 1$, we are done. So let us assume that n is greater than one. Furthermore, let us assume as inductive hypothesis that $D_{i+1,n} + D' \prec D_{1,i}$ holds for every i, $1 \leq i < j \leq n$. We need to show the same relation holds for $i = j$. Now, since d_j dominates the set $D + D'$ we must have $D + D' \prec d_j$ for any admissible '$\prec$.' If we can show $D_{j+1,n} + D' \prec d_j$, we will be done, as otherwise there should be some default d in $D_{1,j-1}$ for which

$d_j \prec d$ holds but $D_{j+1,n} + D' \prec d$ does not, contradicting transitivity. Similarly, if $D_{j+1,n} + D' \prec d_j$ did not hold, we should have $d \prec d_j$ for some d in $D_{1,j-1}$. Furthermore, since $D_{j+1,n} + \{d_j\} + D' \prec D_{1,j-1}$ holds as hypothesis, the latter would imply that either $D_{j+1,n} + D' \prec d$ holds, in contradiction with transitivity, or that $d_j \prec d$ holds, in contradiction with the asymmetry of priority orderings.

Proof (only if part) This part of the proof is slightly more involved. We need to show that if the relation $D' \prec D$ holds for every admissible ordering with a (conditionally) consistent background context K, then D is part of a set that dominates D'. Let us first divide the set D_K of defaults in K between those which participate in a set that dominates D', which we group into a set D_A, from those which do not participate in a set that dominates D'. Furthermore, let

$$D_B = D' - D_A \quad \text{and} \quad D_C = D_K - (D_A + D_B)$$

Note that D_B cannot be empty, otherwise D_A would dominate itself, precluding K from being consistent. Note also, that if two sets dominate D', so will their union. It follows then that D_A dominates D'. Our goal will be to show that D is included in D_A. For that we will show that there is a priority ordering '$\prec$' admissible with K, such that the relation $D' \prec d$ holds only if $d \in D_A$.

Let us say that a priority ordering '$\prec$' in a background context K is admissible within a *range* D and a *restriction* D' iff every set D'' dominated by a default d in D contains a default d' in D', such that $d' \prec d$ holds. The notions of *range* and *restriction* provide a finer measure of the admissibility of a priority ordering. In particular, an admissible priority ordering, must be admissible within a range D_K and a restriction D_K. Furthermore, if a priority relation '$\prec$' is admissible within a range D_1 and a restriction D_2, for two disjoint sets D_1 and D_2 such that $D_1 + D_2 = D_K$, then there must be a priority relation '$\prec$' admissible within a range D_1 and a restriction D_K, such that $d_2 \prec d_1$ holds only if $d_1 \in D_1$ and $d_2 \in D_2$. Indeed, if '$\prec'$' is a priority relation admissible within a range D_1 and a restriction D_2, the relation that results by deleting all pairs $\langle d_1 \notin D_1, d_2 \notin D_2 \rangle$ for which $d_1 \prec' d_2$ holds, remains irreflexive, transitive, and admissible.

Now, let us assume that there is no priority ordering admissible within a range D_C and a restriction D_C, for D_C as above. It is possible to show then, that there must be a non-empty subset D'_C of D_C such that each default $d' \in D'_C$ dominates the set $D'_C + \overline{D_C}$, where $\overline{D_C}$ stands for the set of defaults not in D_C; in this case, $D_A + D_B$. This, however, amounts to say that D'_C *dominates* the set $D_A + D_B$, which by virtue of the dominance of D_A over D' and the inclusion of D_B in D', implies that D'_C dominates D' as well, in contradiction with the maximality of D_A. Thus, there must be a priority ordering '$\prec_C$' admissible within a range D_C and a restriction D_C, such that $d \prec_C d'$ holds only if both d and d' belong to D_C. Furthermore, since K is consistent, there must be a priority ordering '$\prec_A$' admissible within range D_A and restriction D_K, such that $d \prec_A d'$ holds only if d' belongs to D_A. We can thus define a relation '$\prec$' such that

$$d \prec d' \text{ iff } [d \prec_A d'] \text{ or } [d \prec_C d'] \text{ or } [d \in D_C \text{ and } d' \in D_A + D_B]$$

It is simple to show that such a relation is a priority relation, and that it is admissible within a range $D_A + D_C$. Let us assume, on the other hand, that '$\prec$' is not admissible within a range D_B. That is, there is a default d in D_B which dominates a set D'_B for which the relation $D'_B \prec d$ fails to hold. Note that D'_B cannot contain elements from D_C; for, otherwise, the relation $D'_B \prec d$ will certainly hold. Thus, $D'_B \subseteq D_A + D_B$, so d dominates $D_A + D_B$. That means, however, that the set $D_A + \{d\}$ dominates the set D', in contradiction with the assumption that D_A is the maximal such set. So, the ordering '$\prec$' must be admissible within the range D_B as well, and so '$\prec$' must be a priority relation admissible with K. Since $D' \prec D$ holds by hypothesis, and $D' \prec d$ holds only if $d \in D_A$, it follows then that D is part of a set, D_A, which dominates D'. ∎

Theorem 4.5 If E is irrelevant to $p \rightarrow q$ given a background K, then $p \Rightarrow q$ is conditionally entailed by $T = \langle K, E \rangle$.

Proof By a simple inductive argument it is possible to show that if $p \rightarrow q$ preempts an argument D', then $p \rightarrow q$ belongs to a set D'' that dominates D'. Therefore, the argument $\{p \rightarrow q\}$ is protected from every conflicting argument D', and hence, $\{p \rightarrow q\}$ is stable. Since propositions supported by stable arguments are conditionally entailed (Lemma 4.6) and $p \rightarrow q$ supports the material conditional $p \Rightarrow q$, $p \Rightarrow q$ is conditionally entailed. ∎

Theorem 4.6 For finite propositional languages, *all* the rules of $\mathbf{P}$ are *sound* rules of conditional entailment.

Proof Immediate from Theorems 3.1, 4.1 and 4.5. ∎

Theorem 4.7 An argument Δ is *stable* if and only if for every conflict set C_i, $C_i \cap \Delta \neq \emptyset$, there is a *basic defeat pair* $\langle C_j^0, C_j^1 \rangle$ such that $C_j^0 + C_j^1 \subseteq C_i + \Delta$ and $C_j^0 \subseteq C_i - \Delta$.

Proof In the text. ∎

Lemma 5.1 If the collection $\mathcal{B}_0$ of $<$-minimal classes is a basis, it is the smallest basis; i.e., every basis is a superset of $\mathcal{B}_0$.

Proof If $\mathcal{C}$ belongs to $\mathcal{B}_0$, then $\mathcal{C}$ is $<$-minimal, and so, $\mathcal{C}$ must be a minimal class. Therefore, if $\mathcal{B}$ is a basis and $\mathcal{C} \notin \mathcal{B}$, there there must be a class $\mathcal{C}'$ in $\mathcal{B}$ such that $\mathcal{C}' \leq \mathcal{C}$. However, since $\mathcal{C}$ is $<$-minimal, we must have $\mathcal{C}' \not< \mathcal{C}$, and therefore, $\mathcal{C} \leq \mathcal{C}'$, in contradiction with the assumption that $\mathcal{B}$ is a basis. ∎

Theorem 5.1 is a special case of Theorem 5.2 (since $\{\Delta\}$ is a stable cover when Δ is a stable argument).

Theorem 5.2 A proposition p is causally entailed if and only if p is supported by a stable *cover*.

Proof (if part) We show that if $C = \{\Delta_1, \ldots, \Delta_n\}$ is a stable cover, the collection $\mathcal{B}$ of minimal classes that validate one of the sets Δ_i, $i = 1, \ldots, n$, is a basis. We need to consider three cases. If $\mathcal{C}'$ is a minimal class not in $\mathcal{B}$ such that $\mathcal{C}' \leq \mathcal{C}_i$, where $\mathcal{C}_i$ is a class that validates the argument Δ_i, it means that the collection of assumptions Δ' that hold in $\mathcal{C}'$ are protected from Δ_i, in contradiction with the assumption that C is stable. If $\mathcal{C}'$ is a minimal class not in $\mathcal{B}$ and there is no class $\mathcal{C}_i$ in $\mathcal{B}$ such that $\mathcal{C}_i \leq \mathcal{C}'$, it means that the collection of assumptions Δ' that hold in $\mathcal{C}'$ is in conflict with each Δ_j and that no Δ_j is protected from Δ', again in contradiction with the stability of C. Finally, if $\mathcal{C}''$ is a non-minimal class which is not in $\mathcal{B}$, then there will be a minimal class $\mathcal{C}'$ such that $A[\mathcal{C}'] \subset A[\mathcal{C}'']$.[8] Since $\mathcal{C}' \leq \mathcal{C}''$, if $\mathcal{C}' \in \mathcal{B}$ we would be

[8]This form of well-foundedness is a consequence of a result established by Bossu and Siegel [BS85a] that for every non-minimal Herbrand model M of a set of clauses there is always a minimal Herbrand model M' such that $M' \subset M$.

done; otherwise there has to be some class $\mathcal{C}_i$ in $\mathcal{B}$ such that $\mathcal{C}_i \leq \mathcal{C}'$, and therefore, that $\mathcal{C}_i \leq \mathcal{C}''$.

We prove now the 'only if part'. If $\mathcal{B}$ is a basis, let the cover C be given by the maximal collection Δ_i of assumptions sanctioned by each of the classes $\mathcal{C}_i$ in $\mathcal{B}$. We will show that C is stable. Let $\mathcal{C}'$ stand for the class of models that validate an argument Δ' in conflict with each of the arguments Δ_i. It follows then that $\mathcal{C}'$ does not belong to $\mathcal{B}$, and therefore, that some class $\mathcal{C}_i$ in $\mathcal{B}$ is as preferred as $\mathcal{C}'$. This means however that Δ_i is protected from Δ'. Likewise, if Δ' is protected from some Δ_i, it means that there is a set $\Delta'_i \subseteq \Delta_i - \Delta'$ such that the set of assumptions $\Delta' + \Delta'_i$ is consistent and explains the complement of each of the assumptions in $\Delta_i - \Delta'_i$. Therefore, we can define a minimal class $\mathcal{C}'$ that satisfies both Δ' and Δ'_i, for which $\mathcal{C}' \leq \mathcal{C}_i$. However, this is in contradiction with the assumption that $\mathcal{B}$ is a basis, and thus, Δ' cannot be protected from Δ_i. ∎

Proposition 5.1 $\mathcal{C}_M$ is a minimal class of the simple causal theory T if and only if M is a minimal Herbrand model of the logic program $P[T]$.

Proof An atom (resp. an assumption) α holds in a minimal class $\mathcal{C}_M$ iff α belongs (resp. does *not* belong) to M. So, if M violates a rule or a constraint in $P[T]$, $\mathcal{C}_M$ will violate the corresponding constraint in T. Hence if $\mathcal{C}_M$ is a minimal class of T, M is a model of $P[T]$. To show that M must be a *minimal* model, we will show first that if M' is a *minimal* Herbrand model of $P[T]$ then $\mathcal{C}_{M'}$ is a class of T. Let $\mathrm{C}[M']$ refer to the collection of formulas $\mathrm{C}p_i$ for the atoms p_i in M'. Then it is simple to show that the Herbrand interpretation $M' + \mathrm{C}[M']$ must satisfy T if M' satisfies $P[T]$. Therefore, $\mathcal{C}_{M'}$ is a class of T if M' is a minimal Herbrand model of $P[T]$. Now if $\mathcal{C}_M$ is a *minimal* class of T and M is not a *minimal* model of $P[T]$, there must be a model M' of $P[T]$ such that $M' \subset M$. In light of the result above, however, this would contradict the assumption that $\mathcal{C}_M$ is a minimal class. Similarly, if M is a *minimal* Hebrand model of $P[T]$, $\mathcal{C}_M$ will be a *minimal* class of $P[T]$. ∎

Proposition 5.2 A ground atom p is *explained* in the minimal class $\mathcal{C}_M$ of T if and only if p is supported by $P[T]$ in the minimal Herbrand model M of $P[T]$.

Proof We show first that if a set of assumptions Δ supports an atom p in $P = P[T]$ then Δ is an argument for Cp in the theory T (i.e., Δ explains p). Let M be the Herbrand interpretation defined as the collection of ground atoms q such that Cq follows from Δ and T. If Δ is not consistent with T, the result is immediate; otherwise, M must satisfy $\neg p$ and Δ. Moreover, M must satisfy the positive program P^+_Δ as well; otherwise, there has to be a rule $\cdots \wedge \alpha_i \wedge \cdots \wedge \neg\beta_i \wedge \cdots \Rightarrow \mathrm{C}\gamma$ in T such that each $\neg\beta_i$ belongs to Δ, each α_i is explained by Δ, but γ is *not* explained by Δ. Therefore, M must satisfy P^+_Δ and $\neg p$, in contradiction with the assumption that Δ supports p in P.

We prove now that if Δ is an argument for Cp in T then p must be supported by Δ in P. From the result above, if Δ is self-defeating, i.e., Δ supports an atom q in P for $\neg q \in \Delta$, Δ cannot be consistent with T, and therefore, Δ cannot be an argument. Thus, if Δ does not support p, the minimal Herbrand model of P^+_Δ will satisfy both Δ and $\neg p$. Therefore, the model $M' = M + \mathrm{C}[M] + \cup_i\{\beta_i\}$, where the β_i's are the atoms that appear negated in the bodies of the rules in P but do not belong to Δ, must satisfy the causal theory T (since T is open, making the atoms β_i true does not force other atoms to be true). However, since M' is a model of T, Δ and $\neg$Cp, the assumption that Δ is an argument for Cp in T is contradicted.

Since p is explained in a class if there is an argument for p satisfied in the class, and similarly, p is supported by P in a model, if there is a support for p satisfied by the model, Proposition 5.2 follows. ∎

Theorem 5.3 The simple causal theory T causally entails an atom p iff the program $P[T]$ entails p. Likewise, T causally entails Cp iff the program $P[T]$ supports p.

Proof Since any non-minimal class (resp. model) can be removed from a basis, and the preference relation on classes (resp. models) depends only on the explained (resp. supported) and unexplained (resp. unsupported) atoms, the result is immediate from Propositions 5.1 and 5.2. ∎

Proposition 5.3 1) A set of assumptions Δ is consistent with T iff Δ is consistent with $P[T]$. 2) Δ is an argument for an atom p in T iff Δ is an argument for p in $P[T]$. 3) Δ *explains* p in T iff Δ *supports* p.

Proof 1) If Δ is consistent with T, then there is a minimal class $\mathcal{C}_M$ of T where Δ holds, whose gap M is a Herbrand model of $P[T]$ (Proposition 5.1). Therefore, Δ must be consistent with $P[T]$. Applying Proposition 5.1 in the other direction, we get that if Δ is consistent with $P[T]$, Δ must also be consistent with T. 2) Δ is an argument for p in T iff Δ is consistent in T but $\Delta + \{\neg p\}$ is not. This in turn is true if Δ is consistent in $P[T]$ but $\Delta + \{\neg p\}$ is not (part 1), which in turn means that Δ is an argument for p in $P[T]$. 3) Proved as part of Proposition 5.2 above. ∎

Lemma 5.2 A list $\Delta = \{\neg\beta_1, \ldots, \neg\beta_n\}$ is linearly stable iff for every argument Δ' in conflict with $\Delta_i = \{\neg\beta_1, \ldots, \neg\beta_i\}$, $i = 1, \ldots, n$, the relation $\Delta_i \succ \Delta'$ holds.

Proof Immediate from Definition 5.9 of linear stability. ∎

Lemma 5.3 A list of assumptions $\Delta_n = \{\neg\beta_1, \neg\beta_2, \ldots, \neg\beta_n\}$ is linearly stable iff for every argument Δ' and $i = 1, \ldots, n$, [A.1] if Δ' supports β_i, then $\Delta_{i-1}, \Delta' \vdash$ **false** , and [A.2] if Δ implies β_i, then $\Delta_i \succeq \Delta'$.

Proof Assume that Δ_n is linearly stable, and let i be the smallest integer in $[1, n]$ for which Δ_i violates condition [A.1] (Δ_i cannot violate [A.2] because Δ_i is stable and thus $\Delta_i \succeq \Delta'$ holds for every conflicting Δ'). Then, there must be an argument Δ' which supports β_i such that $\Delta_{i-1} + \Delta'$ is consistent. However, this contradicts the stability of Δ_i, as it implies that $\Delta'' = \Delta_{i-1} + \Delta'$ supports β_i and is consistent with Δ_{i-1}, and thus, $\Delta'' \succeq \Delta_i$.

The 'only if' part is a bit more involved. Let us first assume that Δ_n is derivable from [A.1] and [A.2] and let i be the smallest integer in $[1, n]$ such that Δ_i is not stable. If there is an argument Δ' in conflict with Δ_i such that $\Delta' \succeq \Delta_i$, then from the definition of the relation '$\succeq$', there must be a set $\Delta'_i \subseteq \Delta_i$ such that $\Delta'' = \Delta' + \Delta'_i$ is consistent and explains the complement of each assumption in $\Delta_i - \Delta'_i$. However, if j is the smallest integer such that $\neg\beta_j \in \Delta_i - \Delta'_i$, this means that $\Delta_{j-1} \subset \Delta''$, and therefore, that Δ'' supports β_j and is consistent with Δ_{j-1}, in contradiction with the assumption that Δ_j is derivable from [A.1] and [A.2].

We need to show now that if Δ_i is a list of assumptions derivable from [A.1] and [A.2], then $\Delta_i \succeq \Delta'$ holds for any conflicting argument Δ'. We show this by induction. For $i = 1$, Δ' cannot support β_1, otherwise Δ_1 wouldn't be derivable, and therefore, Δ' must imply β_1 from which

$\Delta_1 \succ \Delta'$ follows from [A.2]. Let us now assume $\Delta_j \succeq \Delta'$, for any Δ' in conflict with Δ_j and any j in $[1, n]$. We will show $\Delta_i \succeq \Delta'$ for $i = j+1$. There are two cases to consider. The first, if Δ' *implies* β_i, is trivial, as $\Delta_i \succeq \Delta_i$ follows from [A.2]. In the second, if Δ' is *consistent with* $\neg\beta_i$, we get that $\Delta'' = \Delta' + \{\neg\beta_i\}$ must be in conflict with Δ_{i-1}, and from the inductive hypotheses, that $\Delta_{i-1} \succeq \Delta''$ must hold. Therefore, Δ'' must contain a set Δ''_i such that $\Delta_{i-1} + \Delta''_i$ is consistent and supports the complement of each assumption in $\Delta'' - \Delta''_i$. Moreover, if $\neg\beta_i \in \Delta''_i$, then $\Delta_{i-1} + \Delta''_i$ would be an argument that supports β_i consistent with Δ_{i-1}, contradicting the condition [A.1]. Therefore, $\neg\beta_i \notin \Delta''_i$, and thus, $\Delta_i \succeq \Delta'$. ∎

Theorem 5.4 (Π_1) A list of assumptions $\Delta_n = \{\neg\beta_1, \neg\beta_2, \ldots, \neg\beta_n\}$ is linearly stable iff for every *admissible* Δ' and $i = 1, \ldots, n$, [B.1] if Δ' supports β_i, then $\Delta' + \Delta_{i-1}$ is self-defeating, and [B.2] if $\Delta' + \{\neg\beta_i\}$ is contradicted, then $\Delta' + \Delta_i$ is self-defeating.

Proof We prove the 'only if' part first. Let us assume that Δ_n is linearly stable, and thus derivable from [A.1] and [A.2] above, and let i be the smallest integer in $[1, n]$ such that Δ_i is *not* derivable from [B.1] and [B.2]. Therefore, there has to be an admissible Δ' such that Δ' supports β_i or $\Delta' + \{\neg\beta_i\}$ is contradicted. In the first case, we get from [A.1] that Δ' must be in conflict with Δ_{i-1}, and since Δ_{i-1} must be stable (Lemma 5.3), that $\Delta' + \Delta_{i-1}$ must be self-defeating. In the second case, we get from [A.2] that $\Delta_i \succeq \Delta'$ must hold, and therefore, that $\Delta' + \Delta_i$ must be self-defeating.

To prove the 'if part' we show first that if P is completely stable and conditions [B.1] and [B.2] are satisfied, $\Delta_i + \Delta'$ would be self-defeating iff $\Delta_i \succeq \Delta$, where Δ' is any admissible set of assumptions in conflict with Δ_i. Clearly the second condition implies the first, because there has to be a set $\Delta'_i \subset \Delta'$ such that the union $\Delta_i + \Delta'_i$ is consistent, and supports the complement of each of the assumptions in the non-empty set $\Delta' - \Delta'_i$. Likewise, if $\Delta_i + \Delta'$ is self-defeating and P is completely stable, there must be a subset Δ'_i of $\Delta_i + \Delta'$ such that Δ'_i is not self-defeating and supports each of the assumptions in $(\Delta_i + \Delta') - \Delta'_i$. Moreover, Δ'_i must be admissible; otherwise, since Δ' *is* admissible, there would have to be a smallest j in $[1, n]$ such that $\Delta'_i - \{\neg\beta_{j+1}, \ldots, \neg\beta_n\}$ is contradicted but $\Delta'_i - \{\neg\beta_j, \ldots, \neg\beta_n\}$ is not, meaning that $\Delta'_i - \{\neg\beta_j, \ldots, \neg\beta_n\}$ is self-defeating (because of [B.2]), in contradiction with the selection of Δ'_i. Furthermore, there cannot be an assumption in Δ_i which is *not* in Δ'_i, because otherwise, if $\neg\beta_j$ is the first such assumption, Δ'_i would support β_j, and by [B.2], Δ'_i would have to be self-defeating. Thus, $\Delta'' = \Delta'_i - \Delta_i$ is a subset of $\Delta' - \Delta_i$ such that $\Delta_i + \Delta''$ 1) is not self-defeating, and thus, consistent,[9] and 2) supports the complement of each of the assumptions in $\Delta' - \Delta''$. Therefore, $\Delta_i \succeq \Delta'$ holds.

We can now show that conditions [B.1] and [B.2] imply conditions [A.1] and [A.2], and therefore, that the two pairs of conditions are equivalent. If Δ' is an argument that supports β_i, then by [B.1], $\Delta' + \Delta_{i-1}$ will be self-defeating, and thus, $\Delta' + \Delta_{i-1}$ will be inconsistent. Likewise, if Δ' implies β_i, $\Delta' + \{\neg\beta_i\}$ will be either self-defeating or contradicted (because P is open; see page 204 below). In either case, $\Delta' + \Delta_i$ will be self-defeating, and therefore, from the result above, $\Delta_i \succeq \Delta'$ follows. ∎

Theorem 5.5 (Π_1^-) If the program $P[T]$ encodes the *closure* of a simple causal theory T and no constraints in $P[T]$ are *evidential,* then the list $\Delta_n = \{\neg\beta_1, \ldots, \neg\beta_n\}$ will be linearly stable iff for any Δ' which supports β_i, $1 \leq i \leq n$, $\Delta' + \Delta_{i-1}$ is self-defeating.

Proof The only detail left to prove is that the rebuttals Δ' no longer have to be admissible. For if an unadmissible Δ' supports β_i, Δ' would be self-defeating, and thus the condition '$\Delta' + \Delta_{i-1}$ is self-defeating' will be satisfied automatically. ∎

Theorem 5.6 (Π_2) An atom q is supported by a linear stable argument in the *closure* of a program P, if $\mid\!\approx_P q$ is derivable from the following rules: [1]. If $p \leftarrow\, \in P$, then $\mid\!\approx_P p$, [2]. If $p \leftarrow A \in P$, $\mid\!\approx_P p_i$ for each atom p_i in A, and every support Δ' for $\sim\!p$ is *defeated,* then $\mid\!\approx_P p$.

Proof We prove the result by induction in the length of the derivation of q. If q is derivable in a single step, q must be supported by a linear stable argument (the empty argument). So let us assume that every atom q derivable in less than n steps is supported by a linear stable argument. We need to show that if p is derivable in n steps, then p will also be supported by a linear stable argument. So let

[9] If P is open, a set of assumptions Δ is consistent iff Δ is not self-defeating. See the proof in footnote 12 on page 204 below.

$p \leftarrow \alpha_1, \ldots, \alpha_n, \neg\beta_1, \ldots, \neg\beta_m$ be the last rule used for deriving p, and let Δ stand for union of all the linear stable arguments supporting the atoms derivable in less than n steps. Clearly, Δ is linearly stable. We have to show that $\Delta^* = \Delta + \{\neg\beta_1, \ldots, \neg\beta_m\}$ is linearly stable as well, or in light of Theorem 5.4, that Δ^* is derivable from Π_1. Given the inductive hypothesis and the completeness of Π_1, we only need to focus on the last part of the list Δ^* and show that the union of any rebuttal Δ' that supports one of the β_i's and Δ will be self-defeating.

Since none of the β_i's can appear in the head of a rule in P (explicit 'cancellations' are ruled out), the only way Δ' can support β_i is when $\neg\beta_i$ occurs in a rule $r : q \leftarrow \alpha_1, \ldots, \alpha_n, \neg\beta_1, \ldots, \neg\beta_m$[10] in head-to-head conflict with a rule $r' : \sim q \leftarrow A'$ supported by Δ', and whose priority is not lower than the priority of r.[11] This is in fact the only way β_i could appear as the head of a rule in the *closure* of P. Now, if Δ' is defeated, it means that Δ' supports an atom $\sim s$ which is incompatible with an atom s derivable by Π_2 in less than n steps. This means that the union $\Delta' + \Delta$ is contradicted, and therefore, under the assumptions of the theorem, that $\Delta' + \Delta$ is self-defeating. Then $\Delta^* = \Delta + \{\neg\beta_1, \ldots, \neg\beta_m\}$ is derivable from Π_1, and since each of the positive antecedents α_i is supported by Δ, p is supported by the linear stable argument Δ^*. ∎

Theorem 5.7 An open program P is *completely stable* if P does not contain self-defeating rules and the open disjunctive program P_D obtained from P is *stratified*.

Proof P_D is stratified if the non-disjunctive program P_D^* is stratified. If so, the atoms in P_D^* can be partitioned into strata S_1, S_2, ... such that for every ground rule $\gamma \leftarrow \alpha_1, \ldots, \alpha_n, \neg\beta_1, \ldots, \neg\beta_m$, if γ belongs to S_j, each α_i belongs to some stratum S_k, $k \leq j$, and each β_i belongs to some stratum S_l, $l < j$ [Prz87, ABW87]. Below we will write $p < q$ (resp. $p = q$) if p and q occur in strata S_i and S_j such that $i < j$ (resp. $i = j$).

Since some atoms are renamed in P_D^* (e.g., when there are several atoms in a clique in P, all are mapped into a single atom ξ_i in P_D^*), we will denote the atom in P_D^* which corresponds to the atom a in P as $n(a)$. The mapping $n(\cdot)$ is thus a many-to-one. In particular every

[10] Recall that for Π_2 we are assuming that all rules that include a common assumption have a common body.

[11] Δ' supports a rule $\sim q \leftarrow \alpha'_1, \ldots, \alpha'_n, \neg\beta'_1, \ldots, \neg\beta'_m$ when it supports each positive α'_i and it includes each negative $\neg\beta'_i$.

positive link $a \to b$ in (the dependency graph of) P maps into a positive link $n(a) \to n(b)$ in (the dependency graph of) P_D^*. However, a negative link $a \not\to b$ can either appear as a negative link $n(a) \not\to n(b)$ in P_D^*, or can 'collapse' into a single point when a and b belong to the same clique in P. In the first case, $n(a) < n(b)$, and in the second case, $n(a) = n(b)$.

For a program P, a Herbrand interpretation M is a model of P when M 'hits' every set of assumptions Δ_i *inconsistent* with P (M hits a set Δ when M contains the complement of one of the assumptions in Δ). Moreover, if P is open and does not contain constraints, these sets Δ_i correspond exactly to the sets Δ_i which are *self-defeating.*[12] Since the stable models of P are models of P, we can thus focus on the interpretations that 'hit' each of the *minimal* self-defeating assumptions sets in P. Below we will focus on the interpretation that 'hit' each of the *minimal* self-defeating assumption sets Δ_i contained in an arbitrary set Δ, as we need to show that *any* subprogram P_Δ in P is stable,[13] and thus, that P is *completely* stable.

We will start by partitioning each minimal self-defeating Δ_i in Δ into a *head* H_i and a *body* B_i. The head H_i of Δ_i will be given by the assumptions $\neg\alpha_j$ in Δ_i such that $\Delta_i - \{\neg\alpha_j\}$ supports α_j. Since P does not contain self-defeating rules and P_D^* is stratified, H_i will be non-empty, and in fact, it would contain the complements of the atoms α_j, $\neg\alpha_j \in \Delta_i$, supported by Δ_i (recall that P is open, so positive antecedents and negative antecedents are disjoint). The body B_i of Δ_i will be given by $\Delta_i - H_i$. Since $\Delta_i - \{\neg\alpha_j\}$ is a minimal support for α_j for any assumption $\neg\alpha_j$ in H_i, in the dependency graph of P, the complement of every assumption $\neg\alpha_l$ in Δ_i different than $\neg\alpha_j$ will have to be connected to α_j by a negative link followed by a (possibly) empty chain of positive links. Therefore, either α_j and α_l must belong to the same clique in P, or they must be such that $n(\alpha_j) < n(\alpha_l)$ in P_D^*. Moreover, since the relation '$<$' is asymmetric, $\neg\alpha_l$ and $\neg\alpha_j$ will have to belong to the same clique when both belong to H_i. Since the same

[12]If Δ is consistent with P, there is a model of both P and Δ, and thus, a model of both P_Δ^+ and Δ. Therefore, if Δ is consistent, Δ is not self-defeating. Similarly, if Δ is not self-defeating, there must be a model M of both P_Δ^+ and Δ. Thus, if we add to M all the atoms β_i for negative literals $\neg\beta_i$ in P which do not belong to Δ, the resulting model M' will satisfy both Δ and P (since P is open, making any β_i true will not force others atom to become true). Therefore, Δ will be consistent with P if Δ is not self-defeating.

[13]Recall that P_Δ stand for the ground rule instances in P whose assumptions belong to Δ.

applies to all members of H_i, all the assumptions $\neg\alpha_j$ in H_i will have to belong to the same clique in P, and therefore, all the atoms α_j will be mapped to the same atom in P_D^*. We will call this atom $n(H_i)$. For each assumption $\neg\beta_j$ in the body B_i of Δ_i, on the other hand, we must have $n(\beta_j) < n(H_i)$, since otherwise, $\neg\beta_j$ would have to be in the same clique as the assumptions in H_i, and therefore, $\neg\beta_j$ would belong to H_i and not to B_i.

Provided with the rankings $n(H_i)$ for each of the heads of the minimal self-defeating sets Δ_i in P_Δ, we will define the following sequence of interpretations I_j:

$$I_0 = \emptyset$$

$$I_j = I_{j-1} + \text{ minimal hit set for } C_j[I_{j-1}]$$

where $C_j[I] = \{H_i \,|\, n(H_i) = j \;\&\; \Delta_i \text{ not hit by } I\}$ and a hitting set for $C_j[I]$ is a collection of atoms that hit every assumption set in $C_j[I]$. We will show that the interpretation M defined as the limit of I_j when $j \to \infty$ is *stable model* of P_Δ, and since this applies to any Δ, that P is a completely stable program.

First, M is a model of P_Δ because M hits every minimal self-defeating assumption set Δ_i. Moreover, M is a *minimal* model of P_Δ. Otherwise, if we remove $p \in I_j$ from M, and H_i is a head hit by I_j but not by $I_j - \{p\}$ (there has to be one such H_i, otherwise, I_j would not be a minimal hitting set), we would obtain that the resulting interpretation $M' = M - \{p\}$ does not hit Δ_i. Indeed, I_{j-1} cannot hit Δ_i, otherwise, Δ_i would not belong to $C_j[I_{j-1}]$. Similarly, $M - I_j$ cannot hit Δ_i either, because for every atom q in $M - I_j$, $n(q) > j$ while for every assumption $\neg\beta$ in Δ_i, $n(\beta) \leq j$. In particular, thus, $\neg p$ is the only assumption in Δ_i that is *false* in M, and therefore, since $\neg p$ belongs to the head of Δ_i, p is supported by $\Delta_i - \{\neg p\}$ in M. Since the same applies to all the other atoms in M, M is a stable model of P_Δ. ∎

The following lemma will be used in several of the proofs below. Recall that P_Δ^+ is the positive ground program obtained from P by selecting all the rule instances in P whose assumptions all belong to Δ, and by discarding all the assumptions from the rules that are left. (the transformation is analogous to the one in [GL88]). Likewise, Δ supports p if p is a logical consequence of the program P_Δ^+, and Δ is self-defeating if Δ supports an atom q for an assumption $\neg q$ in Δ. Similarly, Δ is an argument in T if Δ is consistent with T. The notation C$[M]$ is used to denote the collection of formulas Cp_i for atoms p_i in M.

Lemma 6.0 Let T stand for the causal theory $C_1[P]$. Then an argument Δ explains an atom p in the theory T, i.e., $T, \Delta \vdash p$, if and only if Δ supports p in P, i.e., $P^+_\Delta \vdash p$, and Δ is not self-defeating.

Proof If Δ supports p in P but Δ does not explain p in T, we can build a Herbrand interpretation M comprised of all the atoms q that are explained by Δ in T. M does not satisfy p, but as we will show, M does satisfy P^+_Δ, in contradiction with the assumption that p is supported by Δ in P. Let us assume that M does not satisfy P^+_Δ. Then, there has to be a rule

$$r : \gamma \leftarrow \alpha_1, \ldots, \alpha_n, \neg\beta_1, \ldots, \neg\beta_m$$

in P such that each α_i belongs to M, each $\neg\beta_i$ belongs to Δ but γ does not belong to M. However, by the definition of T and the construction of M, this implies that there is a rule

$$r_C : \mathrm{C}\alpha_1 \wedge \cdots \wedge \mathrm{C}\alpha_n \wedge \neg\beta_1 \wedge \cdots \wedge \neg\beta_m \Rightarrow \mathrm{C}\gamma$$

in T such that Δ explains each α_i, Δ includes each $\neg\beta_i$ but Δ does not explain γ, what amounts to a contradiction. Thus, Δ explains p in the causal theory T, if Δ supports p in the program P.

Let us now assume that a consistent Δ explains p in the theory T but Δ does not support p in the program P. Then the minimal Herbrand model M of the positive program P^+_Δ must satisfy both Δ and $\neg p$ (if M does not satisfy Δ, it would mean that Δ is self-defeating, and thus, from the result above, that Δ is not consistent with T). We will show that the interpretation M' defined as $M' = M + \mathrm{C}[M] + \cup_i\{\beta_i\}$, where the β_i's are complements of the assumptions $\neg\beta_i \not\in \Delta$, must be a model of T, Δ and $\neg \mathrm{C}p$, in contradiction with the assumption that Δ explains p in T. Indeed, assume that M' violates a rule in T such as r_C above. That means 1) that each formula Cα_i belongs to M' and thus to C$[M]$, 2) that each assumption $\neg\beta_i$ is satisfied by M' and thus that $\neg\beta_i$ belongs to Δ, and 3) that Cγ does not belong to M' and thus that it does not belong to C$[M]$ either. However, this contradicts the assumption that M satisfies the program P^+_Δ, because P^+_Δ must then contain the positive rule $\gamma \leftarrow \alpha_1, \ldots, \alpha_n$, for which M contains each of the antecedents but not the consequent. Thus, the minimal model of P^+_Δ cannot satisfy $\neg p$ if a consistent Δ explains p in the theory T, and therefore, Δ supports p in the program P.

We are left to show that if Δ is inconsistent in T, then Δ must be self-defeating in P, but this is immediate from the the construction of the interpretation M' above. ∎

Theorem 6.1 If P is stratified, then M is the canonical Herbrand model of P if and only if $\mathcal{C}_M$ is the single preferred class of $C_1[P]$.

Proof When P is stratified, the canonical model M of P is the unique stable model of P [GL88]. In Theorem 6.2 below, we establish that M is a stable model of P iff $\mathcal{C}_M$ is a perfectly coherent class of $C_1[P]$ (i.e., every atom in M is explained in $\mathcal{C}_M$). Since a perfectly coherent class is at least as preferred as any other class, we only have to show here that no class $\mathcal{C}_{M'}$ of $C_1[P]$ is at least as preferred as $\mathcal{C}_M$, if $M' \neq M$. We will write $\alpha_1 < \alpha_2$, for two atoms α_1 and α_2 with predicates p_1 and p_2, respectively, when the dependency graph of P contains a path connecting p_1 to p_2 which includes a negative link. Since P is stratified, the relation '$<$' must be a strict partial order. Now let α be a *minimal* element in $M' - M$ relative to the order '$<$'. For the class $\mathcal{C}_{M'}$ to be as preferred as $\mathcal{C}_M$, the atom α must be explained in $\mathcal{C}_{M'}$, and thus, there must be a minimal set Δ of assumptions $\neg\alpha_1, \ldots, \neg\alpha_n$ that hold in $\mathcal{C}_{M'}$ which explain α. From Lemma 6.0, Δ must support α in P, and therefore, for each of the atoms α_i, $i = 1, \ldots, n$, we must have $\alpha_i < \alpha$. Furthermore, since α does not belong to M, one of the atoms α_i must belong to M, and therefore, to $M - M'$. Since $\mathcal{C}_M$ is perfectly coherent, however, α_i must be explained in $\mathcal{C}_M$, and thus, there must be a minimal set of assumptions $\neg\beta_1, \ldots, \neg\beta_m$ that hold in $\mathcal{C}_M$ which explain α_i. By arguments similar to the ones above, we must have $\beta_j < \alpha_i$, for $j = 1, \ldots, m$, and one such β_j must belong to $M' - M$. However, since $\beta_j < \alpha_i < \alpha$, this contradicts the assumption that α is a minimal element in $M' - M$. Therefore, there is no minimal element in $M' - M$, and $M' = M$. ∎

Theorem 6.2 M is a *stable* model of an arbitrary program P if and only if $\mathcal{C}_M$ is a perfectly coherent class of the causal theory $C_1[P]$.

Proof From the definition of stable models and the notion of support, M is a stable model of P iff the set Δ of assumptions true in M is not self-defeating and supports every atom p in M. By Lemma 6.0 then, Δ must be consistent with $C_1[P]$ and must explain every atom $\beta \in M$. Therefore, $\mathcal{C}_M$ is a class of $C_1[P]$ which is perfectly coherent. Similarly, if $\mathcal{C}_M$ is a perfectly coherent class of $C_1[P]$, the set Δ of assumptions that hold in $\mathcal{C}_M$ (i.e., the assumptions $\neg\beta$ for $\beta \notin M$) must be consistent with $C_1[P]$ and must explain every atom in M. By Lemma 6.0 then, Δ is not self-defeating in P and must support every atom $\beta \in M$. Therefore, M is a stable model of P. ∎

Theorem 6.3 For an acyclic program P, M is the canonical model of P iff $\mathcal{C}_M$ is the single preferred class of $C_1[P]$, $C_2[P]$, and $C_3[P]$.

Proof From Theorem 6.1, M is the canonical model of a stratified program P iff $\mathcal{C}_M$ is the single preferred class of $C_1[P]$ (recall that acyclic programs are stratified). Furthermore every model M' in $\mathcal{C}_M$ has to be a model of both $C_2[P]$ and $C_3[P]$, because p holds in M' iff Cp does (Theorem 6.2). Likewise, every model of $C_2[P]$ and $C_3[P]$ is always a model of $C_1[P]$. As a result, $\mathcal{C}_M$ has to be a perfectly coherent class of $C_2[P]$ and $C_3[P]$, and hence, it must be at least as preferred as any other classes of $C_2[P]$ and $C_3[P]$. To prove the theorem we thus need to show that there is no class $\mathcal{C}_{M'}$ which is at least as preferred as $\mathcal{C}_M$ in either $C_2[P]$ or $C_3[P]$. We proved this earlier for $C_1[P]$ (Theorem 6.1). Let us write $\alpha_1 < \alpha_2$ for two atoms α_1 and α_2, when the dependency graph of P contains a path from α_1 to α_2 (or a path from the predicate p_1 corresponding to α_1 and the predicate p_2 corresponding to α_2). Since P is acyclic, the relation '$<$' is a strict partial order. Thus, if $\mathcal{C}_{M'}$ is a class of $T = C_i[P]$, for $i = 1$, 2 or 3, which is as least as preferred as $\mathcal{C}_M$, and $M' \neq M$, there has to be an atom α in $M' - M$ that is minimal relative to such order. Moreover, since the class $\mathcal{C}_{M'}$ is as preferred as the class $\mathcal{C}_M$, α must be explained in $\mathcal{C}_{M'}$. Therefore, T must contain a rule

$$[\mathrm{C}]\,\alpha_1 \wedge \ldots \wedge [\mathrm{C}]\,\alpha_n \wedge \neg\beta_1 \wedge \ldots \wedge \neg\beta_m \Rightarrow \mathrm{C}\alpha$$

such that every positive literal α_i and negative literal $\neg\beta_j$ hold in $\mathcal{C}_{M'}$ ([C] means that the operator C may or may not occur). Also, since $\alpha_i < \alpha$, for $i = 1, \ldots, n$, every positive antecedent α_i must belong to M, otherwise, α wouldn't be the *minimal* atom in $M' - M$ relative to the ordering '$<$'. Yet, since α does not belong to M, one of the atoms β_i,

$1 \leq i \leq m$, must belong to $M - M'$. So let α' be a minimal element in $M - M'$ such that $\alpha' < \beta_i$ or $\alpha = \beta_i$. Since α' must be explained in $\mathcal{C}_M$, T must contain a rule:

$$[\mathrm{C}]\,\alpha'_1 \wedge \ldots \wedge [\mathrm{C}]\,\alpha'_n \wedge \neg\beta'_1 \wedge \ldots \wedge \neg\beta'_m \Rightarrow \mathrm{C}\alpha'$$

in which every antecedent α'_i and $\neg\beta'_j$ holds in $\mathcal{C}_M$. Furthermore, no β'_j, $1 \leq j \leq m$, may belong to M' since $\beta'_j \notin M$ and $\beta'_j < \alpha' \leq \beta_i < \alpha$. On the other hand, given the minimality of α', every atom α'_k must also belong to M'. So, every antecedent α'_i and $\neg\beta'_j$ of α' must hold in $\mathcal{C}_{M'}$, in contradiction with the assumption that α' does not belong to M'. Thus, $\mathcal{C}_{M'}$ cannot be at least as preferred as $\mathcal{C}_M$, and thus, $\mathcal{C}_M$ is the single preferred class of each $C_1[P]$, $C_2[P]$ and $C_3[P]$. ∎

Theorem 6.4 The causal theories $C_1[P]$, $C_2[P]$, and $C_3[P]$ are equivalent for any program P which is *open*.

Proof We need to show that the three causal theories $C_1[P]$, $C_2[P]$, and $C_3[P]$ have the same classes of minimal models, and that in each class, the same atoms are explained. Both results are consequence of results proven earlier in a different form. We will use T to refer to *any* of the causal theories $C_i[P]$ for $i = 1$, 2 or 3.

1. If p is supported by Δ in P, i.e., $P^+_\Delta \vdash p$, then Cp follows from Δ in T, i.e., $T, \Delta \vdash \mathrm{C}p$. This is obvious if Δ is inconsistent in T. On the other hand, if Δ is consistent and Cp does not follow, we can build an interpretation M that satisfies Δ by collecting all the atoms q such that Cq follows from T and Δ. Since p does not hold in M, M must violate some rule in P^+_Δ. This, however, is not possible, as it implies that there is a rule in T whose positive antecedents are all explained, whose negative antecedents all belong Δ, and whose consequent is not explained.

2. If Δ is an argument for Cp in T, then Δ supports p in P. Otherwise, we can build an interpretation M that satisfies T, Δ and $\neg$Cp, starting with the minimal model M of the program P^+_Δ. Since Δ cannot be self-defeating (otherwise, from 1., Δ would be inconsistent in T), M must satisfy both Δ and $\neg p$. Thus, if we add to M all formulas Cq for $q \in M$, and the complement of all the negative literals $\neg\beta_i \notin \Delta$ which occur in P, we get an interpretation M' that satisfies T and Δ but which does not satisfy

Cp (recall that P is open, and thus, that addition of the atoms β_i cannot force other atom to be true).

3. If M is a model of P then $M + \mathrm{C}[M]$ is a model of T ($\mathrm{C}[M]$ stands for the collection of formulas $\mathrm{C}p_i$ for $p_i \in M$). This is straightforward.
4. If $\mathrm{C}[M] + N$ is a model of T, then N is a model of P. Indeed, if N is not a model of P, since P is open, there must be some self-defeating argument Δ which is not 'hit' by N (see proof of Theorem 5.7). However, from 1., if Δ is self-defeating in P, Δ is inconsistent with T, and therefore, should be hit by $C[M]+N$ and thus by N, because $M \subseteq N$ since $\mathrm{C}p$ implies p.

From 1–4 it follows that $\mathcal{C}_M$ will be a minimal class of T iff M is a minimal model of P, and that p will be explained in $\mathcal{C}_M$ iff p is supported by P in M. In other words, any $T = C_i[P]$, $i = 1, 2, 3$ will have the same minimal classes, and in those classes, the same atoms will be explained. ∎

Theorem 6.5 p is true in the well-founded model of P if and only if p is supported by a list of assumptions Δ derivable from P by Π_0.

Proof The alternating fixpoint semantics of P, shown to be equivalent to the well-founded semantics [Van89], legitimizes all the assumptions that hold in the least fixed point A^* of the transformation $A(\Delta) = S'(S'(\Delta))$, where $S'(\Delta)$ stands for literals $\neg\beta_i$ whose complements are not supported by Δ. In order to show that these assumptions are the same assumptions that are derivable from Π_0, let Δ^0_j, $j = 1, 2, \ldots$ stand for the collection of assumptions derivable from Π_0 in a minimum number of j steps, and let Δ_i stand for the union $\cup_{j=1,i}\Delta^0_j$. Let us also say that an assumption $\neg\beta$ is *rebutted* by a set Δ' of assumptions if Δ' supports β, and that Δ' is *defeated* by a set Δ if Δ rebuts some assumption in Δ'. Then, both $A^1(\emptyset)$ and $\Delta^1(\emptyset)$ are comprised of the assumptions which are not rebutted by any Δ', while $A^i(\emptyset)$ and Δ_i, for $i > 1$, are comprised of the assumptions whose rebuttals Δ' are defeated by $A^{i-1}(\emptyset)$ and Δ_{i-1} respectively. As a result, $A^i(\emptyset) = \Delta_i$, for every i, and since $A^* = A^\infty(\emptyset)$, any atom p supported by assumptions in A^* will be supported by assumptions in Δ_∞, and vice versa. ∎

Bibliography

[ABW87] K. Apt, H. Blair, and A. Walker. Towards a theory of declarative knowledge. In J. Minker, editor, *Foundations of Deductive Databases and Logic Programming*, pages 89–148. Morgan Kaufmann, Los Altos, CA, 1987.

[Ada66] E. Adams. Probability and the logic of conditionals. In J. Hintikka and P. Suppes, editors, *Aspects of Inductive Logic*. North Holland Publishing Company, Amsterdam, 1966.

[Ada75] E. Adams. *The Logic of Conditionals*. D. Reiter, Dordrecht, 1975.

[Ada78] E. Adams. A note comparing probabilistic and modal logics of conditionals. *Theoria*, 43:186–194, 1978.

[All84] J. Allen. Towards a general theory of action and time. *Artificial Intelligence*, 23:123–154, 1984.

[Bac89] F. Bacchus. A modest, but semantically well founded, inheritance reasoner. In *Proceedings IJCAI-89*, pages 1104–1109, Detroit, MI., 1989.

[Bac90] F. Bacchus. *Representing and Reasoning with Probabilistic Knowledge*. MIT Press, Cambridge, Mass., 1990.

[BF87] N. Bidoit and C. Fridevaux. Minimalism subsumes default logic and circumscription in stratified logic programming. In *Proceedings of the Logic in Computer Science Conference*, pages 89–97, 1987.

[BG89] A. Baker and M. Ginsberg. A theorem prover for prioritized circumscription. In *Proceedings IJCAI-89*, pages 463–467, Detroit, MI., 1989.

[BGW91] J. Breese, R. Goldman, and M. Wellman. Knowledge based construction of probabilistic and decision models: An overview. In *Notes of AAAI-91 Workshop on Model Construction*, Anaheim, CA, 1991.

[Bre89] G. Brewka. Preferred subtheories: An extended logical framework for default reasoning. In *Proceedings IJCAI-89*, pages 1043–1049, Detroit, Michigan, 1989.

[BS85a] G. Bossu and P. Siegel. Saturation, non-monotonic reasoning and the closed-world assumption. *Artificial Intelligence*, 25:13–63, 1985.

[BS85b] R. Brachman and J. Schmolze. An overview of the KL-ONE knowledge representation system. *Cognitive Science*, 9:171–216, 1985.

[CDT89] L. Console, D. Dupre, and P. Torasso. A theory of diagnosis for incomplete causal models. In *Proceedings IJCAI-89*, pages 1311–1317, Detroit, Michigan, 1989.

[CG89] E. Charniak and R. Goldman. Plan recognition in stories and life. In *Workshop on Uncertainty in AI*, pages 54–60, Buffalo, NY., 1989.

[CL73] C. Chang and R. Lee. *Symbolic Logic and Mechanical Theorem Proving*. Academic Press, New York, 1973.

[Cla78] K. Clark. Negation as failure. In H. Gallaire and J. Minker, editors, *Logic and Data Bases*, pages 293–322. Plenum Press, New York, 1978.

[CM85] E. Charniak and D. McDermott. *Introduction to Artificial Intelligence*. Addison Wesley, Reading, MA., 1985.

[CS90] E. Charniak and S. Shimony. Probabilistic semantics for cost based abduction. In *Proceedings AAAI-90*, pages 106–111, Boston, MA., 1990.

[DB87] T. Dean and M. Boddy. Incremental causal reasoning. In *Proceedings AAAI-87*, pages 196–201, Seattle, WA., 1987.

[Del87] J. Delgrande. An approach to default reasoning based on a first-order conditional logic. In *Proceedings AAAI-87*, pages 340–345, Seattle, 1987.

[DG84] W. Dowling and J. Gallier. Linear-time algorithms for testing the satisfiability of propositional horn formulae. *Journal of Logic Programming*, 3:267–284, 1984.

[dK86] J. de Kleer. An assumption-based truth maintenance system. *Artificial Intelligence*, 28:280–297, 1986.

[DM87] T. Dean and D. McDermott. Temporal data base management. *Artificial Intelligence*, 32:1–55, 1987.

[Doy79] J. Doyle. A truth maintenance system. *Artificial Intelligence*, 12:231–272, 1979.

[Doy85] J. Doyle. Expert systems and the "myth" of symbolic reasoning. *IEEE Transactions on Software Engineering*, 11:1386–1390, 1985.

[Doy90] J. Doyle. Rationality and its roles in reasoning. In *Proceedings AAAI-90*, pages 1093–1100, Boston, MA, 1990.

[DP91] R. Dechter and J. Pearl. Directed constraint networks: A relational framework for causal modeling. In *Proceedings IJCAI-91*, Melbourne, Australia, 1991.

[Dre88] O. Dressler. Extending the basic ATMS. In *Proceedings ECAI*, pages 385–391, 1988.

[Dye83] M. Dyer. *In Depth Understanding: A Computer Model of Integrated Processing for Narrative Comprehension.* MIT Press, Cambridge, MA., 1983.

[Elk88] C. Elkan. A rational reconstruction of nonmonotonic TMSs. Technical report, Cornell University, 1988.

[ER83] D. Etherington and R. Reiter. On inheritance hierarchies with exceptions. In *Proceedings AAAI-83*, pages 104–108, Washington, D.C., 1983.

[Eth88] D. Etherington. *Reasoning with Incomplete Information.* Pitman, London, 1988.

[Fah79] S. Fahlman. *NETL: A System for Representing and Using Real-World Knowledge.* MIT Press, Cambridge, MA., 1979.

[Fin89] K. Fine. The justification of negation as failure. In J. E. Fenstad *et al*, editor, *Logic, Methodology and Philosophy of Science*, pages 263–301. Elsevier Science Publishers, 1989.

[Gab85] D. Gabbay. Theoretical foundations for non-monotonic reasoning in expert systems. In K. R. Apt, editor, *Logics and Models of Concurrent Systems*, pages 439–457. Springer-Verlag, Heilderberg, 1985.

[Gar88] P. Gardenfors. *Knowledge in Flux: Modeling the Dynamics of Epistemic States.* MIT Press, Cambridge, MA., 1988.

[Gef88] H. Geffner. On the logic of defaults. In *Proceedings AAAI-88*, pages 449–454, St. Paul, MN, 1988.

[Gef89] H. Geffner. Default reasoning, minimality and coherence. In *Proceedings of the First International Conference on Principle of Knowledge Representation and Reasoning*, pages 137–148, Toronto, Ontario, 1989.

[Gef90a] H. Geffner. Causal theories for nonmonotonic reasoning. In *Proceedings AAAI-90*, pages 524–530, Boston, MA, 1990.

[Gef90b] H. Geffner. Conditional entailment: Closing the gap between defaults and conditionals. In *Proceedings of the Third International Workshop on Non-Monotonic Reasoning*, pages 58–72, South Lake Tahoe, CA., 1990. A revised version to appear in the *AIJ*, Fall 1991.

[Gef91] H. Geffner. Beyond negation as failure. In *Proceedings of the Second International Conference on Principle of Knowledge Representation and Reasoning*, pages 218–229, April 1991.

[Gef92] H. Geffner. A practical architecture for causal reasoning. Technical report, IBM T.J. Watson Research Center, 1992. Forthcoming.

[Gel87] M. Gelfond. On stratified autoepistemic theories. In *Proceedings AAAI-87*, pages 207–211, Seattle, Washington, 1987.

[Gel89a] M. Gelfond. Autoepistemic logic and formalization of commonsense reasoning. a preliminary report. In M. Reinfrank *et al.*, editor, *Proceedings of the Second International Workshop on Non-Monotonic Reasoning*, pages 177–186, Berlin, Germany, 1989. Springer Lecture Notes on Computer Science.

[Gel89b] M. Gelfond. Epistemic approach to formalization of commonsense reasoning. Unpublished manuscript, 1989.

[Gin87] M. Ginsberg, editor. *Readings in Nonmonotonic Reasoning*. Morgan Kaufmann, Los Altos, CA., 1987.

[Gin88] M. Ginsberg. Multivalued logics: A uniform approach to reasoning in artificial intelligence. *Computational Intelligence*, 4:265–316, 1988.

[Gin90] M. Ginsberg. A local formalization of inheritance: Preliminary report. In *Proceedings of the Third International Workshop on Non-Monotonic Reasoning*, pages 119–130, South Lake Tahoe, CA., 1990.

[GL88] M. Gelfond and V. Lifschitz. The stable model semantics for logic programming. In *Proceedings of the Fifth International Conference and Symposium on Logic Programming*, pages 1070–1080, Cambridge, Mass., 1988. MIT Press.

[GM90] L. Giordano and A. Martelli. Generalized stable models, truth-maintenance and conflict resolution. In *Proceedings of the Seventh International Conference on Logic Programming*, pages 427–441, Cambridge, Mass., 1990. MIT Press.

[GMP90] M. Goldszmidt, P. Morris, and J. Pearl. A maximum entropy approach to nonmonotonic reasoning. In *Proceedings AAAI-90*, pages 646–652, Boston, MA, 1990.

[Goo55] N. Goodman. *Fact, Fiction and Forecast.* Harvard University Press, Cambridge, MA., 1955.

[GP87] H. Geffner and J. Pearl. A framework for reasoning with defaults. Technical Report TR-94-III, Cognitive Systems Laboratory, UCLA, Los Angeles, CA., 1987. Also in *Knowledge Representation and Defeasible Inference*, H. Kyburg, R. Loui and G. Carlson (Eds), Kluwer, 1990.

[GP89] M. Gelfond and H. Przymusinska. Inheritance reasoning in autoepistemic logic. Technical report, Computer Science Department, University of Texas at El Paso, El Paso, Texas, 1989.

[Gro91] B. Grosof. Generalizing prioritization. In *Proceedings of the Second International Conference on Principle of Knowledge Representation and Reasoning*, pages 289–300, April 1991.

[GS88] M. Ginsberg and D. Smith. Reasoning about action I: A possible worlds approach. *Artificial Intelligence*, 35:165–195, 1988.

[GT84] C. Glymour and R. Thomason. Default reasoning and the logic of theory perturbation. In *Proceedings Mon-Monotonic Reasoning Workshop*, pages 93–102, New Paltz, 1984.

[GV89] H. Geffner and T. Verma. Inheritance = Chaining + Defeat. Technical Report TR-129, Cognitive Systems Lab., UCLA, Los Angeles, CA., 1989. Condensed version in *Methodologies for Intelligent Systems 4*, Z. Ras and L. Saitta (Eds), North Holland, 1989.

[Har86] G. Harman. *Change in View.* MIT Press, Cambridge, Mass., 1986.

[Hau87] B. Haugh. Simple causal minimization for temporal persistence and projection. In *Proceedings of the AAAI-87*, pages 218–223, Seattle, Washington, 1987.

[Hau88] B. Haugh. Tractable theories of multiple defeasible inheritance in ordinary nonmonotonic logics. In *Proceedings AAAI-88*, pages 421–426, St. Paul, Minnesota, 1988.

[HBH88] E. Horvitz, J. Breese, and M. Henrion. Decision theory in expert systems and AI. *Int. J. of Approximate Reasoning*, 2:247–302, 1988.

[Hew72] C. Hewitt. Description and theoretical analysis of planner: a language for proving theorems and manipulating models in a robot. Technical Report TR-258, MIT, AI Lab., Cambridge, Mass., 1972.

[HM85] S. Hanks and D. McDermott. Temporal reasoning and default logics. Technical report, Department of Computer Science, Yale University, 1985.

[HM86] S. Hanks and D. McDermott. Default reasoning, non-monotonic logics, and the frame problem. In *Proceedings AAAI-86*, pages 328–333, Philadelphia, 1986.

[HM87] S. Hanks and D. McDermott. Non-monotonic logics and temporal projection. *Artificial Intelligence*, 33:379–412, 1987.

[HSME88] J. Hobbs, M. Stickel, P. Martin, and D. Edwards. Interpretation as abduction. In *Proceedings of the 26th Annual Meeting of the ACL*, pages 95–103, Buffalo, NY., 1988.

[HTT87] J. Horty, R. Thomason, and D. Touretzky. A skeptical theory of inheritance. In *Proceedings AAAI-87*, pages 358–363, Seattle, Washington, 1987.

[Jef83] R. Jeffrey. *The Logic of Decision.* University of Chicago Press, Chicago, 2nd edition, 1983.

[Jun89] U. Junker. A correct non-monotonic ATMS. In *Proceedings IJCAI-89*, pages 1049–1054, Detroit, Michigan, 1989.

[Kau87] H. Kautz. *A Formal Theory of Plan Recognition.* PhD thesis, University of Rochester, Rochester, N.Y., May 1987 1987.

[KKW89] T. Krishnaprasad, M. Kiefer, and D. Warren. On the circumscriptive semantics of inheritance networks. In Z. Ras and L. Saitta, editors, *Methodologies for Intelligent Systems 4*. North Holland, New York, N.Y., 1989.

[Kle89] D. Klein. Interpretive value analysis. Technical Report RC-15278, IBM T.J. Watson Research Center, Yorktown Heights, NY, 1989.

[KLM90] S. Kraus, D. Lehmann, and M. Magidor. Preferential models and cumulative logics. *Artificial Intelligence*, 44:167–207, 1990.

[KM89] K. Konolige and K. Myers. Representing defaults with epistemic concepts. *Computational Intelligence*, 5:32–44, 1989.

[KM90] A.C. Kakas and P. Mancarella. Generalized stable models: A semantics for abduction. In *Proceedings ECAI*, pages 385–391, 1990.

[Kol84] J. Kolodner. *Retrieval and Organizational Strategies in Conceptual Memory.* Lawrence Erlbaum Associates, Hillsdale, N.J., 1984.

[Kon88] K. Konolige. On the relation between default logic and autoepistemic logic. *Artificial Intelligence*, 35:343–382, 1988.

[Kon90] K. Konolige. A general theory of abduction. Unpublished manuscript, 1990.

[Kow79] R. Kowalski. Algorithm = Logic + Control. *Communications of the ACM*, 22:424–436, 1979.

[KS86] R. Kowalski and M. Sergot. A logic-based calculus of events. *New Generation Computing*, 4:67–95, 1986.

[Kyb83] H. Kyburg. The reference class. *Philosophy of Science*, 50:374–397, 1983.

[LB87] H. Levesque and R. Brachman. Expressiveness and tractability in knowledge representation and reasoning. *Computational Intelligence*, 3:78–93, 1987.

[Leh89] D. Lehmann. What does a conditional knowledge base entail? In *Proceedings of the First International Conference on Principles of Knowledge Representation and Reasoning*, pages 212–222, Toronto, Ontario, 1989. Morgan Kaufmann.

[Lev87] H. Levesque. All I know: An abridged report. In *Proceedings AAAI-87*, pages 426–431, Seattle, WA., 1987.

[Lew73] D. Lewis. *Counterfactuals.* Harvard University Press, Cambridge, MA, 1973.

[Lif85] V. Lifschitz. Computing circumscription. In *Proceedings IJCAI-85*, pages 121–127, Los Angeles, CA, 1985.

[Lif87] V. Lifschitz. Formal theories of action. In *Proceedings of the 1987 Workshop on the Frame Problem in AI*, pages 35–57, Kansas, 1987.

[Lif88a] V. Lifschitz. Circumscriptive theories: a logic-based framework for knowledge representation. *Journal of Philosophical Logic*, 17:391–441, 1988.

[Lif88b] V. Lifschitz. On the declarative semantics of logic programs. In J. Minker, editor, *Foundations of Deductive Databases and Logic Programming*, pages 177–192. Morgan Kaufmann, Los Altos, CA., 1988.

[LL89] K. Laskey and P. Lehner. Assumptions, beliefs and probabilities. *Artificial Intelligence*, 41:65–77, 1989.

[Llo84] J. Lloyd. *Foundations of Logic Programming.* Springer-Verlag, New York, 1984.

[LM88] D. Lehmann and M. Magidor. Rational logics and their models: a study in cumulative logic. Technical report, Dept. of Computer Science, Hebrew University, Jerusalem 91904, Israel, November 1988.

[Lou87a] R. Loui. Defeat among arguments: A system of defeasible inference. *Computational Intelligence*, 3(3):100–107, 1987.

[Lou87b] R. Loui. Real rules of inference. *Communication and Cognition*, 1987.

[LS89] C. Langlotz and E. Shortliffe. Logical and decision-theoretic methods for planning under uncertainty. *AI Magazine*, 10(1):39–47, 1989.

[LV90] E. Laenens and D. Vermeir. A fixpoint semantics for ordered logic. *Journal of Logic and Computation*, 1(2):159–185, 1990.

[Mak89] D. Makinson. General theory of cumulative inference. In M. Reinfrank *et al.*, editor, *Proceedings of the Second International Workshop on Non-Monotonic Reasoning*, pages 1–18, Berlin, Germany, 1989. Springer Lecture Notes on Computer Science.

[Mal88] J. Maloney. In praise of narrow minds: the frame problem. In J. Fetzer, editor, *Aspects of Artificial Intelligence*, pages 55–80. Kluwer Academic Publishers, 1988.

[Mar86] W. Marek. Stable theories in autoepistemic logic. Technical report, University of Kentucky, Lexignton, KY., 1986.

[McC68] J. McCarthy. Programs with commonsense. In M. Minsky, editor, *Semantic Information Processing*. MIT Press, Cambridge, MA., 1968.

[McC80] J. McCarthy. Circumscription—a form of non-monotonic reasoning. *Artificial Intelligence*, 13:27–39, 1980.

[McC86] J. McCarthy. Applications of circumscription to formalizing commonsense knowledge. *Artificial Intelligence*, 28:89–116, 1986.

[McC87] J. McCarthy. Generality in artificial intelligence. *Communications of the ACM*, 30, 1987.

[McD82] D. McDermott. A temporal logic for reasoning about processes and plans. *Cognitive Science*, 6:101–155, 1982.

[McD87] D. McDermott. Logic, problem solving and deduction. *Annual Review of Computer Science*, 2:187–229, 1987.

[MD80] D. McDermott and J. Doyle. Non-monotonic logic I. *Artificial Intelligence*, 13:41–72, 1980.

[MH69] J. McCarthy and P. Hayes. Some philosophical problems from the standpoint of artificial intelligence. In B. Meltzer and D. Mitchie, editors, *Machine Intelligence 4*, pages 463–502. American Elsevier, New York, 1969.

[Moo85a] R. Moore. A formal theory of knowledge and action. In J. Hobbs and R. Moore, editors, *Formal Theories of the Commonsense World*. Ablex Publishing Co., Norwood, N.J., 1985.

[Moo85b] R. Moore. Semantical considerations on non-monotonic logics. *Artificial Intelligence*, 25:75–94, 1985.

[Mor89] P. Morris. Autoepistemic stable closures and contradiction resolution. In M. Reinfrank *et al.*, editor, *Proceedings of the Second International Workshop on Non-Monotonic Reasoning*, pages 60–73, Berlin, Germany, 1989. Springer Lecture Notes on Computer Science.

[MS88a] L. Morgenstern and L. Stein. Why things go wrong: a formal theory of causal reasoning. In *Proceedings AAAI-88*, pages 519–523, St. Paul, Minnesota, 1988.

[MS88b] K. Myers and D. Smith. The persistence of derived information. In *Proceedings AAAI-88*, pages 496–500, St. Paul, Minnesota, 1988.

[NP88] E. Neufeld and D. Poole. Probabilistic semantics and defaults. In *Proceedings 4th AAAI Workshop on Uncertainty in AI*, pages 275–281, Minneapolis, MN., 1988.

[Nut84] D. Nute. Conditional logic. In D. Gabbay and F. Guenthner, editors, *Handbook of Philosophical Logic*, pages 387–439. D. Reidel, Dordrecht, 1984.

[Nut88a] D. Nute. Defeasible reasoning: A philosophical analysis in Prolog. In J. Fetzer, editor, *Aspects of Artificial Intelligence*, pages 251–287. Kluwer Academic Publishers, 1988.

[Nut88b] D. Nute. Defeasible reasoning and decision support systems. *Decision Support Systems*, 4:97–110, 1988.

[Pea88a] J. Pearl. Embracing causality in default reasoning. *Artificial Intelligence*, 35:259–271, 1988.

[Pea88b] J. Pearl. *Probabilistic Reasoning in Intelligent Systems.* Morgan Kaufmann, Los Altos, CA., 1988.

[Pea89a] J. Pearl. Probabilistic semantics for nonmonotonic reasoning: A survey. In *Proceedings of the First Int. Conf. on Principles of Knowledge Representation and Reasoning*, pages 505–516, Toronto, Canada, 1989.

[Pea89b] J. Pearl. Reasoning with belief functions: A critical assessment. Technical Report TR-136, Cognitive Systems Lab., UCLA, Los Angeles, CA., 1989.

[Pea90] J. Pearl. System Z: A natural ordering of defaults with tractable applications to non-monotonic reasoning. In R. Parikh, editor, *Theoretical Aspects of Reasoning about Knowledge*, pages 121–135, San Mateo, CA, 1990. Morgan Kaufmann.

[Pei55] C. Peirce. *Abduction and Induction.* Dover, New York, 1955.

[Pit88] J. Pitts, editor. *Theories of Explanation.* Oxford University Press, New York, N. Y., 1988.

[Pol87] J. Pollock. Defeasible reasoning. *Cognitive Science*, 11:481–518, 1987.

[Pol88a] J. Pollock. Defeasible reasoning and the statistical syllogism. Unpublished manuscript, 1988.

[Pol88b] J. Pollock. Oscar: a general theory of reasoning. Unpublished manuscript, 1988.

[Poo85] D. Poole. On the comparison of theories: Preferring the most specific explanation. In *Proceedings of IJCAI-85*, pages 144–147, Los Angeles, 1985.

[Poo87] D. Poole. Defaults and conjectures: hypothetical reasoning for explanation and prediction. Technical Report CS-87-4, University of Waterloo, 1987.

[Poo90] D. Poole. Dialectics and specificity: Conditioning in logic-based hypothetical reasoning (preliminary report). In *Proceedings of the Third International Workshop on Non-Monotonic Reasoning*, pages 201–209, South Lake Tahoe, CA., 1990.

[PP89] H. Przymusinska and T. Przymusinski. Semantic issues in deductive databases and logic programs. In A. Banerji, editor, *Sourcebook on the Formal Approaches in Artificial Intelligence.* North Holland, Amsterdam, 1989.

[PR90] Y. Peng and J. Reggia. *Abductive Inference Methods for Diagnostic Problem Solving*. Springer-Verlag, 1990.

[Prz87] T. Przymusinski. On the declarative semantics of stratified deductive databases and logic programs. In J. Minker, editor, *Foundations of Deductive Databases and Logic Programming*, pages 193–216. Morgan Kaufmann, Los Altos, CA, 1987.

[Prz89] T. Przymusinski. Every program has a natural stratification and an iterated fixed point model. In *Proceedings of the Eighth Symposium on Principles of Database Systems*, pages 11–21, 1989.

[RC83] R. Reiter and G. Criscuolo. Some representational issues in default reasoning. *Int. J. of Computers and Mathematics*, 9:1–13, 1983.

[RDB89] M. Reinfrank, O. Dressler, and G. Brewka. On the relation between truth maintenance and autoepistemic logic. In *Proceedings IJCAI-89*, pages 1206–1212, Detroit, Michigan, 1989.

[Rei80] R. Reiter. A logic for default reasoning. *Artificial Intelligence*, 12:81–132, 1980.

[Rei84] R. Reiter. Towards a logical reconstruction of relational database theory. In M. Brodie, J. Mylopoulos, and J. W. Schmidt, editors, *On Conceptual Modelling*, pages 163–189. Springer-Verlag, New York, 1984.

[Rei87a] R. Reiter. Nonmonotonic reasoning. *Annual Review of Computer Science*, 2:147–186, 1987.

[Rei87b] R. Reiter. A theory of diagnosis from first principles. *Artificial Intelligence*, 32:57–95, 1987.

[Rou75] P. Roussell. Prolog, Manuel de reference et d'utilisation. Technical report, Groupe d'Intelligence Artificielle, U.E.R. de Marseille, France, 1975.

[SA77] R. Schank and R. Abelson. *Scripts, Plans, Goals and Understanding*. Laurence Erlbaum Associates, Hillsdale, N.J., 1977.

[San88] E. Sandewal. An approach to non-monotonic entailment. In Z. Ras and L. Saitta, editors, *Methodologies for Intelligent Systems 3*, pages 391–397. North Holland, New York, N.Y., 1988.

[She87] J. Shepherson. Negation in logic programming. In J. Minker, editor, *Foundations of Deductive Databases and Logic Programming*, pages 19–88. Morgan Kaufmann, Los Altos, CA, 1987.

[Sho86] Y. Shoham. Chronological ignorance: time, non-monotonicity, necessity and causal theories. In *Proceedings AAAI-86*, pages 389–393, Philadelphia, 1986.

[Sho88] Y. Shoham. *Reasoning about Change: Time and Causation from the Standpoint of Artificial Intelligence*. MIT Press, Cambridge, Mass., 1988.

[SL90] G. Simari and R. Loui. Confluence of argument systems: Poole's rules revisited. In *Proceedings of the Third International Workshop on Non-Monotonic Reasoning*, pages 223–232, South Lake Tahoe, CA., 1990.

[Sow84] J. Sowa. *Conceptual Structures: Information Proceeding in Mind and Machine*. Addison-Wesley, Reading, MA., 1984.

[Spo88] W. Spohn. A general non-probabilistic theory of inductive reasoning. In *Proceedings 4th Workshop on Uncertainty*, pages 315–322, St. Paul, 1988.

[THT87] D. Touretzky, J. Horty, and R. Thomason. A clash of intuitions: The current state of non-monotonic multiple inheritance systems. In *Proceedings of IJCAI-87*, pages 476–482, Milano, Italy, 1987.

[Tou86] D. Touretzky. *The Mathematics of Inheritance Systems.* Pitman, London, 1986.

[Van89] A. Van Gelder. The alternating fixpoint of logic programs with negation (Extended Abstract). In *Proceedings Eight Symposium on Principles of Database Systems*, pages 1–10, 1989.

[VRS88] A. Van Gelder, K. Ross, and J. S. Schlipf. Unfounded sets and well-founded semantics for general logic programs. In *Proceedings of the Seventh Symposium on Principles of Database Systems*, pages 221–230, 1988.

[Wel90] M. Wellman. *Formulation of Tradeoffs in Planning under Uncertainty.* Pitman, London, 1990.

[WH91] M. Wellman and M. Henrion. Qualitative intercausal relations, or explaining "explaining away". In *Proceedings of the Second International Conference on Principle of Knowledge Representation and Reasoning*, pages 535–546, April 1991.

[Wil83] R. Wilensky. *Planning and Understanding: A Computational Approach to Human Reasoning.* Addison-Wesley, Reading, MA, 1983.

[Win88] M. Winslett. Reasoning about action using a possible models approach. In *Proceedings AAAI-88*, pages 89–93, St. Paul, Minnesota, 1988.

[Wit91] C. Witteveen. Skeptical reason maintenance is tractable. In *Proceedings of the Second International Conference on Principle of Knowledge Representation and Reasoning*, pages 570–580, April 1991.

[Zad87] W. Zadrozny. A theory of default reasoning. In *Proceedings AAAI-87*, pages 385–390, Seattle, Washington, 1987.

Index

The MIT Press, with Peter Denning as general consulting editor, publishes computer science books in the following series:

ACL-MIT Press Series in Natural Language Processing
Aravind K. Joshi, Karen Sparck Jones, and Mark Y. Liberman, editors

ACM Doctoral Dissertation Award and Distinguished Dissertation Series

Artificial Intelligence
Patrick Winston, founding editor
J. Michael Brady, Daniel G. Bobrow, and Randall Davis, editors

Charles Babbage Institute Reprint Series for the History of Computing
Martin Campbell-Kelly, editor

Computer Systems
Herb Schwetman, editor

Explorations with Logo
E. Paul Goldenberg, editor

Foundations of Computing
Michael Garey and Albert Meyer, editors

History of Computing
I. Bernard Cohen and William Aspray, editors

Logic Programming
Ehud Shapiro, editor; Fernando Pereira, Koichi Furukawa, Jean-Louis Lassez, and David H. D. Warren, associate editors

The MIT Press Electrical Engineering and Computer Science Series

Research Monographs in Parallel and Distributed Processing
Christopher Jesshope and David Klappholz, editors

Scientific and Engineering Computation
Janusz Kowalik, editor

Technical Communication and Information Systems
Ed Barrett, editor